PUFF...

Editor: Kaye Webb

JOCK OF THE BUSHVELD

'It must be *all true*! And don't leave out *anything*!'

It was to meet this demand of a youthful but exacting audience that the author first told the story of Jock's life in the hunter's paradise of the African bush.

Jock is a bull-terrier. When he is born he is the ugliest of a litter of six; but he grows up to be the wisest and bravest of them all. With his master he shares the excitement of a transport rider's life in the early days of the Transvaal gold rush; they become close companions and all Jock's skill and intelligence are needed in many thrilling and dangerous encounters with big game. Through the story of Jock and his master a vivid picture of the Bushveld unfolds as together they discover its birds and beasts and men.

This tale has become a classic among animal stories and today it is as fresh and exciting as when it was first told.

It is published here in a new abridged edition to enable the younger reader to enjoy the book fully on his own without adult help or explanation. The original marginal illustrations have been retained but their layout is different. The illustrations at the end of the book have been added.

SIR PERCY FITZPATRICK

JOCK OF
THE BUSHVELD

ILLUSTRATIONS BY E. CALDWELL

ABRIDGED BY DOLORES FLEISCHER

PUFFIN BOOKS

Puffin Books, Penguin Books Ltd, Harmondsworth, Middlesex, England
Penguin Books, 625 Madison Avenue, New York, New York 10022, U.S.A.
Penguin Books Australia Ltd, Ringwood, Victoria, Australia
Penguin Books Canada Ltd, 41 Steelcase Road West, Markham, Ontario, Canada
Penguin Books (N.Z.) Ltd, 182–190 Wairau Road, Auckland 10, New Zealand

—

First published 1907
This new abridged edition first published by Kestrel Books 1975
Published in Puffin Books 1976

—

Copyright © Percy FitzPatrick Memorial Trust, 1975

—

Made and printed in Great Britain
by Richard Clay (The Chaucer Press), Ltd
Bungay, Suffolk
Set in Linotype Pilgrim

Contents

Jock of the Bushveld

Paradise Camp

Seedling's Place

PILGRIM'S
REST

GRASKOP

Mac Mac Falls

THE BERG

HIGHVELD

THE EDGE OF THE BERG

BUSH FIRE

LOWVELD

LYDENBURG

SABIE

JOCK'S BIRTHPLACE

SPITZKOP

SHIP MOUNTAIN

CROCODILE RIVER

T R A N S V

CROCO

KAAPMUID

ELANDS RIVER

THE LAST HUNT

Portuguese Road

KAAPR RIVER Low's Creek

Fig Tree Creek

KAAP

R

BARBERTON

T

S W

TRANSPORT ROUTES

TSETSE FLY BELT

MINING SITES

Miles 10   5   0   10   20   30

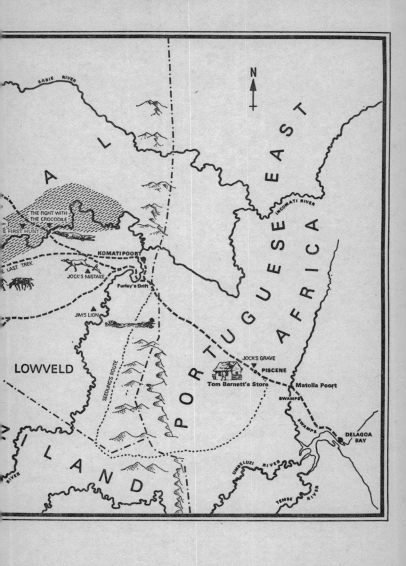

The Background

BEFORE the turn of the twentieth century, when the lure of gold brought men from all corners of the earth to the Transvaal, a young man from Cape Town came to the Lydenburg gold-fields to seek his fortune. He had left his home and family, his secure but dull job in a bank, and was equipped with nothing more than a stout heart, a keen brain, a sense of adventure and a willingness to work.

But work was scarce and after trying his hand at prospecting and store-keeping there came a chance to go transport-riding. At that time supplies for the mining camps were brought by ox-wagon from Delagoa Bay, through the Lowveld and up the precipitous escarpment to the gold-fields on the Highveld. The distances were not great by today's standards, but the transport riders had to manage heavily laden wagons, pulled by spans of fourteen or sixteen oxen, along roads that were mere tracks, across rivers, over primitive drifts, and finally up the frightening pass to the top of the Berg.

It is difficult for us to understand the slow pace at which life moved; that a day's trek of fifteen to eighteen miles was considered a good achievement; that it took at least a week to travel a hundred miles. And all the while the men with the wagons, white men and black, had to be fed.

The wagons were loaded to capacity with goods to be sold on the gold-fields, so it was neither practical nor profitable to carry much food. The transport riders took with them tea, sugar, salt and meal, but to provide meat they had to hunt as they travelled along. They were fortunate to be moving through country where game was plentiful and of great variety, and they found time between 'treks', when oxen and men were resting, to go shooting for the pot.

So this young man, in his early twenties, who had led a sheltered town life and who knew little of the bush, had to learn to hunt. He must have realized that it would not be easy for a beginner, in that wild country; he must also have known that to have a good hunting dog would be a great advantage in the Bushveld.

He found a puppy, and with great patience, care, affection and understanding he trained him to be perhaps the greatest hunting dog of them all, Jock. They learnt to hunt together and a wonderful bond of understanding grew up between them. Jock became his companion in everything and, in a simple life devoid of any kind of entertainment, the hunting became a relaxation and diversion from the hard work with the wagons.

Many years afterwards, when Percy FitzPatrick had his own children, he used to tell them bed-time stories of his life in the bush with Jock. 'It must be *all true*! and don't leave out *anything*!' was the instruction from his keenest of critics, 'The Little People'. For them he wrote this book; and to them he dedicated it. Round the story of a dog he wove a pattern of the life of a transport rider in an Africa still untamed and largely untrodden by man; he recorded a vivid picture of a way of life which was unique to a certain place and time and which has gone for ever. He left too a 'tribute of remembrance and affection' to those who made the old life and who pioneered the way for the ones who came after.

DOLORES FLEISCHER

Johannesburg, 1973

Jess

GOOD dogs were not easy to get – I had tried hard enough for one before starting, but without success – and good hunting dogs were as rare as good men, good horses and good front oxen.

A lot of qualities are needed in the make-up of a good hunting dog: size, strength, quickness, scent, sense and speed – and plenty of courage. They were very very difficult to get.

There was only one dog in our camp, and she was not an attractive one. She was a bull-terrier with a dull brindled coat – black and grey in shadowy stripes. She had small cross-looking eyes and uncertain always-moving ears. She was bad tempered and most unsociable, but she was as faithful and as brave a dog as ever lived. She never barked; never howled when beaten for biting strangers or going for the cattle; and was very silent, very savage and very quick. She belonged to my friend Ted, and never left his side day or night. Her name was Jess.

Jess was not a favourite, but everybody respected her, partly because she would not stand any nonsense – no pushing, patting or punishment, and very little talking to – and partly because she was so faithful and plucky. She was not a hunting dog, but on several occasions had helped to pull down wounded game. She had no knowledge or skill, and was only fierce and brave, and there was always the risk that she would be killed. She would listen to Ted, but to no one else. One of us might have shouted his lungs out, but it would not have stopped her from giving chase the moment she saw anything, and keeping on till she was too dead beat to move any further.

The first time I saw Jess we were having dinner, and I gave her a bone – putting it down close to her and saying, 'Here! good dog!' As she did not even look at it, I moved it right under her nose. She gave a low growl, and her little eyes turned on me for just one look as she got up and walked away.

There was a snigger of laughter from some of the others, but nobody said anything, and it seemed wiser to ask no questions just then. Afterwards, when we were alone, one of them told me Ted had trained her not to feed from any one else, adding, 'You must not feed another man's dog; a dog has only one master!'

We respected Jess greatly; but no one knew quite how much we respected her until the memorable day near Ship Mountain.

We had rested through the heat of the day under a big tree on the bank of a little stream. About sundown, just before we were ready to start, some other wagons passed, and Ted, knowing the owner, went on with him intending to rejoin us at the next outspan. As he jumped on to the passing wagon he called to Jess, and she ran out of a patch of soft grass under one of the big trees behind our wagons. She answered his call instantly, but when she saw him moving off on the other wagon she sat down in the road and watched him anxiously for some seconds, then ran on a few steps in her curious quick silent way and again stopped, giving swift glances alternately towards Ted and towards us. Ted remarked laughingly that she evidently thought he had made a mistake by getting on to the wrong wagon, and that she would follow presently.

After he had disappeared she ran back to her patch of grass and lay down, but in a few minutes she was back

again squatting in the road looking with that same anxious worried expression after her master. Thus she went to and fro for the quarter of an hour it took us to inspan, and each time she passed we could hear a faint anxious little whine.

The oxen were inspanned and the last odd things were being put up when one of the boys came to say that he could not get the guns and water-barrel because Jess would not let him near them. There was something the matter with the dog, he said; he thought she was mad.

Knowing how Jess hated natives we laughed at the notion, and went for the things ourselves. As we came within five yards of the tree where we had left the guns there was a

rustle in the grass, and Jess came out with her swift silent run, appearing as unexpectedly as a snake does, and with some odd suggestion of a snake in her look and attitude. Her head, body and tail were in a dead line, and she was crouching slightly as for a spring; her ears were laid flat back, her lips twitched constantly, showing the strong white teeth, and her cross, wicked eyes had such a look of remorseless cruelty in them that we stopped as if we had been turned to stone.

She never moved a muscle or made a sound, but kept those eyes steadily fixed on us. We moved back a pace or two and began to coax and wheedle her, but it was no good. For a minute we stood our ground, and then the hair on her back and shoulders began very slowly to stand up. That was enough: we cleared off. It was a mighty uncanny appearance.

The position was too ridiculous, and we were at our wits' end – for Jess held the camp. The boys declared the dog was mad, and we began to have very uncomfortable suspicions that they were right; but we decided to make a last attempt, and surrounding the place approached from all sides. But the suddenness with which she appeared before we got into position so demoralized the boys that they bolted, and we gave it up, owning ourselves beaten. We turned to watch her as she ran back for the last time, and as she disappeared in the grass we heard distinctly the cry of a very young puppy. Then the secret of Jess's madness was out.

We had to send for Ted, and when he returned a couple of hours later Jess met him out on the road in the dark where she had been watching half the time ever since he left. She jumped up at his chest giving a long tremulous whimper of welcome, and then ran ahead straight to the nest in the grass.

He took a lantern and we followed, but not too close. When he knelt down to look at the puppies she stood over them and pushed herself in between him and them. When he put out a hand to touch them she pushed it away with her nose, whining softly in protest and trembling with excitement – you could see she would not bite, but she hated him to touch her puppies. Finally, when he picked one up she gave a low cry and caught his wrist gently, but held it.

That was Jess, the mother of Jock!

The Pick of the Puppies

THERE were six puppies, and as the wagons were empty we fixed up a roomy nest in one of them for Jess and her family. There was no trouble with Jess; nobody interfered with her, and she interfered with nobody. The boys kept clear of her, but we used to take a look at her and the puppies as we walked along with the wagons. So, by degrees she got to know that we would not harm them, and she no longer wanted to eat us alive if we went near and talked to her.

Five of the puppies were strong, yellow little chaps with dark muzzles – just like their father, as Ted said. Their father was an imported bull-terrier, and was always spoken of as the best dog of the breed that had ever been in the country. I never saw him, so I do not really know what he was like – perhaps he was not a yellow dog at all. But, whatever he was, he had at that time a great reputation because he was 'imported', and there were not half a dozen imported dogs in the whole of the Transvaal then.

Many people used to ask what breed the puppies were – I suppose it was because poor, cross, faithful old Jess was not much to look at, and because no one had a very high opinion of yellow dogs in general. They used to smile in a queer way when they asked the question, but when we answered that their father was an *imported* dog, the smile disappeared. They would give a whistle of surprise and immediately begin to examine the five yellow puppies, remark up their ears and noses and legs, and praise them up until we were all as proud as if they had belonged to us.

Jess looked after her puppies and knew nothing about the remarks that were made, but I often looked at the faithful old thing with her dark brindled face, cross-looking eyes and always-moving ears, and thought it jolly hard lines that nobody had a good word for her. It seemed rough on her that every one should be glad there was only one puppy at all like the mother – the sixth one, a poor miserable little rat of a thing about half the size of the others. He was not yellow like them, nor dark brindled like Jess, but a sort of dirty pale half-and-half colour with some dark, faint, wavy lines all over him, as if he had tried to be brindled and failed; and he had a dark, sharp, wizened, little muzzle that looked shrivelled up with age.

Most of the fellows said it would be a good thing to drown the odd one because he spoilt the litter and made them look as though they were not really thoroughbred, and because he was such a miserable rat he was not worth saving anyhow. But in the end he was allowed to live. I believe no one fancied the job of taking one of Jess's puppies away from her. Moreover, as any dog was better than none, I had offered to take him rather than let him be drowned. Ted had old friends to whom he had already promised the pick of the puppies, so when I came along it was too late, and all he could promise me was that if there should be one over I might have it.

As they grew older and were able to crawl about they were taken off the wagons when we outspanned and put on the ground. Jess got to understand this at once, and she used to watch us quite quietly as we took them in our hands to put them down or lift them back again.

When they were two or three weeks old a man came to the wagons who talked a great deal about dogs, and appeared to know what had to be done. He said that the puppies' tails ought to be docked, and that a bull-terrier would be no class at all with a long tail, but you should on no account clip his ears. I thought he was speaking of fox-terriers, and that with bull-terriers the position was the other way round. But as he said it was 'the thing' in England, and nobody contradicted him, I shut up. We found out afterwards that he had made a mistake; but it was too

late then, and Jess's puppies started life with long ears and short tails.

I felt sure from the beginning that all the yellow puppies would be claimed and that I should have to take the odd one, or none at all. So I began to look upon him as mine already, and to take an interest in him and look after him. I felt sorry for him because he was small and weak, and the other five big puppies used to push him away from his food and trample on him; and when they were old enough to play they used to pull him about by his ears and pack on to him – three or four to one – and bully him horribly. Many a time I rescued him, and many a time gave him a little preserved milk and water with bread soaked in it when the others had shouldered him out and eaten everything.

I began to notice little things about him that no one else noticed, and got to be quite fond of the little beggar – in

a kind of way. Perhaps I grew fond of him simply because, finding him lonely and with no one else to depend on, I befriended him; and perhaps it was because he was always cheerful and plucky and it seemed as if there might be some good stuff in him after all.

Those were the things I used to think of sometimes when feeding the little outcast. The other puppies would tumble over him and take his food from him; they would bump into him when he was stooping over the dish of milk and porridge, and his head was so big and his legs so weak that he would tip up and go heels over head into the dish. We were always picking him out of the food and scraping it off him : half the time he was wet and sticky, and the other half covered with porridge and sand, baked hard by the sun.

One day just after the wagons had started, as I took a final look round the outspan place to see if anything had been forgotten, I found the little chap – who was only about four inches high – struggling to walk through the long grass. He was not big enough or strong enough to push his way through – even the stems of the down-trodden grass tripped him – and he stumbled and floundered at every step; but he got up again each time with his little tail standing straight up, his head erect and his ears cocked. He looked such a ridiculous sight one could only laugh.

What he thought he was doing, goodness only knows. He looked as proud and important as if he owned the whole world. The poor little chap could not see a yard in that grass; and in any case he was not old enough to see much, or understand anything, for his eyes still had that bluish blind look that all very young puppies have. But he was

marching along as full of confidence as a general at the head of his army. How he fell out of the wagon no one knew. Perhaps the big puppies tumbled him out; or he may have tried to follow Jess; or have climbed over the tail-board to see what was the other side, for he was always going off exploring by himself. His little world was small – only the bedplank of the wagon and the few square yards of the ground on which they were dumped at the outspans – but he took it as seriously as any explorer who ever tackled a continent.

The others were a bit more softened towards the odd puppy when I caught up to the wagons and told them of his valiant struggle to follow. And the man who had docked the puppies' tails allowed, 'I believe the Rat's got pluck, whatever else is the matter with him, for he was the only one that didn't howl when I snipped them. The little cuss just gave a grunt and turned round as if he wanted to eat me. Pity he's such an awful-looking mongrel.'

But no one else said a good word for him. He was really beneath notice, and if ever they had to speak about him they called him 'The Rat'. There is no doubt about it he was extremely ugly, and instead of improving as he grew older, he became worse. Yet I could not help liking him and looking after him, sometimes feeling sorry for him, sometimes being tremendously amused and sometimes really admiring him.

He was extraordinarily silent. While the others barked at nothing, howled when lonely and yelled when frightened

or hurt, the odd puppy did none of these things. In fact, he began to show many of Jess's peculiarities. He hardly ever barked, and when he did it was not a wild excited string of barks, but little suppressed muffled noises, half bark and half growl, and just one or two at a time – and he did not appear to be afraid of anything.

One day one of the oxen, sniffing about the outspan, caught sight of him all alone, and filled with curiosity came up to examine him, as a hulking silly old tame ox will do. It moved towards him slowly and heavily with its ears spread wide and its head down, giving great big sniffs at this new object, trying to make out what it was. 'The Rat' stood quite still with his stumpy tail cocked up and his head a little on one side, and when the huge ox's nose was about a foot from him he gave one of those funny abrupt little barks. It was as if the object had suddenly 'gone off' like a cracker, and the ox nearly tumbled over with fright. But even when the great mountain of a thing gave a clumsy plunge round and trotted off, 'The Rat' was not the least frightened. He was startled, and his tail and ears flickered for a second, but stiffened up again instantly, and with another of those little barks he took a couple of steps for-

ward and cocked his head on the other side. That was his way.

He was not a bit like the other puppies. If anyone fired off a gun or cracked one of the big whips the whole five would yell at the top of their voices and would start running, scrambling and floundering as fast as they could towards the wagon, without once looking back to see what they were running away from. The odd puppy would drop his bone with a start or would jump round; his ears and tail would flicker up and down for a second; then he would slowly bristle up all over, and with his head cocked first on one side and then on the other, stare hard with his half-blind bluish puppy eyes in the direction of the noise. But he never ran away.

And so, little by little, I got to like him in spite of his awful ugliness. And it really was awful! The other puppies grew big all over, but the odd one at that time seemed to grow only in one part — his tummy! The poor little chap was born small and weak; he had always been bullied and crowded out by the others, and the truth is he was half-starved. Thus, as soon as he could walk about and pick up things for himself he made up for lost time, and filled up his middle piece to an alarming size before the other parts of his body had time to grow. At that time he looked more like a big tock-tockie beetle than a dog.

Besides the balloon-like tummy he had stick-out bandy legs, very like a beetle's too, and a neck so thin that it made the head look enormous, and you wondered how the neck ever held it up. But what made him so supremely ridiculous was the way he walked about as if he was always thinking of his dignity. He had that puffed-out and stuck-up air of importance that you only see in small people and bantam cocks, who are always trying to appear an inch taller than they really are.

When the puppies were about a month old, and could feed on porridge or bread soaked in soup or gravy, they got to be too much for Jess. She used to leave them for hours at a time and hide in the grass so as to have a little peace and sleep.

Puppies are always hungry, so they soon began to hunt about for themselves, and would find scraps of meat and porridge or old bones; and if they could not get anything else, would try to eat the raw-hide nekstrops and reins. Then the fights began. As soon as one puppy saw another busy on anything, he would walk over towards him and, if strong enough, fight him for it. All day long it was nothing but wrangle, snarl, bark and yelp. Sometimes four or five would be at it in one scrum; because as soon as one heard a row going on he would trot up hoping to steal the bone while the others were busy fighting.

It was then that I noticed other things about the odd puppy. No matter how many packed on to him, or how they bit or pulled him, he never once let out a yelp. With four or five on top of him you would see him on his back, snapping right and left with bare white teeth, gripping and worrying them when he got a good hold of anything, and all the time growling and snarling with a fierceness that was really comical.

Before many days passed, it was clear that some of the other puppies were inclined to leave 'The Rat' alone, and that only two of them – the two biggest – seemed anxious

to fight him, and could take his bones away. The reason soon became apparent : instead of wasting his breath in making a noise, or wasting strength in trying to tumble the others over, 'The Rat' simply bit hard and hung on. Noses, ears, lips, cheeks, feet and even tails – all came handy to him. Anything he could get hold of and hang on to was good enough, and the result generally was that in about half a minute the other puppy would leave everything and clear off yelling.

When either of the big puppies tackled the little fellow the fight lasted much longer. Even if he were tumbled over at once, as generally happened, and the other one stood over him barking and growling, that did not end the fight. As soon as the other chap got off him he would struggle up and begin again; he would not give in. The other puppies seemed to think that once you were tumbled over you ought to give up the bone. But the odd puppy had just one rule: 'Stick to it.'

So it was not very long before even the two big fellows gave up interfering with him. They found there was nothing to be gained by fighting him. They might roll him over time after time, but he came back again and worried them so persistently that it was quite impossible to enjoy the bone – they had to keep on fighting for it.

At first I drew attention to these things, but there was no encouragement from the others; they merely laughed at the attempt to make the best of a bad job. Once, when I had described how well he had stood up to Billy's pup, Robbie caught up 'The Rat' and, placing him on the table, said: 'Hats off to the Duke of Wellington on the field of Waterloo.' That seemed to me the poorest sort of joke to send five grown men into fits of laughter. He stood there on the table with his head on one side, one ear standing up, and his stumpy tail twiddling – an absurd picture of friendliness, pride and confidence; yet he was so ugly and ridiculous that my heart sank, and I whisked him away.

After that I stopped talking about him, and made the most of the good points he showed, and tried to discover more. It was the only consolation for having to take the leavings of the litter.

*

Then there came a day when something happened which might easily have turned out very differently, and there would have been no stories and no Jock to tell about – and the best dog in the world would never have been my friend and companion.

The puppies had been behaving very badly, and had stolen several nekstrops and chewed up parts of one or two big whips; the drivers were grumbling about all the damage done and all the extra work it gave them. Ted, exasperated by the worry of it all, announced that the puppies were quite old enough to be taken away; those who had picked puppies must take them at once and look after them, or let someone else have them.

When I heard him say that my heart gave a little thump from excitement, for I knew the day had come when the great question would be settled once and for all. Here was a glorious and unexpected chance. Perhaps one of the others would not or could not take his, and I might get one of the good ones ... I thought of very little else all day long, wondering if any of the good ones would be left – and if so which?

In the afternoon Ted came up to where we were all lying in the shade and startled us with the momentous announcement:

'Billy Griffiths can't take his pup!'

Every man of us sat up. Billy's pup was the first pick, the champion of the litter, the biggest and strongest of the lot. Several of the others said at once that they would exchange theirs for this one; but Ted smiled and shook his head.

'No,' he said, 'you had a good pick in the beginning.' Then he turned to me and added : 'You've only had leavings. You can have Billy's pup.'

It seemed too good to be true. Not even in my wildest imaginings had I fancied myself getting the pick of the lot. I hardly waited to thank Ted before going off to look at my champion. He was a fine big fellow, well built and strong, and looked as if he could beat all the rest put together. His legs were straight; his neck sturdy; his muzzle dark and shapely; his ears equal and well carried; and in the sunlight his yellow coat looked quite bright, with occasional glints of gold in it.

As I put him back again with the others the odd puppy, who had stood up and sniffed at me when I came, licked my hand and twiddled his tail with the friendliest and most independent air – as if he knew me quite well and was glad to see me – and I patted the poor little chap as he waddled up. I had forgotten him in the excitement of getting Billy's pup. But the sight of him made me think of his funny ways, his pluck and independence, and of how he had not a friend in the world except Jess and me; and I felt downright sorry for him.

I picked him up and talked to him; and when his wizened little face was close to mine, he opened his mouth as if laughing, and shooting out his red tongue dabbed me right on the tip of my nose in pure friendliness. The poor little fellow looked more ludicrous than ever. He had been feeding again and was as tight as a drum; his skin was so tight one could not help thinking that if he walked over a mimosa thorn and got a scratch on the tummy he would burst like a toy balloon.

I put him back with the other puppies and returned to the tree where Ted and the rest were sitting. As I came up there was a shout of laughter, and – turning round to see what had provoked it – I found 'The Rat' at my heels. He had followed me and was trotting and stumbling along, tripping every yard or so, but getting up against with head erect, ears cocked and his stumpy tail twiddling away, just as pleased and proud as if he was doing what a dog is supposed to do – that is, follow his master wherever he goes.

All the old jokes were fired off at me again, and I had no peace for quite a time. They all had something to say: 'I'll back "The Rat"!' 'He is going to take care of you!' 'He is afraid you'll get lost!' and so on; and they were still chaffing about it when I grabbed 'The Rat' and took him back again.

The poor friendless Rat! He was uglier than before and yet I could not help liking him. I fell asleep that night thinking of the two puppies – the best and the worst in the litter. No sooner had I gone over all the splendid points in Billy's pup – and made up my mind that he was certainly the finest I had ever seen – than the friendly, wizened little face, the half-cocked ears and the head on one side, the cocky little stump of a tail, and the comical dignified plucky look of the odd puppy would all come back to me. The thought of how he had licked my hand and twiddled his tail at me, and how he dabbed me on the nose, and then the manful way in which he had struggled after me through the grass, all made my heart go soft towards him – and I fell asleep not knowing what to do.

When I woke up in the morning, my first thought was of the odd puppy. What would he feel like if – after looking on me as really belonging to him – he was to be left behind or given away to anyone who would take him? From the way he had followed me the night before it was clear he was looking after me – and the other fellows thought the same thing.

We used to make our first trek at about three o'clock in the morning, so as to be outspanned by sunrise. Walking along during that morning trek I recalled all the stories that the others had told of miserable puppies having grown into wonderful dogs, and of great men who had been very ordinary children; and at breakfast I took the plunge.

'Ted,' I said, bracing myself for the laughter, 'if you don't mind, I'll stick to "The Rat".'

If I had fired off a gun under their noses they would have been much less startled. Robbie made a grab for his plate as it slipped from his knees. The others stopped eating and drinking, held their beakers of steaming coffee well out of the way to get a better look at me, and when they saw it was seriously meant there was a chorus of:

'Well, I'm hanged.'

I took him in hand at once – for now he was really mine – and brought him over for his saucer of soaked bread and milk to where we sat at breakfast.

Beside me there was a rough camp table – a luxury sometimes indulged in while camping or trekking with empty wagons – on which we can put our tinned milk, treacle and such things to keep them out of reach of the ants, grasshoppers, Hottentot-gods, beetles and dust. I put the puppy and his saucer in a safe place under the table out of the way of stray feet, and sank the saucer into the sand so that when he trod in it he would not spill the food; for puppies are quite as stupid as they are greedy, and seem to think that they can eat faster by getting further into the dish. He appeared to be more ravenous than usual, and we were all amused by the way the little fellow craned his thin neck out further and further until he tipped up behind, and his nose bumping into the saucer see-sawed him back again. He finished it all and looked round briskly at me, licking his lips and twiddling his stumpy tail.

Well, I meant to make a dog of him, so I gave him another lot. He was just like a little child – he thought he was very hungry still and could eat any amount more; but it was not possible. The lapping became slower and more laboured, with pauses every now and then to get breath or lick his lips and look about him, until at last he was fairly beaten. He could only look at it, blink and lick his chops. Knowing that he would keep on trying, I took the saucer away. He was too full to object or to run after it. He was too full to move. He stood where he was, with his legs well spread and his little body blown out like a balloon, and finished licking the drops and crumbs off his face without moving a foot.

He had been standing very close to the leg of the table, but not quite touching it, when he finished feeding. Even after he had done washing his face and cleaning up generally, he

stood there stock still for several minutes, as though it was altogether too much trouble to move. One little bandy hind leg stuck out behind the table-leg, and the bulge of his little tummy stuck out in front of it; so that, when at last he decided to make a move, the very first little lurch brought his hip up against the table-leg.

In an instant the puppy's appearance changed completely. The hair on his back and shoulders bristled; his head went up erect; one ear stood up straight and the other at half cock; and his stumpy tail quivered with rage. He evidently thought that one of the other puppies had come up behind to interfere with him. He was too proud to turn round and appear to be nervous. With head erect he glared hard straight in front of him, and, with all the little breath that he had left after his big feed, he growled ferociously in comical gasps. He stood like that, not moving an inch, with the front foot still ready to take that step forward. Then, as nothing more happened, the hair on his back gradually went flat again; the fierceness died out of his face; and the growling stopped.

After a minute's pause, he again very slowly and carefully began to step forward. Of course exactly the same thing happened again, except that this time he shook all over with

rage, and the growling was fiercer and more choky. One could not imagine anything so small being in so great a rage. He took longer to cool down, too, and much longer before he made the third attempt to start. But the third time it was all over in a second. He seemed to think that this was more than any dog could stand, and that he must put a stop to it. The instant his hip touched the leg, he whipped round with a ferocious snarl – his little white teeth bared and gleaming – and bumped his nose against the table-leg.

I cannot say whether it was because of the shout of laughter from us, or because he really understood what had happened, that he looked so foolish. He just gave one crestfallen look at me and with a feeble wag of his tail waddled off as fast as he could.

Then Ted nodded over at me, and said: 'I believe you have got the champion after all!'

And I was too proud to speak.

Jock's Schooldays

AFTER that day no one spoke of 'The Rat' or 'The Odd Puppy', and even 'The Duke of Wellington' ceased to be a gibe. They still laughed at his ridiculous dignity, and they loved to tease him to see him stiffen with rage and hear his choky little growls – but they liked his independence and admired his tremendous pluck. So they respected his name when he got one.

And his name was 'Jock'.

It is probably the best thing that could have happened to Jock that as a puppy he was small and weak, but full of pluck. It compelled him to learn how to fight. It made him clever, cool and careful, for he could not afford to make mistakes. When he fought he meant business. He went for a good spot, bit hard and hung on for all he was worth; then, as the enemy began to slacken, he would start vigorously worrying and shaking. I often saw him shake himself off his feet, because the thing he was fighting was too heavy for him.

The day Jock fought the two big puppies – one after the

other – for his bone, and beat them off, was the day of his independence. We all saw the tussle and cheered the little chap. After that he had no more puppy fights, and thenceforth was cock of the walk.

One by one the other puppies were taken away by their new masters, and before Jock was three months old he and Jess were the only dogs with the wagons. Then he went to school, and like all schoolboys learnt some things very quickly – the things that he liked – and some things he learnt very slowly, and hated them just as a boy hates extra work in playtime.

When I poked about with a stick in the banks of dongas to turn out mice and field-rats for him, or when I hid a partridge or a hare and made him find it, he was as happy as could be. But when I made him lie down and watch my gun or coat while I pretended to go off and leave him, he did not like it. And as for his lessons in manners! Well, he simply hated them.

There are some things which a dog in that sort of life simply must learn or you cannot keep him. The first of these is not to steal. Every puppy will help himself until he is taught not to; and your dog lives with you and can get at everything. At the outspans the grub-box is put on the ground, open for each man to help himself. If you make a stew, or roast the leg of a buck, the big three-legged pot is put down handy and left there. If you are lucky enough to have some tinned butter or condensed milk, the tins are opened and stood on the ground – and if you have a dog thief in the camp, nothing is safe.

There was a dog with us once – a year or two later – who was the worst thief I ever knew. He was a one-eyed pointer with feet like a duck's, and his name was Snarleyow. He looked the most foolish and most innocent dog in the world, and was so timid that if you stumbled as you passed him he would instantly start howling and run for the horizon. The first bad experience I had of Snarley was on one of the little hunting trips which we sometimes made in those days, away from the wagons. We travelled light on these occasions, and, except for some tea and a very little flour and salt, took no food. We lived on what we shot and of course kept 'hunter's pot'.

'Hunter's pot' is a perpetual stew. You make one stew, and keep it going as long as necessary, maintaining a full pot by adding to it as fast as you take any out. Scraps of everything go in: any kind of meat – buck, bird, pig, hare

– and if you have such luxuries as onions or potatoes, so much the better; then, to make the soup strong, the big bones are added – the old ones being fished out every day and replaced by a fresh lot. When allowed to cool it sets like brawn, and a hungry hunter wants nothing better.

We had had a good feed the first night of this trip and had then filled the pot up, leaving it to simmer as long as the fire lasted. We expected to have cold pie set in jelly – but without the pie-crust – for early breakfast next morning before going off for the day; but, to our amazement, in the morning the pot was empty. There were some strange natives – camp followers – hanging on to our trail for what they could pick up, and we suspected them. There was a great row, but the boys denied having touched the pot, and we could prove nothing.

That night we made the fire close to our sleeping-place and moved the natives further away, but next morning the pot was again empty – cleaned and polished as if it had been washed out. While we, speechless with astonishment and anger, were wondering who the thief was and what we should do with him, one of the hunting boys came up and pointed to the prints of a dog's feet in the soft white ashes of the dead fire. There was only one word: 'Snarleyow'. The thief was lying fast asleep comfortably curled up on his master's clothes. There could be no mistake about those big splayed footprints, and in about two minutes Snarleyow was getting a first-class hammering, with his head tied inside the three-legged pot for a lesson.

After that he was kept tied up at night; but Snarleyow was past curing. We had practically nothing to eat but what we shot, and nothing to drink but bush tea – that is, tea made from a certain wild shrub with a very strong scent. It is not nice, but you drink it when you cannot get any-

thing else. We could not afford luxuries then, but two days before Ted's birthday he sent a runner off to Komati Drift to buy a small tin of ground coffee and a tin of condensed milk for his birthday treat. It was to be a real feast that day, so he cut the top off the tin instead of punching two holes and blowing the milk out, as we usually did in order to economize and keep out the dust and insects. What we could not use in the coffee we were going to spread on our 'doughboys' instead of butter and jam. It was to be a real feast!

The five of us sat down in a circle and began on our hunter's pot, saving the good things for the last. While we were still busy on the stew, there came a pathetic heart-breaking yowl from Snarleyow. We looked round just in time to see him, his tail tucked between his legs and his head high in the air, bolting off into the bush as hard as he could lay legs to the ground, with the milk tin stuck firmly on to his nose. The greedy thief in trying to get the last scrap out had dug his nose and top jaw too far in, and the jagged edges of the tin had gripped him. The last we saw of our birthday treat was the tin flashing in the sunlight on Snarley's nose as he tore away howling into the bush.

Snarleyow came to a bad end: his master shot him as

he was running off with a ham. He was a full-grown dog when he came to our camp, and too old to learn principles and good manners.

Dogs are like people. What they learn when they are young, whether of good or of evil, is not readily forgotten. I began early with Jock, and tried to help him. It is little use punishing a dog for stealing if you take no trouble about feeding him. I taught Jock not to touch food in camp until he was told to 'take it'.

The lesson began when he got his saucer of porridge in the morning. He must have thought it cruel to have that put in front of him, and then to be held back or tapped with a finger on the nose each time he tried to dive into it. At first he struggled and fought to get at it; then he tried to back away and dodge round the other side; then he became dazed, and, thinking it was not for him at all, wanted to walk off and have nothing more to do with it. In a few days, however, I got him to lie still and take it only when I patted him and pushed him towards it; and in a very little time he got on so well that I could put his food down without saying anything and let him wait for permission. He would lie down with his head on his paws and his nose right up against the saucer, so as to lose no time when the order came; but he would not touch it until he heard 'Take it'. He never moved his head, but his little browny dark eyes, full of childlike eagerness, used to be turned up sideways and fixed on mine. I believe he watched my lips; he was so quick to obey the order when it came.

When he grew up and had learned his lessons there was no need for these exercises. He got to understand me so well that when I nodded or moved my hand in a way that meant 'all right', he would go ahead. By that time too he was dignified and patient. It was only in his puppyhood that he used to crouch close to his food and tremble with impatience.

There was one lesson that he hated most of all. I used to balance a piece of meat on his nose and made him keep it there until the word to take it came. Time after time he

would close his eyes as if the sight of the meat was more than he could bear; and his mouth would water so from the savoury smell that long streels of dribble would hang down on either side.

It seems unnecessary and even cruel to tantalize a dog in that way, but it was not. It was education; and it was true kindness. It taught him to understand his master, and to be obedient, patient and observant; it taught him not to steal; it saved him from much sickness, and perhaps death by teaching him not to feed on anything he could find; it taught him manners and made it possible for him to live with his master and be treated like a friend.

Good feeding, good care and plenty of exercise soon began to make a great change in Jock. He ceased to look like a beetle – grew bigger everywhere, not only in one part as he had done at first. His neck grew thick and strong, and his legs straightened up and filled out with muscle.

There was one change which came more slowly and seemed to me much more wonderful. After his morning feed, if there was nothing to do, he used to go to sleep in some shady place, and I remember well one day watching him as he lay. His bit of shade had moved away and left him in the bright sunshine. As he breathed and his ribs rose and fell, the tips of the hairs on his side and back caught the sunlight and shone like polished gold, and the wavy dark lines seemed more distinct and darker, but still very soft. In fact, I was astonished to see that in a certain light Jock looked quite handsome. That was the first time I noticed the change in colour, and it made me remember a remark made by an old hunter who had offered to buy Jock – the real meaning of which I did not understand at the time.

'The best dog I ever owned was a golden brindle,' said the old man thoughtfully, after I had laughed at the idea of selling my dog. I had got so used to thinking that he was only a faded wishy-washy edition of Jess that the idea of his colour changing did not occur to me then, and I never suspected that the old man could see how he would turn out. But the touch of sunlight opened my eyes that day. After that whenever I looked at Jock the words 'golden brindle' came back to my mind, and I pictured him as he was going to be – and as he really did grow up – having a coat like burnished gold with soft, dark, wavy brindles in it and that snow-white V on his chest.

Jock had many things to learn besides the lessons he got

from me – the lessons of experience which nobody could teach him.

On trek there were always new places to see, new roads to travel, and new things to examine, tackle or avoid. He learnt something fresh almost every day. He learnt, for instance, that, although it was shady and cool under the wagon, it was not good enough to lie in the wheel track –

not even for the pleasure of feeling the cool iron tyre against your back or head as you slept. One day he had done it and the wheel had gone over his foot; and it might just as easily have been his back or head. Fortunately the sand was soft and his foot was not crushed, but he was very lame for some days, and had to travel on the wagon.

He learned a good deal from Jess: among other things that it was not necessary to poke his nose up against a snake in order to find out what it was. He knew that Jess would fight anything, and when one day he saw her back hair go up and watched her sheer off the footpath wide into the grass, he did the same. When we had shot the snake, both he and Jess came up very, very cautiously and sniffed at it, with every hair on their bodies standing up.

He found out for himself that it was not a good idea to turn a scorpion over with his paw. The vicious little tail with a thorn in it whipped over the scorpion's back, and Jock had such a foot that he must have thought a scorpion worse than two wagons. He was a very sick dog for some days. After that, whenever he saw anything that he did not understand, he would watch it very carefully from a little way off and notice what it did and what it looked like, before trying experiments.

So, little by little, Jock got to understand plenty of things that no town dog would ever know, and he got to know – by what we call instinct – whether a thing was dangerous or safe, even though he had never seen anything like it before. That is how he knew that lions were about – and that they were dangerous – when he heard or scented them. You may well wonder how to tell whether the scent or the cry belonged to a hyena which he must avoid, or to a buck which he might hunt, when he had never seen either a hyena or a buck. But he did know. He also knew that no dog could safely go outside the ring of the camp fires when hyena or lion was about.

I used to take Jock with me everywhere so that he could

44

learn everything that a hunting dog ought to know; and above all things learn that he was my dog, and be able to understand all that I wanted to tell him. So while he was still a puppy, whenever he stopped to sniff at something new or to look at something strange, I would show him what it was. But if he stayed behind to explore while I moved on, or if he fell asleep and did not hear me get up from where I had sat down to rest, or went off the track on his own account, I used to hide away from him and let him hunt about until he found me.

At first he used to be quite excited when he missed me, but after a little time he got to know what to do and would sniff along the ground and canter away after me – always finding me quite easily. Even if I climbed a tree to hide from him he would follow my track to the foot of the tree, sniff up the trunk as far as he could reach standing up against it, and then peer into the branches. If he could not see me from one place, he would try another – always with his head tilted a bit on one side. He never barked at these times; but as soon as he saw me his ears would drop, his mouth wide open with a red tongue lolling out and the stump of a tail would twiddle away to show how pleased he was. Sometimes he would give a few little whimpery grunts. He hardly ever barked. When he did I knew there was something worth looking at.

Jock was not a quarrelsome dog, and he was quick to learn and very obedient, but in one connection I had great difficulty with him for quite a little time. He had a sort of private war with the fowls, and it was due to the same cause as his war with the other puppies: they interfered with him.

Now everyone knows what a fowl is like : it is impudent, inquisitive, selfish, always looking for something to eat and has no principles. The fowls tried to steal Jock's food, and he would not stand it. His way of dealing with them was not good for their health. Before I could teach him not to kill, and before the fowls would learn not to steal, he had finished half a dozen of them one after another, with just one bite and a shake. He would growl very low as they came up and, without lifting his head from the plate, watch them with his little eyes turning from soft brown to shiny black; and when they came too near and tried to snatch just one mouthful – well, one jump, one shake and it was all over.

In the end he learned to tumble them over and scare their wits out without hurting them; and they learned to give him a very wide berth.

I used always to keep some fowls with the wagons, partly to have fresh meat if we ran out of game, but mainly to have fresh eggs, which were a very great treat; and as a rule it was only when a hen turned obstinate and would not lay that we ate her. I used to have one old rooster and six or eight hens. The hens changed from time to time – as we ate them – but the rooster remained.

He was a game cock and a bit like Jock in some things. That is why I fancy perhaps Jock and he were friends in a kind of way. But Jock could not get on with the others. They were constantly changing. New ones who had to be taught manners were always coming; so he just lumped them together and hated fowls. He taught them manners, but they taught him something too – at any rate one of them did. One of the biggest surprises and best lessons Jock ever had was given him by a hen while he was still a growing-up puppy.

He was beginning to fancy that he knew a good deal, and

like most young dogs was very inquisitive. At that time he was very keen on hunting mice, rats and bush squirrels, and had even fought and killed a meerkat after the plucky little rikkitikki had bitten him rather badly through the lip. He was still much inclined to poke his nose in or rush onto things instead of sniffing round about first.

However, he learned to be careful, and an old hen helped to teach him. The hens usually laid their eggs in the coop because it was their home, but sometimes they would make nests in the bush at the outspan places. One of the hens had done this, and the bush she had chosen was very low and dense. No one saw the hen make the nest and no one saw her sitting on it, for the sunshine was so bright everywhere else, and the shade of the bush so dark that it was impossible to see anything there. While we were at breakfast Jock, who was bustling about everywhere as a puppy will, must have scented the hen or have seen this brown thing in the dark shady hole.

The hen was sitting with her head sunk right down into her chest, so that he could not see any head, eyes or beak –

just a sort of brown lump. Suddenly we saw Jock stand stock-still, cock up one ear, put his head down and his nose out, hump up his shoulders a bit and begin to walk very slowly forward in a crouching attitude. He lifted his feet so slowly and so softly that you could count five between each step. We were all greatly amused and thought he was pointing a mouse or a locust, and we watched him.

He crept up like a boy 'showing off' until he was only six inches from the object, giving occasional cautious glances back at us to attract attention. Just as he got to the hole the hen let out a vicious peck on the top of his nose and at the same time flapped over his head, screaming and cackling for dear life. It was all so sudden and so surprising that she was gone before he could think of making a grab at her; and when he heard our shouts of laughter he looked as foolish as if he understood all about it.

The First Hunt

JOCK'S first experience in hunting was on the Crocodile river not far from the spot where long afterwards we had the great fight with The Old Crocodile.

In the summer when the heavy rains flood the country the river runs 'bank high', hiding everything — reeds, rocks, islands and stunted trees. In the rainless winter when the water is low and clear the scene is not so grand but it is quiet, peaceful and much more beautiful. There is an infinite variety in it then. The river sometimes winds along in one deep channel, but more often forks out into two or three streams in the broad bed. The loops and lacings of the divided water carve out islands and spaces of all shapes and sizes — banks of clean white sand or of firm damp mud — on which tall green reeds with yellow-tasselled tops shoot up like crops of kaffir corn.

Get up on some vantage point upon the high bank and look down there one day in the winter of the tropics as the heat and hush of noon approach, and it will seem indeed a place to rest and dream. As you sit silently watching and thinking, where all the world is so infinitely still, you will notice that one reed down among all those countless thousands is moving. It bows slowly and gracefully a certain distance, and with a quivering shuddering motion straightens itself still more slowly and with evident difficulty, until at last it stands upright again like the rest – but still all a-quiver while they do not move a leaf. Just as you are beginning to wonder what the reason is, the reed bows slowly again, and again struggles back; and so it goes on as regularly as the swing of a pendulum. Then you know that, down at the roots where you cannot see it, something attached to this reed is dragging in the stream and pulling it over – and swinging back to do it again each time the reed lifts it free.

But the behaviour of that one reed has stopped your dreaming and made you look about more carefully. Then you find that there is hardly a spot where, if you watch for a few minutes, you will not see something moving. A tiny field-mouse climbing one reed will sway it over; a river rat gnawing at the roots will make it shiver and rustle; little birds hopping from one to another will puzzle you; and a lagavaan turning in his sunbath will make half a dozen sway outwards.

All feeling that it is a place to rest and dream leaves you. You are wondering what goes on down below the green and gold where you can see nothing. Then your eye catches a bigger, slower, continuous movement in another place; for twenty yards from the bank to the stream you see the tops of the reeds silently and gently parting and closing again as something down below works its way along without the faintest sound. The place seems too quiet, too uncanny and mysterious, too silent, stealthy and treacherous for you to sit still in comfort. You must get up and do something.

We were spending a couple of days on the river bank to make the most of the good water and grazing, and all through the day some one or other would be out pottering about among the reeds, gun in hand, to keep the pot full and have some fun. There is always good shooting along the rivers in a country where water is scarce. Partridges, bush-pheasants and stembuck were plentiful along the banks and among the thorns, but the reeds themselves were the home of thousands of guinea-fowl, and you could also count on duiker and rietbok as almost a certainty there.

But it is not only man that is on the watch for game at the drinking places. The beasts of prey – lions, leopards, hyenas, wild dogs and jackals, and lastly pythons and crocodiles – know that the game must come to water, and they lie in wait near the tracks or the drinking places. That is what makes the mystery and charm of the reeds; you never know what you will put up. The lions and leopards had deserted the country near the main drifts and followed the big game into more peaceful parts. But the reeds were still the favourite shelter and resting-place of the crocodiles; and there were any number of them left.

There is nothing that one comes across in hunting more horrible and loathsome than the crocodile. Nothing that rouses the feeling of horror and hatred as it does. Nothing that so surely and quickly gives the sensation of 'creeps in the back' as the noiseless apparition of one in the water just where you least expected anything; or the discovery of one silently and intently watching you with its head resting flat on a sand-pit – the thing you had seen half a dozen times before and mistaken for a small rock.

Many things are hunted in the Bushveld; but only the crocodile is hated. There is always the feeling that this hideous, cowardly, cruel thing – with its look of a cunning smile in the greeny glassy eyes and great wide mouth – will mercilessly drag you down-down-down to the bottom of some deep still pool, and hold you there till you drown. Utterly helpless yourself to escape or fight, you cannot even call, and if you could, no one could help you there. It is all done in silence. A few bubbles come up where a man went down – and that is the end of it.

We all knew about the crocodiles and were prepared for them, but when you are fresh at the game and get interested in a hunt it is not very easy to remember all the things you have been warned about.

It was on the first day at the river that one of our party, who was not a very old hand at hunting, came in wet and muddy and told us how a crocodile had scared the wits out of him. He had gone out after guinea-fowl, he said, but as he had no dog to send in and flush them, the birds simply played with him. They would not rise but kept running in the reeds a little way in front of him, just out of sight. He could hear them quite distinctly, and thinking to steal a march on them took off his boots and got on to the rocks.

Stepping bare-footed from rock to rock where the reeds were thin, he made no noise at all and got so close up that he could hear the little whispered chink-chink-chink that they give when near danger.

The only chance of getting a shot at them was to mount one of the big rocks from which he could see down into the reeds; and he worked his way along a mud-bank towards one. A couple more steps from the mud-bank on to a low black rock would take him to the big one.

Without taking his eyes off the reeds where the guinea-fowl were he stepped cautiously on to the low black rock, and in an instant was swept off his feet, tossed and tumbled over and over, into the mud and reeds; and there was a noise of furious rushing and crashing as if a troop of elephants were stampeding through the reeds. He had stepped on the back of a sleeping crocodile.

There was much laughter over this and the breathless earnestness with which he told the story; and Jim and his circus crocodile became the joke of the camp.

*

Although we laughed and chaffed about Jim's experience, I fancy we were all very much on the look-out for rocks that looked like crocs and crocs that looked like rocks.

One of the most difficult lessons that a beginner has to learn is to keep cool. The great, silent bush is so lonely; the strain of being on the look-out all the time is so great; the uncertainty as to what may start up – anything from a partridge to a lion – is so trying, that the beginner is wound up like an alarm clock and goes off at the first touch. He will fire without looking or aiming at all; jerk the rifle as he fires; forget to change the sight after the last shot; forget to cock his gun or move the safety catch; forget to load, forget to fire at all. Nothing is impossible – nothing too silly.

I had started out this day with the determination to keep cool, but, once into the reeds, Jim's account of how he had stepped on the crocodile put all other thoughts out of my mind. Most of my attention was given to examining suspicious-looking rocks as we stole silently and quietly along.

Jock was with me, as usual. I always took him out even then – not for hunting, because he was too young, but in order to train him. He was still only a puppy, about six months old, and had never tackled or even followed a wounded buck, so that it was impossible to say what he would do. He had seen me shoot a couple and had wanted to worry them as they fell; but that was all. He was quite obedient and kept his place behind me; and, although he trembled with excitement when he saw or heard anything, he never rushed in or moved ahead of me without permission. The guinea-fowl tormented him that day. He could scent and hear them, and was constantly making little runs forward, half crouching and with his nose back and tail dead level, one ear full-cocked and the other half-up.

For about half an hour we went on in this way. There was plenty of fresh duiker spoor to show us that we were in a likely place, one spoor in particular being so fresh in the mud that it seemed only a few minutes old. We were following this one very eagerly but very cautiously, and evidently Jock agreed with me that the duiker must be near, for he took no more notice of the guinea-fowl; and I, for my part, forgot all about crocodiles and suspicious-looking rocks. There was at that moment only one thing in the world for me, and that was the duiker.

We crept along noiselessly in and out of the reeds, round rocks and mudholes, across small stretches of firm mud or soft sand, so silently that nothing could have heard us. Finally we came to a very big rock, with the duiker spoor fresher than ever going close round it down stream. The rock was a long sloping one, polished smooth by the floods and very slippery to walk on. I climbed it in dead silence, peering down into the reeds and expecting every moment to see the duiker.

The slope up which we crept was long and easy, but that on the down-stream side was much steeper. I crawled up to the top on hands and knees, and raising myself slowly, looked carefully about, but no duiker could be seen; yet Jock was sniffing and trembling more than ever, and it was quite clear that he thought we were very close up. Seeing nothing in front or on either side, I stood right up and turned to look back the way we had come and examine the reeds on that side. In doing so a few grains of grit crunched under my foot, and instantly there was a rush in the reeds behind me. I jumped round to face it, believing that the crocodile was grabbing at me from behind, and on the polished surface of the rock my feet slipped and shot from under me. Both bare elbows bumped hard on the rock, jerking the rifle out of my hands; and I was launched like a torpedo right into the mass of swaying reeds.

When you think you are tumbling on to a crocodile there is only one thing you want to do – get out as soon as possible. How long it took to reach the top of the rock again, goodness only knows! It seemed like a lifetime. But the fact is I was out of those reeds and up that rock in time to see the duiker as it broke out of the reeds, raced up the bank, and disappeared into the bush with Jock tearing after it as hard as ever he could go.

One call stopped him, and he came back to me looking very crestfallen and guilty, no doubt thinking that he had behaved badly and disgraced himself. But he was not to blame at all. He had known all along that the duiker was there – having had no distracting fancies about crocodiles – and when he saw it dash off and his master instantly jump in after it, he must have thought that the hunt had at last begun and that he was expected to help.

After all that row and excitement there was not much use in trying for anything more in the reeds – and indeed I had had quite enough of them for one afternoon. So we wandered along the upper banks in the hope of finding something where there were no crocodiles, and it was not long before we were interested in something else and able to forget all about the duiker.

Before we had been walking many minutes, Jock raised his head and ears and then lowered himself into a half-crouching attitude and made a little run forward. I looked promptly in the direction he was pointing and about two hundred yards away saw a stembuck standing in the shade of a mimosa bush, feeding briskly on the buffalo grass. It was so small and in such bad light that the shot was too difficult for me at that distance, and I crawled along behind bushes, ant-heaps and trees until we were close enough. The ground was soft and sandy, and we could get along

easily enough without making any noise; but all the time, while thinking how lucky it was to be on ground so soft for the hands and knees, and so easy to move without being heard, something else was happening.

With eyes fixed on the buck I did not notice that in crawling along on all-fours, the muzzle of the rifle dipped regularly into the sand, picking up a little in the barrel each time. There was not enough to burst the rifle, but the effect was surprising. Following on a painfully careful aim, there was a deafening report that made my head reel and buzz; the kick of the rifle on the shoulder and cheek left me blue for days; and when my eyes were clear enough to see anything the stembuck had disappeared.

I was too disgusted to move, and sat in the sand rubbing my shoulder and thanking my stars that the rifle had not burst. There was plenty to think about, to be sure, and no hurry to do anything else, for the noise of the shot must have startled every living thing for a mile round.

It is not always easy to tell the direction from which a report comes when you are near a river or in broken country or patchy bush; and it is not uncommon to find that a shot which has frightened one animal away from you has startled another and driven it towards you. That is what happened in this case.

As I sat in the shade of the thorns with the loaded rifle across my knees there was the faint sound of a buck cantering along in the sand. I looked up, and only about twenty yards from me a duiker came to a stop, half fronting me. There it stood looking back over its shoulder and listening intently, evidently thinking that the danger lay behind it. It was hardly possible to miss that, and as the duiker rolled over, I dropped my rifle and ran to make sure of it.

Of course, it was dead against the rules to leave the rifle behind. But it was simply a case of excitement again : when the buck rolled over everything else was forgotten! I knew the rule perfectly well – reload at once and never part with your gun. Unfortunately I did not remember it when it would have been useful.

As I ran forward the duiker tumbled, struggled and rolled over and over, then got up and made a dash, only to dive head foremost into the sand and somersault over. But in a second it was up again and racing off, again to trip and plunge forward on to its chest with its nose outstretched sliding along the soft ground. The bullet had struck it in the shoulder, and the broken leg was tripping it and bringing it down; but, the little fellow, scrambling once more to its feet, was off on three legs at a pace that left me far behind.

Jock, remembering the mistake in the reeds, kept his place behind, and I in the excitement of the moment neither saw nor thought of him until the duiker, gaining at every jump, looked like vanishing for ever. Then I remembered and, with a frantic wave of my hand, shouted, 'After him, Jock.'

He was gone before my hand was down, and faster than I had ever seen him move, leaving me ploughing through the heavy sand far behind. Past the big bush I saw them again, and there the duiker did as wounded game so often do: taking advantage of cover it changed direction and turned away for some dense thorns.

But that suited Jock exactly. He took the short cut across to head it off and was close up in a few more strides. He caught up to it, raced up beside it, and made a jump at its throat, but the duiker darted away in a fresh direction, leaving him yards behind. Again he was after it and tried the other side, but the buck was too quick, and again he missed and overshot the mark in his jump. He was in such deadly earnest he seemed to turn in the air and get back again and once more was close up – so close that the flying heels of the buck seemed to pass each side of his ears. Then he made his spring from behind, catching the duiker high up on one hind leg, and the two rolled over together, kicking and struggling in a cloud of dust. Time after time the duiker got on its feet, trying to get at him with its horns or to break away again; but Jock, although swung off his feet and rolled on, did not let go his grip. In grim silence he hung on while the duiker plunged, and, when it fell, tugged and worried as if to shake the the life out of it.

What with the hot sun, the heavy sand, and the pace at which we had gone, I was so pumped that I finished the last hundred yards at a walk, and had plenty of time to see what was going on. But even when I got up to them the struggle was so fierce and the movements so quick that for

some time it was not possible to get hold of the duiker to finish it off.

At last came one particularly bad fall, when the buck rolled over on its back, and then Jock let go his grip and made a dash for its throat. But again the duiker was too quick for him. With one twist it was up and round facing him on its one knee. It dug, thrust and swept with its black spiky horns so vigorously that it was impossible to get at its neck. As Jock rushed in the head ducked and the horns flashed round so swiftly that it seemed as if nothing could save him from being stabbed through and through; but his quickness and cleverness were a revelation to me. If he could not catch the duiker, it could not catch him. They were in a way too quick for each other, and they were a long way too quick for me.

Time after time I tried to get in close enough to grab one of the buck's hind legs, but it was not to be caught. While Jock was at it fast and furious in front, I tried to creep up quietly behind – but it was no use. The duiker kept facing Jock with horns down, and whenever I moved it swung round and kept me in front also.

Finally I tried a run straight in, and then it made another dash for liberty. On three legs, however, it had no chance, and in another minute Jock had it again, and down they came together, rolling over and over. Each time it got its feet to the ground to rise Jock would tug sideways and roll it over again. The duiker struggled hard, but Jock hung on until I got up to them. Catching the buck by the head, I held it down with my knee on its neck and my Bushman's Friend in hand to finish it.

There was, however, still another lesson for us both to learn that day: neither of us knew what a buck can do with its hind feet when it is down.

The duiker was flat on its side. Jock, thinking the fight was over, had let go. Before I could move the supple body doubled up, and the feet whizzed viciously at me right over its head. The little pointed cloven feet are as hard and sharp as horns and will tear the flesh like claws. By good luck the kick only grazed my arm, but although the touch was the lightest it cut the skin and little beads of blood shot up marking the line like the scratch of a thorn. Missing my arm the hoof struck full on the handle of the Bushman's Friend and sent it flying out of reach. And it was not merely one kick. Faster than the eye could follow them the little feet whizzed and the legs seemed to buzz round like the spokes of a wheel.

Holding the horns at arm's length in order to dodge the kicks, I tried to pull the duiker towards the knife; but it was too much for me, and with a sudden twist and a wrench it freed itself and was off again.

All the time Jock was moving round and round panting

and licking his chops, stepping in and stepping back, giving anxious little whimpers, and longing to be at it again – but not daring to join in without permission. When the duiker broke away, however, he waited for nothing, and was on to it in one spring – again from behind; and this time he let go as it fell, and jumping free of it, had it by the throat before it could rise. I ran to them again, but the picking up of the knife had delayed me and I was not in time to save Jock the same lesson that the duiker had just taught me.

Down on its side, with Jock's jaws locked in its throat once more, the duiker doubled up and used its feet. The first kick went over Jock's head and scraped harmlessly along his back; but the second caught him at the point of the shoulder, and the razor-like toe ripped his side right to the hip. Then the dog showed his pluck and cleverness. His side was cut open as if it had been slashed by a knife, but he never flinched or loosened his grip for a second. He seemed to go at it more furiously than ever, but more cleverly and warily. He swung his body round clear of the whizzing feet, watching them with his little beady eyes fixed sideways and the gleaming whites showing in the corners. He tugged away incessantly and vigorously, keeping the buck's neck

stretched out and pulling it round in a circle backwards so that it could not possibly double its body up enough to kick him again; and before I could catch the feet to help him, the kicks grew weaker, the buck slackened out, and Jock had won.

The sun was hot, the sand was deep and the rifle was hard to find. It was a long way back to the wagons, and the duiker made a heavy load. But the end of that first chase seemed so good that nothing else mattered. The only thing I did mind was the open cut on Jock's side. But he minded nothing : his tail was going like a telegraph needle; he was panting with his mouth open from ear to ear; and his red tongue was hanging out and making great slapping licks at his chops from time to time. He was not still for a second, but kept walking in and stepping back in a circle round the duiker and looking up at me and then down at it, as if he was consulting me as to whether it would not be a good thing to have another go in and make it all safe.

He was just as happy as a dog could be, and perhaps he was proud of the wound that left a straight line from his shoulder to his hip, and showed up like a cord under the golden brindle as long as he lived – a memento of his first real hunt.

In the Heart of the Bush

WHEN the hen pecked Jock on the nose, she gave him a useful lesson in the art of finding out what you want to know without getting into trouble. As he got older, he also learned that there were only certain things which concerned him and which it was necessary for him to know. A young dog begins by thinking that he can do everything, go everywhere and know everything – but a hunting dog has to learn to mind his own business as well as to understand it. Some dogs turn sulky or timid or stupid when they are checked, but an intelligent dog with a stout heart will learn little by little to leave other things alone, and grow steadily keener on his own work.

There was no mistake about Jock's keenness. When I took down the rifle from the wagon he did not go off into ecstasies of barking, as most sporting dogs will do. He would give a quick look up and, with an eager little run towards me, give a whimper of joy and make two or three bounds as if wanting to stretch his muscles and loosen his joints; then he would shake himself vigorously as though he had just come out of the water, and, with a soft suppressed 'Woo-woo-woo' full of contentment, drop silently into his place at my heels and give his whole attention to his work.

He was the best of companions, and through the years that we hunted together I never tired of watching him. There was always something to learn, something to admire, something to be grateful for, and very often something to laugh at – in the way in which we laugh only at those whom we are fond of.

It was the struggle between Jock's intense keenness and his sense of duty that most often raised the laugh. He knew that his place was behind me; but probably he also knew that nine times out of ten he scented or saw the game long before I knew there was anything near; and naturally he wanted to be in front or at least abreast of me to show me whatever there was to be seen.

He noticed, just as surely and as quickly as any human being could, any change in my manner. Nothing escaped him, for his eyes and ears were on the move the whole time. It was impossible for me to look for more than a few seconds in any one direction, or to stop or even to turn my head to listen, without being caught by him. His bright, brown eyes were everlastingly on the watch: from me to the bush, from the bush back to me.

When we were after game, and he could scent or see it, he would keep a foot or two to the side of me so as to have a clear view; and when he knew by my manner that I thought there was game near, he kept so close up that he would often bump against my heels as I walked, or run right into my legs if I stopped suddenly. Often when stalking buck very quietly and cautiously, thinking only of what was in front, I would get quite a start by feeling something bump up against me behind. At these times it was impossible to say anything without risk of scaring the game, and I got into a habit of making signs with my hand which he understood quite as well.

Sometimes, after having crawled up, I would be in the act of aiming when he would press against me. Nothing puts one off so much as a touch or the expectation of being jogged when in the act of firing. I used to get angry with him then, but dared not breathe a word. I would lower my head slowly, turn round and give him a look. He knew quite well what it meant. Down would go his ears instantly, and he would back away from me a couple of steps, drop his stump of a tail and wag it in a feeble deprecating way, and open his mouth into a sort of foolish laugh. That was his apology!

It was quite impossible to be angry with him, he was so keen and he meant so well; and when he saw me laughing

softly at him, he would come up again close to me, cock his tail a few inches higher and wag it a bit faster.

There is a great deal of expression in a dog's tail. It will generally tell you what his feelings are. That is certainly how I knew what Jock was thinking about once when lost in the veld — and it showed me the way back.

*

It is easy enough to lose oneself in the Bushveld. The Berg stands up some thousands of feet inland on the west, looking as if it had been put there to hold up the Highveld. Between the foothills and the sea lies the Bushveld, stretching for hundreds of miles north and south. From the height and distance of the Berg it looks as flat as the floor, but in many parts it is very much cut up by deep rough dongas, sharp rises and depressions, and numbers of small kopjes. Still, it has a way of looking flat, because the hills are small, and very much alike; and because hill and hollow are

66

covered and hidden mile after mile by small trees of a wonderful sameness, just near enough to prevent you from seeing more than a few hundred yards at a time.

Nearly everyone who goes hunting in the Bushveld gets lost some time or other – generally in the beginning before he has learned to notice things. Some have been lost for many days until they blundered on to a track by accident, or were found by a search party. Others have been lost and, finding no water or food, have died. Others have been killed by lions, and only a boot or a coat, or – in one case that I know of – a ring found inside a lion, told what had occurred. Others have been lost and nothing more ever heard of them.

There is no feeling quite like that of being lost – helplessness, terror and despair! But no one, who has not seen it, would believe the effect that this terror – and the demoralization which it causes – can have on a sane man's senses.

How, you will ask, can it be possible to cross a big dusty road twenty or thirty feet wide without seeing it? Impossible, quite impossible, you think. But it is a fact and I have witnessed it twice myself, once in Mashonaland and once on the Delagoa road. I saw men – tired, haggard and wild-eyed, staring in front of them, never looking at the ground, pressing on, on, on – actually cross well-worn wagon roads. They came from hard veld into a sandy wheelworn track, kicked up a cloud of dust as they passed, and were utterly blind to the fact that they were walking across the roads they had been searching for – in one case for ten hours and in the other for three days. When we called to them they had already crossed and were disappearing again into the bush. In both cases the sound of the human voice and the relief of being 'found' made them collapse. The knees seemed to give way : they could not remain standing.

When the camp is away in the trackless bush, it needs a good man always to find the way home after a couple of hours' chase with all its twists and turns and doublings. But when camp is made on a known road it seems impossible for anyone to be hopelessly lost. If the road runs east and west, knowing on which side you left it, you have only to walk north or south steadily and you must strike it again. There is only one rule to remember: When you have lost your way, don't lose your head.

The man who loses his head is really lost. He cannot think, remember, reason or understand. And the strangest thing of all is that he often cannot even *see* properly. He fails to see the very things that he most wants to see, even when they are as large as life before him.

We were out hunting once in a mounted party, but to spare a tired horse I went on foot. Among our party there was one who was very nervous. He had been lost once for six or eight hours, and, being haunted by the dread of being lost again, his nerve was all gone. He would not go fifty yards without a companion. In the excitement of the chase, however, this dread was forgotten for a moment, and he became separated from the rest.

The strip of wood where I was waiting was four or five miles long but only one to three hundred yards wide. Between the stems of the trees I could see our camp and wagons in the open a quarter of a mile away. Shots faintly heard in the distance told me that the others were on to something and I took cover behind a big stump and waited. For over half an hour, however, nothing came towards me and, believing that the game had broken off another way, I was about to return to camp when I heard the tapping of galloping feet; and soon afterwards I saw a man on horse-back. He was leaning forward and thumping the exhausted horse with his rifle and his heels to keep up its staggering gallop. I looked about quickly to see what it was that he was chasing, but there was nothing; so I stepped out into the open and waited for him to come up. I stood quite still, and he galloped past within ten yards of me.

'What's up, sportsman?' I called. The words brought him

up, white-faced and terrified, and he half slid, half tumbled off the horse, gasping out, 'I was lost, I was lost.'

I turned him round where he stood, and through the trees showed him the wagons and cattle grazing near by – but he was too dazed to understand or explain anything.

There are many kinds of men. That particular kind is not the kind that will ever do for veld life : they are for other things and other work. You will laugh at them at times – but see it! See it – and realize the suspense, the strain and the terror. And there will come the little chilling thought that the strongest, the bravest and the best have known something of it too.

*

Buggins, who was with us in the first season, showed us, as in a play, how you can be lost; how you can walk for ever in one little circle, as though drawn to a centre by magnetic force; and how you can miss seeing things in the bush. In his case there was no tragedy : there was much laughter and – to me – a wonderful revelation.

Buggins – that was his pet name – was returning to England, to a comfortable home, admiring sisters and a rich indulgent father, after having sought his fortune unsuccessfully on the gold-fields for fully four months. He was good-natured, unselfish and credulous; he was no hunter but he was a good shot and not a bad fellow. But he had one fault – he 'yapped' : he talked till our heads buzzed. He used to sleep contentedly all through the night treks and come up fresh as a daisy and full of accumulated chat at the morning outspan, just when we were wanting to get some sleep.

We had had a very long early morning trek and the wagons were drawn up a few yards off the road. The day was hot and still, the grass sweet and plentiful and the cattle soon filled themselves and lay down to sleep. The boys did the same, and we, when breakfast was over, got into the shade of the wagons, some to sleep and others to smoke.

We knew well enough what to expect, so Jimmy, who understood Buggins well, told him pleasantly that he could 'sleep, shoot or shut up'. To shut up was impossible, and to sleep again was difficult, even for Buggins. So, with a good-natured laugh, he took the shot-gun, saying that he 'would potter around a bit and give us a treat'. Well, he did!

We had outspanned on the edge of an open space in the thorn bush. There are plenty of them to be found in the Bushveld – spaces a few hundred yards in diameter, like open park land, where not a single tree breaks the expanse

of wavy grass. The wagons with their greyish tents and bucksails and dusty wood-work stood in the fringe of the trees where this little arena touched the road, and into it sallied Buggins.

He had been gone for more than half an hour when we heard a shot, and a few minutes later Jimmy's voice roused us.

'What the dickens is Buggins doing?' he asked in a tone so puzzled and interested that we all turned to watch. According to Jimmy, he had been walking about in an erratic way for some time on the far side of the open ground – going from one end to the other and then back again, then disappearing for a few minutes in the bush and reappearing again to manœuvre in the open. Now he was walking about at a smart pace, looking from side to side apparently searching for something.

We could see the whole of the arena as clearly as you can see a cricket-field from the railings – but we could see nothing to explain Buggins's manœuvres. Next we saw him face the thorns opposite, raise his gun very deliberately, and fire into the top of the trees.

'Green pigeons,' said Jimmy firmly, and we all agreed that Buggins was after specimens for stuffing. But either our guess was wrong or his aim was bad, for after standing dead still for a minute he resumed his vigorous walk.

By this time Buggins fairly fascinated us. Even the boys had roused each other and were watching him. Away he went at once off to our left, and there he repeated the per-

formance. But, again he made no attempt to pick up anything and showed no further interest in whatever it was
that he had fired at. He turned right about face and walked
across the open ground in our direction until he was only a
couple of hundred yards away. There he stopped and began
to look about him and, making off some few yards in another direction, climbed on to a fair-sized ant-heap five or
six feet high. Balancing himself cautiously on this he deliberately fired off both barrels in quick succession. Then
the same idea struck us all together, 'Buggins is lost' came
from several – all choking with laughter.

Jimmy got up and, stepping out into the open beside the
wagon, called, 'Say, Buggins, what in thunder *are* you
doing?'

To see Buggins slide off the ant-heap and shuffle shame-
facedly back to the wagon before a gallery of four white
men and a lot of natives, all cracking and crying with
laughter, was a sight never to be forgotten.

So far I had never lost my way out hunting. The experiences of other men and warnings from the old hands had
made me very careful. But day after day and month after
month went by without accident or serious difficulty, and
then the same old thing happened: familiarity bred contempt. Each day I went further and more boldly off the
road, and grew more confident and careless.

The very last thing that would have occurred to me on
this particular day was that there was any chance of being
lost or any need to take note of where we went. For many
weeks we had been hunting in exactly the same sort of
country – but not of course in the same part – and I did not
give the matter a thought at all.

Lost in the Veld

WE were outspanned near some deep shaded water-holes, and at about three o'clock I took my rifle and wandered off in the hope of dropping across something for the larder and having some sport during the three hours before the evening trek would begin; and as there was plenty of spoor of many kinds the prospects seemed good enough.

We had been going along slowly, it may be for half an hour, without seeing more than a little stembuck scurrying away in the distance, when I noticed that Jock was rather busy with his nose, sniffing about in a way that looked like business. He was not sure of anything, that was clear, because he kept trying in different directions; not as you see a pointer do, but very seriously, silently and slowly, moving at a cautious walk for a few yards and then taking a look about.

The day was hot and still, as usual at that time of the year, and any noise would be easily heard, so I had stopped to give Jock a chance of ranging about. At the moment we were in rather open ground, and finding that Jock was still very suspicious I moved on towards where the bush was thicker and we were less likely to be seen from a distance. As we got near the better cover there was a rasping, squawky cry in a cockatoo's voice, 'Go 'way; go 'way; go 'way!' and one of those ugly big-beaked Go 'way birds came sailing up from behind and flapped on to the trees we were making for.

No doubt they have another name, but in the Bushveld they were known as Go 'way birds, because of this cry and because they are supposed to warn the game when an enemy is coming. I do not believe they care a rap about the game; they only want to worry you. Often one of them will make up its mind to stick to you, and you can turn, twist and double as many ways as you like, but as soon as you begin to walk on again the wretched thing will fly over your head and perch twenty yards or so in front of you, screeching out 'Go 'way' at the top of its voice. There it will sit ready to fly off again as you come on, its ugly head on one side and big hooked bill like an aggressive nose, watching you mercilessly. They seem to know that you cannot shoot them without making more row and doing more harm than they do.

I stood still for a few minutes to give this one a chance to fly away, and when it would not do so, but kept on screeching and craning its neck at me, I threw a stone at it. It ducked violently and gave a choking hysterical squawk of alarm and anger as the stone whizzed close to its head; then flying on to another tree a few yards off, screamed away more noisily than ever. Evidently the best thing to do was to go ahead taking no notice of the creature and trusting that it would tire and leave me alone. So I walked off briskly.

There was a slight rustling in the bush ahead of us as I stepped out, and then the sound of feet. I made a dash for the chance of a running shot, but it was too late, and all we saw was half a dozen beautiful kudu disappearing among the tree stems.

I turned towards that Go 'way bird. Perhaps he did not like the look on my face or the way I held the rifle; for he gave one more snarling shriek, as if he was emptying himself for ever of his rage and spite, and flapped away.

Jock was standing like a statue, leaning slightly forward but with head very erect, jaws tightly closed, eyes looking straight in front, as bright as black diamonds.

It was a bad disappointment, for that was the first time we had fairly and squarely come upon kudu. However, it was still early and the game had not been scared, but had gone off quietly. So, hoping for another chance, we started off at a trot along the fresh spoor.

A big kudu bull stands as high as a bullock, and although they have the small shapely feet of an antelope the spoor is heavy enough to follow at a trot except on stony ground. Perhaps they know this, for they certainly prefer the rough hard ground when they can get it.

We went along at a good pace, but with many short breaks to make sure of the spoor in the stony parts; and it was pretty hot work, although clothing was light for hunting. A rough flannel shirt, open at the throat, and moleskin trousers dyed with coffee – for khaki was unknown to us then – was the usual wear; and we carried as little as possible. Generally a water-bottle filled with unsweetened cold tea and a cartridge belt were all we took beside the rifle. This time I had less than usual. Meaning to be out only for a couple of hours at most and to stick close to the road, I had pocketed half a dozen cartridges and left both bandolier and water-bottle behind.

It was not long before we came upon the kudu again; but they were on the watch. They were standing in the fringe of some thick bush, broadside on but looking back full at us, and as soon as I stopped to aim the whole lot disappeared with the same easy movement, just melting away in the bush.

If I had only known it, it was a hopeless chase for an inexperienced hunter. They were simply playing with me. When they allowed us to catch up to them time after time, it was not because they did not expect us. They were keeping in touch with us so that we could not surprise them. Whenever they stopped it was always where they could see us coming through the thinner bush for a long way and where they themselves could disappear in the thick bush in a couple of strides. Moreover, with each fresh run they

changed their direction with the object of making it difficult for us to follow them up, and with the deliberate purpose of eventually reaching some favourite and safe haunt of theirs.

An old hand might have known this; but a beginner goes blindly along the spoor – exactly where they are expecting him. The chase was long and tiring, but there was no thought of giving it up. Each time they came in sight we got keener and more excited, and the end seemed nearer and more certain. I knew what the six animals were – four cows, one young bull and a magnificent old fellow with a glorious head and great spiral horns. I had the old bull marked down as mine, and knew his every detail : his splendid bearing, strong shaggy neck with mane to the withers and bearded throat; the soft grey dove-colour of the coat with its white stripes; the easy balancing movement in carrying the massive horns as he cantered away; and the trick of throwing them back to glide them through the bush.

The grace and poise in the movement of the kudu bull's head as he gallops is one of his distinctions above the other antelopes. One notes the same supple balancing movement in the native girls bearing their calabashes of water upon their heads. The movements of the kudu's body are softened into mere undulations, and the head with its immense

spiral horns seems to sail along almost as though it were bearing the body below.

The last run was a long and hard one, and the kudu seemed to have taken matters seriously and made up their minds to put a safe distance between us and them. The spooring was often difficult and the pace hot. I was wet through from the hard work, and so winded that further efforts seemed almost impossible; but we plodded away – the picture of the kudu bull luring me on, and Jock content with any chase. Without him the spoor would have been lost long before. It was in many places too faint and scattered for me to follow, but he would sniff about quietly, and, by his contented looks back at me and brisk wagging of that stumpy tail, show that he was on it again – and off we would go on another tired straggling trot. But at last even his help was not enough. We had come to the end of the chase, and not a spoor, scratch or sign of any sort was to be seen.

Time had passed unnoticed, and it was only when it became clear that further search would be quite useless that I looked at my watch and found it was nearly five o'clock. That was rather a shock, for it seemed reasonable to think that, as we had been out for pretty nearly two hours – and going fast for most of the time – it would take almost as long to get back again.

I had not once noticed our direction or looked at the sun, yet when it came to make for camp again the idea of losing the way never occurred to me. I had not the slightest doubt about the way we had come, and it seemed the natural thing to go back the same way.

A short distance from where we finally gave up the chase there was a rise crowned by some good-sized rocks and bare of trees. It was not high enough to be fairly called a kopje, but I climbed it on chance of getting a view of the surrounding country – to see, if possible, how far we had come. The rise was sufficient, however, to give a view. There was nothing to be seen, and I sat down on the highest rock to rest for a few minutes and smoke a cigarette.

It is over twenty years since that day, but that cigarette is not forgotten and the little rise where we rested is still, to me, Cigarette Kopje. I was so thoroughly wet from the heat and hard work that the matches in the breast pocket of my shirt were all damp, and the heads came off most of them before one was gently coaxed into giving a light. Five minutes' rest was enough. We both wanted a drink, but there was no time then to hunt for water in such a dry part as that, so off we started for camp and jogged along for a good time, perhaps half an hour. Then little by little I began to feel some uncertainty about the way and to look about from side to side for reminders.

The start back had been easy enough. That part of the ground where we had lost the spoor had been gone over very thoroughly and every object was familiar. But further back, where we had followed the spoor at a trot for long stretches and I had hardly raised my eyes from the ground before me, it was a very different matter. I forgot all about those long stretches in which nothing had been noticed except the kudu spoor, and was unconsciously looking out

for things in regular succession which we had passed at quite long intervals.

Of course, they were not to be found, but I kept on look-ing out for them — first feeling annoyed, then puzzled, then worried. Something had gone wrong, and we were not going back on our old tracks. Several times I looked about for the kudu spoor as a guide. But it might be anywhere over a width of a hundred yards, and it seemed a waste of precious time to search the dry, grass-grown, leaf-strewn ground for that.

At the first puzzled stop I tried to recall some of the more noticeable things we had passed during the chase. There were two flat-topped mimosa, looking like great rustic tables on a lawn, and we had passed between them; there was a large ant-heap, with a twisty top like a crooked mud chimney, behind which the kudu bull had calmly stood watching us approach; then a marula tree with a fork like a giant catapult stick; and so on with a score of other things, all coming readily to mind.

That was what put me hopelessly wrong. I began to look for particular objects instead of taking one direction and keeping to it. Whenever a flat-topped thorn, a quaint ant-heap, a patch of tambookie grass, or a forked marula came in sight, I would turn off to see if they were the same we had passed coming out. It was hopeless folly, of course, for in that country there were hundreds and thousands of such things all looking very much alike. You could walk yourself to death zig-zagging about from one to another and never get any nearer home. When it comes to doing that sort of thing your judgement is gone and you have lost your head – and the worst of it is you do not know it.

As the sun sank lower I hurried on faster, but never long in one line – always turning this way and that to search for the particular marks I had in mind. At last we came to four trees in a line, and my heart gave a great jump, for these we had certainly passed before. In order to make quite sure I hunted for kudu spoor. There was none to be seen, but on an old molehill there was the single print of a dog's foot.

'Ha, Jock's!' I exclaimed aloud, and Jock himself, at the sound of his name, stepped up briskly and sniffed at his own spoor. Close beside it there was the clear mark of a heeled boot, and there were others further on. There was no doubt about it, they were Jock's and mine, and I could have given a whoop of delight – but a chilly feeling came over me when I realized that the footprints were *leading the same way as we were going*, instead of the opposite way. What on earth did it mean?

I laid the rifle down and sat on an old stump to think it out. After puzzling over it for some minutes, I came to the conclusion that, by some stupid blunder, I must have turned round somewhere and followed the line of the kudu, instead

of going back on it. The only thing to be done was to right about face and go faster than ever.

At that moment I had not a shadow of doubt about the way; yet the simple fact is we were not then on the kudu trail at all. Having made a complete circle, we had come on to our own trail at the molehill and were now doing the circle the second time – but the reverse way now.

The length of my shadow stretching out before me as we started from the molehill was a reminder of the need for

Map of 'Lost in the Veld'

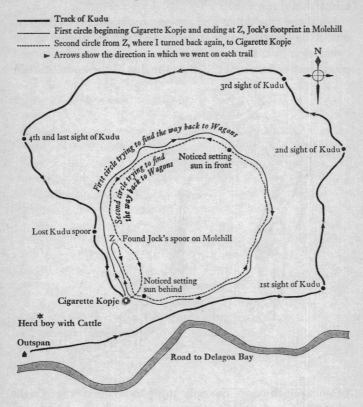

——— Track of Kudu
——— First circle beginning Cigarette Kopje and ending at Z, Jock's footprint in Molehill
.... Second circle from Z, where I turned back again, to Cigarette Kopje
► Arrows show the direction in which we went on each trail

N

3rd sight of Kudu

4th and last sight of Kudu

First circle trying to find the way back to Wagons

2nd sight of Kudu

Second circle to find the way back to Wagons

Noticed setting
sun in front

Lost Kudu spoor

Z Found Jock's spoor on Molehill

Noticed setting
sun behind

1st sight of Kudu

Cigarette Kopje

Herd boy with Cattle

Outspan

Road to Delagoa Bay

haste, and we set off at a smart double. A glance back every
few minutes to make sure that we were returning the way
we had come was enough. On we sped, confident for my
part that we were securely on the line of the kudu and
going straight for the wagons.

It is very difficult to say how long this lasted before once
more a horrible doubt arose. It was when we had done half

the circle that I was pulled up as if struck in the face. The setting sun shining in my eyes as we crossed an open space stopped me. As the bright gold-dust light of the sunset met me full, I remembered that it was my long shadow *in front* of me as we started from the molehill that had urged me to hurry on. We had started due east: we were going dead west!

What on earth was wrong? There were the trees and spaces we had passed, a blackened stump, an ant-bear hole – all familiar. And yet ... and yet, as I went on – no longer trotting and full of hope but walking heavily and weighted with doubt – the feeling of uncertainty grew, until I really did not know whether the familiar-looking objects and scenes were indeed old acquaintances, or merely imagination playing tricks in a country where every style and sample was copied a thousand times over.

A few minutes later I again caught sight of the sunset glow – it was on my direct right. It meant that the trail had taken another turn, while I could have sworn we were holding a course straight as an arrow. It was all a hopeless tangle. I was lost then – and knew it.

It was not the dread of a night out in the bush – for after many months of roughing it, that had no great terrors for me – but the hopeless feeling of being lost and the anxiety and uncertainty about finding the road again, that gnawed at me. I wondered when they would begin to look for me, if they would light big fires and fire shots, and if it would be possible to see or hear the signals. The light would not last much longer. The dimness, the silence and the hateful doubts about the trail made it more and more difficult to recognize the line. So I thought it was time to fire a signal shot.

There was no answer. It was silly to hope for one, for even if it had been heard they would only have thought that I was shooting at something. Yet the clinging to hope was so strong that every twenty yards or so I stopped to listen for a reply; and when, after what seemed an eternity, none came, I fired another.

When you shoot in the excitement of the chase the noise of the report does not strike you as anything out of the way. But a signal shot when you are alone and lost seems to fill the world with sound and to shake the earth itself. It has a most chilling effect, and the feeling of loneliness becomes acute as the echoes die away and still no answer comes.

Another short spell of tip-toe walking and intent listening, and then it came to me that one shot as a signal was useless. I should have fired more and at regular intervals. I felt in my pocket: there were only four cartridges there and one in the rifle. There was night before me, with the hyenas and the lions. There was the food for tomorrow, and perhaps more than tomorrow! Two shots were all that could be spared, and I looked about for some high and open ground where the sound would travel far and wide.

On ahead of us to the right the trees seemed fewer and the light stronger, and there I came upon some rising ground bare of bush. It was not much for my purpose, but it was higher than the rest and quite open, and there were some rocks scattered about the top. The same old feeling of mixed remembrance and doubt came over me as we climbed it : it looked familiar and yet different. Was it memory or imagination?

But there was no time for wonderings. From the biggest rock, which was only waist high, I fired off two of my precious cartridges, and stood like a statue listening for the reply. The silence seemed worse than before. The birds had gone to roost. Even the flies had disappeared. There was no sound at all but the beat of my own heart and Jock's panting breath.

There were three cartridges and a few damp matches left. There was no sun to dry them now, but I laid them out carefully on the smooth warm rock, and hoped that one at least would serve to light our camp fire. There was no time to waste. While the light lasted I had to drag up wood for the fire and pick a place for the camp — somewhere where the rocks behind and the fire in front would shelter us from the lions and hyenas, and where I could watch and listen for signals in the night.

There was plenty of wood near by, and thinking anxiously of the damp matches I looked about for dry tindery grass so that any spark would give a start for the fire. As

I stooped to look for the grass I came on a patch of bare ground between the scattered tufts, and in the middle of it there lay a half-burnt match. Such a flood of relief and hope surged up that my heart beat up in my throat. Where there were matches there had been men! We were not in the wilds, then, where white men seldom went — not off the beaten track, perhaps not far from the road itself.

You must experience it to know what it meant at that moment. It drew me on to look for more! A yard away I found the burnt end of a cigarette, and before there was time to realize why that should seem queer, I came on eight or ten matches with their heads knocked off.

For a moment things seemed to go round and round. I sat down with my back against the rock and a funny choky feeling in my throat. I knew they were my matches and cigarette, and that we were exactly where we had started from hours before, when we gave up the chase of the kudu.

I began to understand things then : why places and land-marks seemed familiar; why Jock's spoor in the molehill had pointed the wrong way; why my shadow was in front and behind and beside me in turns. We had been going round in a circle. Why, this was the fourth time we had been on or close to some part of this same rise that day, each time within fifty yards of the same place. It was the second time I had sat on that very rock. And there was nothing odd or remarkable about that either, for each time I had been looking for the highest point to spy from and had naturally picked the rock-topped rise – but I had not recognized it.

It seems incredible that one could be so near and not see or understand. Why should one walk in circles instead of taking a fairly straight line? How was it possible to pass Cigarette Kopje and not recognize it? The answer is that the bush does not allow you to see much and things do not look the same unless seen from the same point. When coming towards Cigarette Kopje from a new side it must have looked quite different – and besides that, I had not been expecting it, not looking for it, not even thinking of it. As for walking in circles, it is my belief that most people just like most horses, have a natural leaning or tendency towards one side or the other, and, unless checked, unconsciously in-dulge it.

All at once it seemed as if my eyes were opened and all was clear at last. I knew what to do : just make the best of it for the night; listen for shots and watch for fires; and if by morning no help came, then strike a line due south for the road and follow it up until we found the wagons. The relief of really understanding was so great that the thought of a night out no longer worried me.

There was enough wood gathered, and I stretched out on the grass to rest as there was nothing else to do. We were both tired out, hot, dusty and very thirsty, but it was too late to hunt for water then. I was lying on my side chewing a grass stem, and Jock lay down in front of me a couple of feet away. It was a habit of his. He liked to watch my face, and often when I rolled over to ease one side and lie on the other, he would get up when he found my back turned to him and come round deliberately to the other side and sling himself down in front of me again. There he would

lie with his hind legs sprawled on one side, his front legs straight out, and his head resting on his paws. He would lie like that without a move, his little dark eyes fixed on mine all the time until the stillness and the rest made him sleepy, and he would blink and blink, like a drowsy child, fighting against sleep until it beat him.

In the loneliness of that evening I looked into his steadfast resolute face with its darker muzzle and bright faithful eyes that looked so soft and brown when there was nothing to do, but got so beady black when it came to fighting. I felt very friendly to the comrade who was little more than a puppy still – and he seemed to feel something too. As I lay there chewing the straw and looking at him, he stirred his stump of a tail in the dust an inch or so from time to time, to let me know that he understood all about it and that it was all right as long as we were together.

But an interruption came. Jock suddenly switched up his head, put it a bit sideways as a man would do, listening over his shoulder with his nose rather up in the air. I watched him, and thinking that it was probably only a buck out to feed in the cool of the evening, I tickled his nose with the long straw, saying, 'No good, old chap; only three cartridges left. We must keep them.'

No dog likes to have his nose tickled. It makes them sneeze and many dogs get quite offended, because it hurts their dignity. Jock was not offended but he got up and, as if

to show me that I was frivolous and not attending properly to business, turned away from me and with his ears cocked began to listen again.

He was standing slightly in front of me and I happened to notice his tail. It was not moving. It was drooping slightly and was perfectly still. He kept it like that as he stepped quietly forward on to another sloping rock overlooking a side where we had not yet been. Evidently there was something there, but he did not know what, and he wanted to find out.

I watched him, much amused by his calm business-like manner. He walked to the edge of the rock and looked out. For a few minutes he stood stock-still with his ears cocked and his tail motionless – then his ears dropped and his tail wagged gently from side to side.

Instinctively I understood and I jumped up, thinking, 'He sees something that he knows: he is pleased.' As I walked over to him, he looked back at me with his mouth open and tongue out, his ears still down and tail wagging – he was smiling all over, in his own way. I looked out over his head and there, about three hundred yards off, were the oxen peacefully grazing and the herd boy in his red coat lounging along behind them.

Shame at losing myself and dread of the others' chaff kept me very quiet, and all they knew for many months was that we had had a long fruitless chase after kudu and hard work to get back in time.

I had had my lesson, and did not require to have it rubbed in and be roasted as Buggins had been. Only Jock and I knew all about it; but once or twice there were anxious nervous moments when it looked as if we were not the only ones in the secret. The big Zulu driver, Jim Makokel' – always interested in hunting and all that concerned Jock – asked me as we were inspanning what I had fired the last two shots at. As I pretended not to hear or to notice the question, he went on to say how he had told the other boys that it must been a klipspringer on a high rock or a monkey or a bird, because the bullets had whistled over the wagons. I told him to inspan and not talk so much, and moved round to the other side of the wagon.

That night I slept hard, but woke up once dreaming that several lions were looking down at me from the top of a big flat rock and Jock was keeping them off.

Jock was in his usual place beside me, lying against my blankets. I gave him an extra pat for the dream, thinking, 'Good old boy; we know all about it, you and I, and we're not going to tell. But we've learned some things that we won't forget.' And as I dropped off to sleep again I felt a few feeble sleepy pats against my leg, and knew it was Jock's tail wagging 'Good night'.

The Impala Stampede

NOT all our days were spent in excitement – far, far from it. For six or seven months the rains were too heavy, the heat too great, the grass too rank, and the fever too bad in the Bushveld for anyone to do any good there. So for more than half of the year we had no hunting to speak of, as there was not much to be done above the Berg.

But even during the hunting season there were many off-days and long spells when we never fired a shot. The work with the wagons was hard when we had full loads. The trekking was slow and at night, so that there was always something to do in the daytime – repairs to be done, oxen to be doctored, grass and water to be looked for and so on; and we had to make up sleep when we could.

So Jock and I had many a long spell when there was no hunting; many a bad day when we worked hard but had no sport; and many a good day when we got what we were after and nothing happened that would interest anyone else.

Every hunt was exciting and interesting for us, even those in which we got nothing. To tell all that happened would be to tell the same old story many times over – but, indeed, it would not be possible to tell all, for there were some things which only Jock knew.

After the fight with the duiker there was never any doubt as to what he would do if allowed to follow up a wounded animal. It made a deal of difference in the hunting to know that he could be trusted to find it and hold on or bay it until I could get up. The bush was so thick that it was not possible to see more than a very few hundred yards at best, and the country was so dry and rough that if a wounded animal once got out of sight only an expert tracker had any chance of finding it again.

Jock soon showed himself to be better than the best of trackers. Besides never losing the trail he would either pull down the buck or, if too big for that, attack and worry even the biggest of them to such an extent that they would have to keep turning on him to protect themselves. He would thus give me the chance to catch up.

But the first result of my confidence in him was some perfectly hopeless chases. Whenever a bullet struck with a thud, I – the enthusiastic beginner – thought that it must have wounded the buck. Once you get the idea that the buck is hit, there is hardly anything that the buck can do which does not seem to you to prove that it is wounded. It bounds into the air, races off suddenly, or goes away quite slowly; it switches its tail or shakes its head; it stops to look back, or does not stop at all; the spoor looks awkward and scrappy; the rust on the grass looks like dry blood. All these things will, in fact, mean exactly what you want them to mean.

Poor old Jock had a few hard chases after animals which I thought were wounded but were not hit at all – not many, however, for he soon got hold of the right idea and was a better judge than his master. He went off the instant he was sent, but if there was nothing wounded – that is, if he could not pick up a 'blood spoor' – he would soon show it by casting across the trail, instead of following hard on it. I knew then that there was nothing in it.

Often he would come back of his own accord, and when

he returned from these wild-goose chases he would come up to me with his mouth wide open and tongue out, a bit blown, and stand still with his front legs wide apart. He would look up at me with a peculiar look in his eyes and not a movement in his ears or tail and never a turn of his head to show the least interest in anything else. I got to know that look quite well, and to me it meant, 'No good: you were quite wrong. You missed the whole lot of them.'

What always seemed to me so curious and full of meaning was that he never once looked back in the direction of the

unwounded game, but seemed to put them out of his mind altogether as of no further interest.

It was very different when he got on to the trail of a wounded buck and I had to call him off – as was sometimes necessary when the chase looked hopeless or it was too late to go further. He would obey, of course, but he would follow me in a sort of sideways trot, looking back over his shoulder all the time. Whenever there was a stop, he would turn right round and stare intently in the direction of the game, with his little tail moving steadily from side to side and his hind legs crouched as if ready to spring off the instant he got permission.

Twice I thought he was lost for ever through following

wounded game. The first occasion was also the first time that we got among the impala and saw them in numbers.

There is no more beautiful and fascinating sight than that of a troop of impala really on the move and jumping in earnest. The height and distance that they clear is simply incredible. Every hunter has seen a whole troop, old and young, following the example of the leader, clear a road or donga twenty feet wide, apparently in an effortless stride. It is a fine sight, and the steady stream of buck makes an arch of red and white bodies over the road, like the curve

of a great wave. Then suddenly you see one animal – for no apparent reason – take off away back behind the others, shoot up, and sail high above the arch of all the rest, and with head erect and feet comfortably gathered, land far beyond them. Something is wrung from you – a word, a gasp – and you stand breathless with wonder and admiration until the last one is gone. You have forgotten to shoot; but they have left you something better than a trophy – a picture that will fill your mind whenever you hear the name Impala.

Something of this I carried away from my first experience among them. There were a few minutes of complete bewilderment, a scene of the wildest confusion, and flashes of incident that go to make a great picture which it is impossible to forget. But then there followed many hours of keen anxiety when I believed that Jock was gone for ever.

*

We had gone out after breakfast, striking well away from the main road until we got among the thicker thorns, where there was any amount of fresh spoor and we were quite certain to find a troop sooner or later. The day was so still, the ground so dry and the bush so thick that the chances were the game would hear us before we could get near enough to see them. Several times I heard sounds of rustling bush or feet cantering away – something had heard us and made off unseen. So I dropped down into the sandy bed of a dry donga and used it as a stalking trench. From this it was easy enough to have a good look around every hundred yards or so without risk of being heard or seen.

We had been going along cautiously in this way for some time when, peering over the bank, I spied a single impala

half hidden by a scraggy bush. It seemed queer that there should be only one, as their habit is to move in troops. But there was nothing else to be seen. Indeed it was only the flicker of an ear on this one that had caught my eye. Nothing else in the land moved.

Jock climbed the bank also, following so closely that he bumped against my heels, and when I lay flat actually crawled over my legs to get up beside me and see what was on. Little by little he got into the way of imitating all I did, so that after a while it was hardly necessary to say a word or make a sign to him. He lay down beside me and raised his head to look just as he saw me do.

He was all excitement, trembling like a wet spaniel on a cold day, and instead of looking steadily at the impala as I was doing and as he usually did, he was looking here, there and everywhere. It seemed almost as if he was looking at things – not for them. It was my comfortable belief at the moment that he had not yet spotted the buck, but was looking about anxiously to find out what was interesting me. It turned out, as usual, that he had seen a great deal more than his master had.

The stalking looked very easy. A few yards further up the donga there was excellent cover in some dense thorns, behind which we could walk boldly across open ground to within easy range of the buck and get a clear shot. We reached the cover all right, but I had not taken three steps into the open space beyond, before there was a rushing and scrambling on every side of me. The place was a whirlpool of racing and plunging impala. They came from every side and went in every direction as though caught suddenly in an enclosure and, mad with fear and bewilderment, were trying to find a way out. How many there were it was quite impossible to say. The bush was alive with them. The dust they kicked up, the noise of their feet, their curious sneezy snorts and their wild confusion completely bewildered me. Not one stood still. Never for a moment could I see any single animal clearly enough or long enough to fire at it: another would cross it; a bush would cover it as I aimed; or it would leap into the air, clearing bushes, bucks and everything in its way, and disappear again in the moving mass. They seemed to me to whirl like leaves in a wind eddy. My eyes could not follow them and my brain swam as I looked.

It was a hot day. There was no breeze at all. Probably the herd had been resting after their morning feed and drink when we came upon them. By creeping up along the donga we had managed to get unobserved right into the middle of the dozing herd, so they were literally on every side of us. At times it looked as if they were bound to stampede over us and simply trample us down in their numbers; for in their panic they saw nothing, and no one appeared to know what or where the danger was. Time and again, as I singled one out and tried to aim, others would come racing straight for us, compelling me to switch round to face them – only to find them swerve with a dart or a mighty bound when within a few paces of me.

What Jock was doing during that time I do not know. It was all such a whirl of excitement and confusion that there are only a few clear impressions left on my mind. One is of a buck coming through the air right at me, jumping over the backs of two others racing across my front. I can see now the sudden wriggle of its body and the look of terror in its eyes when it saw me and realized that it was going to land almost at my feet. I tried to jump aside, but it was not necessary: with one touch on the ground it shot slantingly past me like a ricochet bullet. Another picture that always comes back is that of a splendid ram clearing the first of the dense thorn bushes that were to have been my cover in stalking. He flew over it outlined against the sky in the easiest, most graceful and most perfect curve imaginable. It came back to me afterwards that he was eight or ten yards from me, and yet I had to look up into the sky to see his white chest and gracefully gathered feet as he cleared the thorn bush like a soaring bird.

One shot, out of three or four fired in desperation as they were melting away, hit something. The unmistakable thud of the bullet told me so. That time it was the real thing, and when you hear the real thing you cannot mistake it. The wounded animal went off with the rest and I followed, with Jock ahead of me hot on the trail.

A hundred yards further on, where Jock with his nose to the ground had raced along between some low stones and a marula tree, I came to a stop – bush all round me, not a living thing in sight, and all as silent as the grave. On one of the smooth hot stones there was a big drop of blood, and a few yards on I found a couple more. Here and there along the spoor there were smears on the long yellow grass, and it was clear enough, judging by the height of the blood-marks from the ground, that the impala was wounded in the body – probably far back, as there were no frothy bubbles to show a lung shot. I knew that it would be a long chase unless Jock could head the buck off and bay it. But unless he could do this at once, he was so silent in his work that there was little chance of finding him.

The trail became more and more difficult to follow. The blood was less frequent, and the hot sun dried it so quickly that it was more than I could do to pick it out from the red streaks on the grass and many coloured leaves. So I gave it up and sat down to smoke and wait.

Half an hour passed, and still no Jock. Then I wandered about whistling and calling for him – calling until the sound of my own voice became quite uncanny, the only sound in the immense silence. Two hours passed in useless calling and listening, searching and waiting, and then I gave it up altogether and made back for the wagons, trying to hope that Jock had struck the road somewhere and had followed it to the outspan – instead of coming back on his own trail through the bush to me.

But there was no Jock at the wagons. My heart sank, although I was not surprised. It was nearly four hours since he had disappeared, and it was as sure as anything could be that something extraordinary must have happened or he would have come back to me long before this. There was nothing to be done but to wait and see what would happen. It was perfectly useless to look for him. If alive and well, he was better able to find his way than the best tracker that ever lived. If dead or injured and unable to move, there was not one chance in a million of finding him.

*

There was only one native whom Jock would take any notice of or would allow to touch him – a great big Zulu named Jim Makokel'. Jim was one of the real fighting Zulu breed, and the pride he took in Jock began the day Jock fought the table-leg and grew stronger and stronger to the end. Jim became Jock's devoted champion, and more than once showed that he would face man or beast to stand by him when he needed help.

This day when I returned to the wagons Jim was sitting with the other drivers in the group round the big pot of porridge. I saw him give one quick look my way and heard him say sharply to the others, 'Where is the dog? Where is Jock?'

In a few minutes they all knew what had happened. The other boys took it calmly, saying that the dog would find its way back. But Jim was not calm – it was not his nature. At one moment he would agree with them, swamping them with a flood of reasons why Jock, the best dog in the world, would be sure to come back; and the next – hot with restless excitement – would picture all that the dog might have been doing and all that he might still have to face. Then he would break off to proclaim loudly that everyone ought to go out and hunt for him.

Knowing only too well how useless it would be to search for Jock, I lay down under the wagon to rest and wait.

After half an hour of this Jim could restrain himself no longer. He came over to where I lay and – with a look of severe disapproval and barely controlled indignation – asked me for a gun, saying that he himself meant to go out and look for Jock. It would be nearer the mark to say that he demanded a gun. He was so genuinely anxious and so indignant at what he considered my indifference that it was impossible to be angry; and I let him talk away to me and at me in his excited bullying way. He would take no answer and listen to no reason. So finally, to keep him quiet, I gave him the shot-gun, and off he went, muttering his opinions of everyone else – a great springy striding picture of fierce resolution.

He came back nearly three hours later, silent, morose, hot and dusty. He put the gun down beside me without a word – just a click of disgust – and, as he strode across to his wagon, he called roughly to one of the drivers for the drinking water. Lifting the bucket to his mouth he drank like an ox and slammed it down again without a word of thanks. Then he sat down in the shade of the wagon, filled his pipe, and smoked in silence.

The trekking hour came and passed. But we did not move. The sun went down, and in the quiet of the evening we heard the first jackal's yapping – the first warning of the night. There were still lions and leopards in those parts, and any number of hyenas and wild dogs. The darker it grew and the more I thought of it, the more helpless seemed Jock's chance of getting through a night in the bush to work his way back to the wagons.

It was almost dark when I was startled by a yell from Jim Makokel', and looking round, saw him bound out into the road shouting, 'He has come, he has come! What did I tell you?' He ran out to Jock, stooping to pat and talk to him, and then in a lower voice and with growing excitement went on rapidly, 'See the blood! See it! He has fought: he has killed! Dog of all dogs! Jock, Jock!' His savage song of triumph broke off in a burst of rough tenderness, and he called the dog's name five or six times with every note of affection and welcome in his deep voice.

Jock took no notice of Jim's dancing out to meet him, nor of his shouts, endearments and antics. Slowing his tired trot down to a walk, he came straight on to me, flickered his ears a bit, wagged his tail cordially, and gave my hand a splashy lick as I patted him. Then he turned round in the direction he had just come from, looked steadily out, cocked his ears well up, and moved his tail slowly from side to side. For the next half hour or so he kept repeating this action every few minutes. But even without that I knew that it had been no wild-goose chase, and that miles away in the bush there was something lying dead which he could show me if I would follow him back again to see.

What had happened in the eight hours since he had dashed off in pursuit can only be guessed. That he had pulled down the impala and killed it seemed certain – what a chase and what a fight it must have been to take all that time! The buck could not have been badly wounded or it would have died in far less time than that. What a fight it must have been to kill an animal six or eight times his own weight and armed with such horns and hoofs! But was it only the impala? Or had the hyenas and wild dogs followed up the trail, as they so often do, and did Jock have to fight his way through them too?

He was hollow-flanked and empty, parched with thirst, and so blown that his breath still caught in suffocating chokes. He was covered with blood and sand. His beautiful golden coat was dark and stained. His white front had disappeared. On his chest and throat, on his jaws and ears, down his front legs even to the toes, the blood was caked on him – mostly black and dried but some still red and sticky. He was a little lame in one foreleg, but there was no cut or swelling to show the cause. There was only one mark to be seen: over his right eye there was a bluish line where the hair had been shaved off clean, leaving the skin smooth and unbroken. What did it? Was it horn, hoof, tooth or – what? Only Jock knew.

Hovering round and over me, pacing backwards and forwards between the wagons like a caged animal, Jim, growing more and more excited, filled the air with his talk, his shouts and savage song. Wanting to help, but always in the way, ordering and thrusting the other boys here and there, he worked himself up into a wild frenzy. It was the Zulu fighting blood on fire and he 'saw red' everywhere.

I called for water.

'Water!' roared Jim, 'bring water.' Glaring round he made a spring – stick in hand – at the nearest native. The boy fled in terror, with Jim after him for a few paces, and brought a bucket of water. Jim snatched it from him and with a

resounding thump on the ribs sent the unlucky boy sprawling on the ground.

Jock took the water in great gulpy bites broken by pauses to get his breath again. And Jim paced up and down – talking, talking, talking! Talking to me, to the others, to the natives, to Jock, to the world at large, to the heavens, and to the dead. His eyes glared like a wild beast's and gradually little seams of froth gathered in the corners of his mouth as he poured out his cataract of words, telling of all Jock had done and might have done and would yet do; comparing him with the fighting heroes of his own race, and wandering off into vivid recitals of great battles; seizing his sticks, shouting his war cries, and going through all the mimicry of fight with the wild frenzy of one possessed.

Time after time I called him and tried to quiet him. But he was beyond control and I knew the fit must run its course.

The night closed in and there was quiet once more. The flames of the camp fires had died down. The big thorn logs had burnt into glowing coals like the pink crisp hearts of giant water-melons. Jock lay sleeping, tired out, but even in his sleep came little spells of panting now and then, like the after-sobs of a child that has cried itself to sleep. We lay rolled in our blankets, and no sound came from where the natives slept.

But Jim – only Jim – sat on his rough three-legged stool, elbows on knees and hands clasped together, staring intently into the coals. The fit worked slowly off, and his excitement died gradually away. Now and then there was a fresh burst, but always milder and at longer intervals. Slowly but surely he subsided until at last there were only occasional mutterings of 'Ow, Jock!' followed by the Zulu click, the expressive shake of the head, and that appreciative half grunt, half chuckle, by which they pay tribute to what seems truly wonderful. He wanted no sleep that night. He sat on, waiting for the morning trek, staring into the red coals, and thinking of the bygone glories of his race in the days of the mighty Chaka.

That was Jim, when the fit was on him — transported by some trifling and unforeseen incident from the humdrum of the road to the life he once had lived with splendid recklessness.

Jock's Night Out

JOCK was lost twice. It came about both times through his following up wounded animals and leaving me behind, and happened in the days when our hunting was all done on foot. When I could afford a horse and could keep pace with him that difficulty did not trouble us.

After that day with the impala we had many good days together and many hard ones, and we were both getting to know our way about by degrees. Buck of many kinds had fallen to us, but so far as I was concerned there was one disappointment that was not to be forgotten. The picture of that kudu bull as he appeared for the last time looking over the ant-heap the day we were lost, was always before me. I could not hear the name or see the spoor of kudu without a pang of regret and the thought that never again would such a chance occur.

Kudu, like other kinds of game, were not to be found everywhere. They favoured some localities more than others, and when we passed through their known haunts chances of smaller game were often neglected in the hope of coming across the kudu.

I could not give up whole days to hunting – for we had

to keep moving along with the wagons all the time – or it would have been easy enough in many parts to locate the kudu. As it was, on three or four occasions we did come across them, and once I got a running shot, but missed. Day by day I went out always hoping to get my chance, and when at last the chance did come it was not in the least expected.

*

The herd boy came in one afternoon to say that there was a stembuck feeding among the oxen only a couple of hundred yards away. He had been quite close to it, he said, and it was very tame.

Game, so readily alarmed by the sight of white men, will often take no notice of natives, allowing them to approach to very close quarters. They are also easily stalked under cover of cattle or horses, and much more readily approached on horseback than on foot. The presence of other animals seems to give them confidence or to excite mild curiosity without alarm, and thus distract attention from the man.

In this case the bonny little red-brown fellow was not a bit scared. From time to time he turned his head our way and, with his large but shapely and most sensitive ears thrown forward, examined us frankly while he moved slightly one way or another so as to keep under cover of the oxen and busily continue his browsing.

In and out among seventy head of cattle we played hide-and-seek for quite a while – I not daring to fire for fear of hitting one of the bullocks – until at last he found himself manoeuvred out of the troop. Then, without giving me a chance, he was off into the bush in a few frisky steps. I followed quietly, knowing that as he was on the feed and not scared, he would not go far.

Moving along silently under good cover, I reached a thick scrubby bush and peered over the top of it to search the grass under the surrounding thorn trees for the little red-brown form. I was looking about low down in the russety grass – for he was only about twice the size of Jock – when a movement on a higher level caught my eye. It was just the flip of a fly-tickled ear; but it was a movement where all else was still, and instantly the form of a kudu cow appeared before me. There it stood within fifty yards, the soft grey-and-white looking still softer in the shadow of the

thorns, but as clear to me – and as still – as a figure carved in stone. The stem of a mimosa hid the shoulders, but all the rest was plainly visible as it stood there utterly unconscious of danger.

The tree made a dead shot almost impossible, but the risk of trying for another position was too great, and I fired. The thud of the bullet and the tremendous bound of the kudu straight up in the air told that the shot had gone home. But these things were for a time forgotten in the surprise that followed.

At the sound of the shot twenty other kudu jumped into life and sight before me. The one I had seen and shot was one of a herd all dozing peacefully in the shade, and, strangest of all, it was the one that was farthest from me. To the right and left of this one, at distances from fifteen to thirty yards from me, the magnificent creatures had been standing, and I had not seen them. It was the flicker of this one's ear alone that had caught my eye. My bewilderment was complete when I saw the big bull of the herd start off twenty yards on my right front and pass away like a streak in a few sweeping strides.

It was a matter of seconds only and they were all out of sight – all except the wounded one, which had turned off from the others. For all the flurry and confusion I had not lost sight of her, and noting her tucked-up appearance and shortened strides set Jock on her trail, believing that she would be down in a few minutes.

It is not necessary to go over it all again. It was much the same as the impala chase. I came back tired, disappointed and beaten, and without Jock. It was only after darkness set in that things began to look serious. When it came to midnight, with the camp wrapped in silence and in sleep, and there was still no sign of Jock, things looked very black indeed.

I heard his panting breath before it was possible to see anything. It was past one o'clock when he returned.

*

As we had missed the night trek to wait for Jock I decided to stay on where we were until the next evening and to have another try for the wounded kudu, with the chance of coming across the troop again.

By daybreak Jock did not seem much the worse for his night's adventures – whatever they were. There were no marks of blood on him this time. There were some scratches, which might have been caused by thorns during the chase, and odd-looking grazes on both hind quarters near the hip-bones, as though he had been roughly gravelled there. He seemed a little stiff, and flinched when I pressed his sides and muscles, but he was as game as ever when he saw the rifle taken down.

The kudu had been shot through the body, and even without being run to death by Jock must have died in the night, or have lain down and become too cold and stiff to move. If not discovered by wild animals there was a good chance of finding it untouched in the early morning; but after sunrise every minute's delay meant fresh risk from the aasvogels. There is very little which, if left uncovered, will escape their eyes. You may leave your buck for help to bring the meat in, certain that there is not one of these creatures in sight. You return in half an hour to find nothing but a few bones, the horns and hoofs, a rag of skin, and a group of disgusting gorged vultures – all smeared, torn and feather-strewn from their voracious struggles.

In the cloudless winter sky – a dome of spotless polished steel – nothing, you would think, can move unseen. Yet they are there. In the early morning, from their white-splashed eyries on some distant mountain, they slide off like a launching ship into their sea of blue; striking the currents of the upper air, they sweep round and upwards in immense circles, their huge motionless wings carrying them higher and higher until they are lost to human sight.

Lie on your back in some dense shade where no side-lights strike in, but where an opening above forms a sort of natural telescope to the sky, and you may see tiny specks where nothing could be seen before. Take your field-glasses: the specks are vultures circling up on high! Look again, and far, far above you will see other specks – and for aught you know, there may be others still beyond. How high are they? And what can they see from there? Who knows? But this is sure, that within a few minutes scores will come swooping down in great spiral rushes where not one was visible before.

In the dewy cool of the morning we soon reached the place where Jock had left me behind the evening before, and from there on he led the way. It was much slower work then. As far as I was concerned, there was nothing to guide me, and it was impossible to know what he was after. Did he understand that it was not fresh game but the wounded kudu that I wanted? And, if so, was he following the scent of the old chase or merely what he might remember of the way he had gone? It seemed impossible that scent could lie in that dry country for twelve hours; yet it was clearly nose more than eyes that guided him. He went ahead soberly and steadily, and once when he stopped completely, to sniff at a particular tuft of grass, I found out what was helping him. The grass was well streaked with blood – quite dry it is true, still it was blood.

A mile or so on we checked where the grass was trampled and the ground scored with spoor. The heavy spoor was all in a ring four or five yards in diameter. Outside this the grass was also flattened, and there I found a dog's footprints. But it had no further interest for Jock. While I was examining it he picked up the trail and trotted on.

We came upon four or five other rings where they had fought. Then for a matter of a hundred yards or more it looked as if they had fought and tumbled all the way. Jock was some distance ahead of me, trotting along quietly, when I saw him look up, give that rare growling bark of his – one of suppressed but real fury – lower his head, and charge. Then came heavy flapping and scrambling and the wind of huge wings, as twenty or thirty great lumbering aasvogels flopped along the ground with Jock dashing furiously about among them – taking flying leaps at them as they rose, his jaws snapping like rat-traps as he missed them.

On a little open flat of hard-baked sand lay the stripped frame of the kudu. The head and leg-bones were missing. Meat-stripped fragments were scattered all about. Fifty yards away among some bushes Jock found the head – and still further afield were remains of skin and thigh-bones crushed almost beyond recognition.

No aasvogel had done this. It was hyenas' work. The high-shouldered slinking brute, with jaws like a stone-crusher, alone cracks bones like those and bigger ones which even the lion cannot tackle. I walked back a little way and found the scene of the last stand, all harrowed bare. There was no spoor of kudu or of Jock to be seen there – only prints innumerable of wild dogs, hyenas and jackals, and some traces of where the carcass had been dragged by them in the effort to tear it asunder.

I looked at Jock. The mane on his neck and shoulders which had risen at the sight of the vultures was not flat yet. He was sniffing about slowly and carefully on the spoor of the hyenas and wild dogs; and he looked 'fight' all over. But what it all meant was beyond me. I could only guess – just as you will – what had happened out in the silent ghostly bush that night.

The Kudu Bull

I LEFT the scene of torn carcass and crunched bones, consumed by regrets and disappointment. Each fresh detail only added to my feeling of disgust, but Jock did not seem to mind. He jumped up briskly as soon as I started walking in earnest, as though he recognized that we were making a fresh start, and he began to look forward immediately.

The little bare flat where the kudu had fallen for the last time was at the head of one of those depressions which collect the waters of the summer floods. Changing gradually into shallow valleys, they are eventually scoured out and become the dongas – dry in winter but full charged with muddy flood in summer – which drain the Bushveld to its rivers. Here and there are deep pools which, except in years of drought, last all through the winter. These are the drinking places of the game. I followed this one down for a couple of miles without any definite purpose until the sight of some greener and denser wild figs suggested that there might be water, and perhaps a rietbuck or a duiker near by. As we reached the trees Jock showed unmistakable signs of interest in something, and with the utmost caution I moved from tree to tree in the shady grove towards where it seemed the water-hole might be.

There were bushy wild plums flanking the grove, and beyond them the ordinary scattered thorns. As I reached this point, and stopped to look out between the bushes on to the more open ground, a kudu cow walked quietly up the slope from the water – but before there was time to raise the rifle her easy stride had carried her behind a small mimosa tree. I took one quick step out to follow her up and found myself face to face at less than a dozen yards with a grand kudu bull. For a fraction of a second we looked straight into each other's eyes; then, as if by magic, he was round and going from me with the overwhelming rush of speed and strength and weight combined. A whirlwind of dust and leaves marked his course, and through it I fired, unsteadied by excitement and hardly able to see. Then the right hind-leg swung out and the great creature sank for a moment, almost to the ground.

There had been no time to aim, and the shot – a real snap shot – was not at all a bad one. I fired again as the kudu recovered himself, but he was then seventy or eighty yards away and partly hidden at times by trees and scrub. He struck up the slope, following the line of the troop through the scattered thorns. Running hard and dropping quickly to my knee for steadier aim, I fired again and again – but each time a longer shot and more obscured by the intervening bush; and no tell-tale thud came back to cheer me on.

Forgetting last night's experience, forgetting everything except how we had twice chased and twice lost them, seeing only another and the grandest prize slipping away, I sent Jock on and followed as fast as I could. Once more the kudu came in sight – just a chance at four hundred yards as he reached an open space on rising ground. Jock was already closing up, but still unseen, and the noble old fellow turned full broadside to me as he stopped to look back. Once more

I knelt, gripping hard and holding my breath to snatch a moment's steadiness, and fired. But I missed again, and as the bullet struck under him he plunged forward and disappeared over the rise at the moment that Jock, dashing out from the scrub, reached his heels.

The old Martini carbine had one bad fault: years of rough and careless treatment in all sorts of weather – for it was only a discarded old Mounted Police weapon – had told on it, and both in barrel and breech it was well pitted with rust scars. One result of this was that it was always jamming, and unless the cartridges were kept well greased

the empty shells would stick and the ejector fail to work. This was almost sure to happen when the carbine became hot from quick firing. It jammed now, and fearing to lose sight of the chase I dared not stop a second, but ran on, struggling from time to time to wrench the breech open.

Reaching the place where they had disappeared, I saw with intense relief and excitement Jock and the kudu having it out less than a hundred yards away. The kudu's leg was broken right up in the ham, and it was a terrible handicap for an animal so big and heavy, but his nimbleness and quickness were astonishing. Using the sound hind-legs as a pivot he swung round, always facing his enemy. Jock was in and out, here, there and everywhere, as a buzzing fly torments one on a hot day. Indeed, to the kudu just then he was the fly and nothing more. He could only annoy his big enemy, and was playing with his life to do it. Sometimes

he tried to get round; sometimes pretended to charge straight in, stopping himself with all four feet spread – just out of reach; then like a red streak he would fly through the air with a snap for the kudu's nose.

It was a fight for life, for the kudu, in spite of his wound, easily held his own. No doubt he had fought out many a life and death struggle to win and hold his place as lord of the herd and knew every trick of attack and defence. Maybe, too, he was blazing with anger and contempt for this persistent little gad-fly that worried him so and kept out of reach.

Sometimes he snorted and feinted to charge; at other times backed slowly, giving way to draw the enemy on. Then, with a sudden lunge the great horns swished like a scythe with a tremendous reach out, easily covering the spot where Jock had been a fraction of a second before.

There were pauses too in which he watched his tormentor steadily, with occasional impatient shakes of the head; or, raising it to full height, towered up a monument of splendid and contemptuous indifference, looking about with big, angry but unfrightened eyes for the herd – his herd – that had deserted him. Or with a slight toss of his head he would walk limpingly forward, forcing the ignored Jock before him; then, interrupted and annoyed by a flying snap at his nose, he would spring forward and strike with the sharp cloven fore-foot – zip-zip-zip – at Jock as he landed. Any one of the vicious flashing stabs would have pinned him to the earth and finished him – but Jock was never there.

Keeping what cover there was I came up slowly behind them, struggling and using all the force I dared, short of smashing the lever, to get the empty cartridge out. At last one of the turns in the fight brought me in view, and the kudu dashed off again. For a little way the pace seemed as great as ever, but it soon died away. The driving power was gone. The strain and weight on the one sound leg and the tripping of the broken one were telling, and from then on I was close enough to see it all.

In the first rush the kudu seemed to dash right over Jock – the swirl of dust and leaves and the bulk of the kudu hiding him. Then I saw him close abreast, looking up at it and making furious jumps for its nose, alternately from one side and the other, as they raced along together. The kudu holding its nose high and well forward, as they do when on the move, with the horns thrown back almost horizontally, was out of his reach and galloped heavily on completely ignoring his attacks.

At the fourth or fifth attempt by Jock a spurt from the kudu brought him cannoning against its shoulder, and he was sent rolling unnoticed yards away. He scrambled instantly to his feet, but found himself again behind.

Jock had learned one very clever trick while following a rietbuck which I had wounded in the same way. He had made several tries at its nose and throat, but the buck was going too strongly and was out of reach. Racing up behind he flew at the dangling broken leg, caught it at the shin, and thrusting his feet well out, simply dragged until the buck slowed down, and then began furiously tugging sideways. The crossing of the legs brought the wounded animal down immediately and Jock had it by the throat before it could rise again. He had already used this device successfully several times, but so far only with the smaller buck. This day he did what I should have thought to be impossible for a dog three or four times his size.

Realizing that attack in front was useless, he went for the broken leg. It swung about in wild eccentric curves, but at the third or fourth attempt he got it and hung on, and with all fours spread he dragged along the ground. The first startled spring of the kudu jerked him into the air, but there was no let go now. Although dragged along the rough ground and dashed about among the scrub – sometimes swinging in the air, and sometimes sliding on his back – he pulled from side to side in futile attempts to throw the big animal.

Ineffectual and even hopeless as it looked at first, Jock's attempts soon began to tell. The kudu made wild efforts to get at him, but with every turn he turned too, and did it so vigorously that the staggering animal swayed over and had to plunge violently to recover its balance. So they turned, this way and that, until a wider plunge swung Jock off his feet, throwing the broken leg across the other one. Then, with feet firmly planted, Jock tugged again, and the kudu trying to regain its footing was tripped by the crossed legs and came down with a crash.

As it fell Jock was round and fastened on the nose. But it was no duiker, impala or rietbuck that he had to deal with this time. The kudu gave a snort of indignation and shook its head. As a terrier shakes a rat, so it shook Jock, whipping the ground with his swinging body, and with another indignant snort and toss of the head flung him off, sending him skidding along the ground on his back.

The kudu had fallen on the wounded leg and failed to rise with the first effort. Jock while still slithering along the ground on his back was tearing at the air with his feet in his mad haste to get back to the attack, and as he scrambled up, he raced in again with head down and the little eyes black with fury. He was too mad to be wary, and my heart stood still as the long horns went round with a swish. One black point seemed to pierce him through and through, showing a foot out the other side, and a jerky twist of the head sent him whirling like a tip-cat eight or ten feet in the air. It had just missed him, passing under his stomach next to the hind-legs; but, until he dropped with a thud and, tearing and scrambling to his feet, raced in again, I felt certain he had been gored through.

The kudu was up again then. I had rushed in with rifle clubbed, with the wild idea of stunning it before it could rise, but was met by the lowered horns and unmistakable signs of charging – and I beat a retreat quite as speedy as my charge.

It was a running fight from then on. The instant the kudu turned to go Jock was on to the leg again, and nothing could shake his hold. I had to keep at a respectful distance, for the bull was still good for a furious charge. Even with Jock hanging on, he eyed me in the most unpromising fashion whenever I attempted to head him off or even to come close up.

The big eyes were blood-shot then, but there was no look of fear in them – they blazed with baffled rage. Impossible as it seemed to shake Jock off or to get away from us, and in spite of the broken leg and loss of blood, the furious attempts to beat us off did not slacken. It was a desperate running fight, and right bravely he fought it to the end.

Partly barring the way in front were the whitened trunks and branches of several trees struck down by some storm of the year before. Running ahead of the kudu I made for these, hoping to find a stick straight enough for a ramrod to force the empty cartridge out. As I reached them the kudu made for me with half a dozen plunges that sent me flying off for other cover. But the broken leg swayed over one of the branches, and Jock with feet planted against the tree

hung on. The kudu, turning furiously on him, stumbled, floundered, tripped, and came down with a crash amongst the crackling wood.

Once more like a flash Jock was over the fallen body and had fastened on the nose – but only to be shaken worse than before. The kudu literally flogged the ground with him, and for an instant I shut my eyes. It seemed as if the plucky dog would be beaten into pulp. The bull tried to chop him with its fore-feet, but could not raise itself enough, and at each pause Jock – with his watchful eyes ever on the alert

– dodged his body round to avoid the chopping feet without letting go his hold. Then with a snort of fury the kudu, half rising, gave its head a wild upward sweep, and shook. As a springing rod flings a fish the kudu flung Jock over its head and on to a low flat-topped thorn-tree behind. The dog somersaulted slowly as he circled in the air, dropped on his back in the thorns some twelve feet from the ground, and came tumbling down through the branches. Surely the tree saved him, for it seemed as if such a throw must break his back. As it was he dropped with a sickening thump; yet even as he fell I saw again the scrambling tearing movement, as if he was trying to race back to the fight even before he reached ground. Without a pause to breathe or even to look, he was in again and trying once more for the nose.

The kudu lying partly on its side, with both hind-legs hampered by the mass of dead wood, could not rise, but it swept the clear space in front with the terrible horns, and for some time kept Jock at bay. I tried stick after stick for a ramrod, but without success. At last, in desperation at seeing Jock once more hanging to the kudu's nose, I hooked the lever on to a branch and setting my foot against the tree wrenched until the empty cartridge flew out and I went staggering backwards.

In the last struggle, while I was busy with the rifle, the kudu had moved, and it was then lying against one of the fallen trunks. The first swing to get rid of Jock had literally slogged him against the tree. The second swing swept him under it where a bend in the trunk raised it about a foot from the ground, and gaining his foothold there Jock stood fast – with his feet planted firmly and his shoulder humped against the dead tree, he stood this tug-of-war. The kudu with its head twisted back, as caught at the end of a swing, could put no weight to the pull; yet the wrenches it gave to free itself drew the nose and upper lip out like tough rubber and seemed to stretch Jock's neck visibly. I had to come round within a few feet of them to avoid risk of hitting Jock, and it seemed impossible for bone and muscle to stand the two or three terrible wrenches that I saw. The shot was the end. As the splendid head dropped slowly over, Jock let go his hold.

He had not uttered a sound except the grunts that were knocked out of him.

Jim Makokel'

JIM MAKOKEL' was Jock's ally and champion. There was a great deal to like and something to admire in Jim. But taking him all round, I am very much afraid that most people would consider him rather a bad lot. The fact of the matter is he belonged to another period and other conditions. He was simply a great, passionate, fighting savage. Instead of wearing the cast-off clothing of the white man and peacefully driving bullock wagons along a transport road, he should have been decked in his savage finery of leopard skin and black ostrich feathers – showing off the powerful bronzed limbs and body all alive with muscle – and sharing in some wild war-dance; or, equipped with shield and assegais, leading in some murderous fight.

Jim had but one argument and one answer to everything: Fight!

It was his nature, bred and born in him. He was a survival of a great fighting race and in a fighting nation Jim's kraal was known as a fighting one. The turbulent blood that ran in their veins could not settle down into a placid stream merely because the Great White Queen had said, 'There shall be peace!'

Chaka, the 'black Napoleon' whose wars had cost South

Africa over a million lives, had died – murdered by his brother Dingaan. Dingaan, his successor, had been crushed by the gallant little band of Boers under Potgieter for his fiendish massacre of Piet Retief and his men. 'Mpande, the third of the three famous brothers, had come and gone. Ketshwayo, the last of the great Zulu kings, after years of arrogant and unquestioned rule, had loosed his straining impis at the people of the Great White Queen. The awful day of Isandhlwana – where the 24th Regiment died almost to a man – had blooded the impis to madness. But Rorke's Drift and Kambula had followed to tell another tale; and at Ulundi the tides met – the black and the white. And the kingdom and might of the house of Chaka were no more.

Jim had fought at Isandhlwana! He could tell of an umfaan sent out to herd some cattle within sight of the British camp to draw the troops out raiding – while the impis crept round by hill and bush and donga behind them; of the fight made by the red-coats as they were attacked hand to hand with stabbing assegais, ten and twenty to one; of one man in blue who was the last to die, fighting with his back to a wagon against scores before him; and how he fell at last, stabbed in the back through the spokes of the wheel by one who had crept up behind.

Jim had fought at Rorke's Drift! Wild with lust of blood, he had gone on with the victory-maddened lot to invade Natal and eat up the little garrison on the way. He could tell how seventy or eighty white men behind a little rampart of biscuit-tins and flour-bags had fought through the long and terrible hours, beating off five thousand of the Zulu best; had fought until the flour-bags and biscuit-tins stood lower than the pile of dead outside, and the Zulu host was beaten and Natal saved that day.

Jim had seen all that – and Ulundi, the Day of Despair! And he knew the power of the Great White Queen and the way that her people fight. But peace was not for him or his kraal. In the fight for leadership when his King, Ketsh-

wayo, was gone, Jim's kraal had been surrounded one night and massacred. Jim had fought his way out, wounded and alone. Without kith or kin, cattle, king, or country, he fled to the Transvaal – to live amongst white men under the Boer Government and to work for the first time in his life!

Wagon-boys – as the drivers were called – often acquired a certain amount of reputation on the road, but it was, as a rule, only a reputation as good or bad drivers. In Jim's case it was different. He was a character and had an individual reputation, which was exceptional in a native. He was known as the best driver, the hardest fighter, the worst drinker and the strongest black man on the road.

His real name was Makolela, but in accordance with a common Zulu habit, it was usually abbreviated to Makokel'. I called him Jim as a rule – Makokel' when relations were strained. The wagon-boys found it safer to use his proper name!

Many men had employed Jim before he came to me, and all had 'sacked' him for fighting, drinking and the unbearable worry he caused. They said that he gave more trouble than his work was worth and it may have been true. He certainly was a living test of patience, purpose and management, but I am glad that Jim never 'got the sack' from me. Why he did not, it is not easy to say. Perhaps the circumstances under which he came to me and the hard knocks of an unkind fate pleaded for him. But it was not that alone. There was something in Jim himself – something good and fine, something that shone out from time to time through his battered face as the soul of a real man.

It was in the first season in the Bushveld that we were outspanned one night on the sand-hills overlooking Delagoa Bay, among scores of other wagons dotted about in little camps – all loading or waiting for loads to transport to the Transvaal. Delagoa was not a good place to stay in, in those days: liquor was cheap and bad; there was very little in the way of law and order; and everyone took care of himself as well as he could. The kraals were close about the town, and the natives of the place were as rascally a lot of thieves and vagabonds as you could find anywhere.

The result was everlasting trouble with the wagon-boys and a chronic state of war between them, the natives and the Arab traders of the place. The boys, with pockets full of wages, haggled and were cheated in the stores, and by the hawkers, and in the canteens; and they often ended up the night with beer-drinking at the kraals or reprisals on their enemies. Every night there were fights and robberies. The natives or Indians would rob and half-kill a wagon-boy; then he in turn would rally his friends, and raid and clear out the kraal or the store. Most of the wagon-boys were Zulus or of Zulu descent, and they were always ready for a fight and would tackle any odds when their blood was up.

It was the third night of our stay, and the usual row was on. Shouts and cries, the beating of tom-toms and shrill ear-piercing whistles, came from all sides – and through it all the dull hum of hundreds of human voices, all gabbling together. Near to us there was another camp of four wagons drawn up in close order, and as we sat talking and wondering at the strange babel in the beautiful calm moonlight night, one sound was ever recurring, coming away out of all the rest with something in it that fixed our attention. It was the sound of two voices from the next wagons. One voice was a native's – a great, deep, bull-throated voice. It was not raised – it was monotonously steady and low – but it carried far, with the ring and the lingering vibration of a big gong.

'Funa 'nyama, Inkos, funa 'nyama!' ('I want meat, Chief, I want meat!') was what the voice kept repeating at intervals of a minute or two, with deadly monotony and persistency.

The white man's voice grew more impatient, louder and angrier, with each refusal – but the boy paid no heed. A few minutes later the request would be made again: 'I am hungry, Baas, I can't sleep. Meat! Meat! Meat!' 'Porridge and bread are for women and piccaninnies. I am a man. I want meat, Baas, meat.' From the white man it was, 'Go to sleep, I tell you!' 'Be quiet, will you?' 'Shut up that row!' 'Be still, you drunken brute, or I'll tie you up!' and 'You'll get twenty-five in a minute!'

It may have lasted half an hour when one of our party said, 'That's Bob's old driver, the big Zulu. There'll be a row tonight. He's with a foreigner chap from Natal now. New chums are always roughest on the black men.'

In a flash I remembered Bob Saunderson's story of the boy who had caught the lion alive: Bob had shot a lioness near the Komati River, but her cubs, pretty well grown, had made off in the grass. One took to the water, and the big Zulu went after it. He swam up behind, and putting his hand on its head ducked it right under. The cub turned as it came up and struck out at him viciously, but he was out of reach. When it turned again to go he ducked it again and it went on like that six or eight times, till the thing was half drowned and had no more fight in it. Then he got hold of it by the tail and swam back with it, still shouting and mad with excitement. I remembered Bob's own words:

'You can say it was only a cub; but it takes a good man to go up naked and tackle a thing like that, with teeth and claws to cut you into ribbons. He was a real fine native, but a terror to drink and always in trouble. I had to sack him. He fairly wore me right out.'

A few minutes later there was a short scuffle, and the boy's voice could be heard protesting in the same deep low tone. They were tying him up to the wagon-wheel for a flogging. Others were helping the white man, but the boy was not resisting.

At the second thin whistling stroke some one said, 'That's

a sjambok he's using, not a nekstrop!' Sjambok, that will cut a bullock's hide! At about the eighth there was a wrench that made the wagon rattle, and the deep voice was raised in protest, 'Ow, *Inkos*!'

It made me choke. It was the first I knew of such things and the horror of it was unbearable. But the man who had spoken before – a good man too, trusted by black and white – said, 'Sonny, you must not interfere between a man and his boys here. It's hard sometimes, but we'd not live a day if they didn't know who was baas.'

I think we counted eighteen; and then everything seemed going to burst.

The white man looked about at the faces close to him – and stopped. He began slowly to untie the outstretched arms and blustered out some threats. But no one said a word!

*

The noises died down as the night wore on, until the stillness was broken only by the desultory barking of a dog or the crowing of some awakened rooster who had mistaken the bright moonlight for the dawn. But for me there was one other sound for which I listened into the cool of the morning with the quivering sensitiveness of a bruised nerve. Sometimes it was a long catchy sigh, and sometimes it broke into a groan just audible, like the faintest rumble of most distant surf. Twice in the long night there came the

same request to one of the boys near him, uttered in a deep clear unshaken voice and in a tone that was civil but firm, and strangely moving from its quiet indifference.

'*Landela manzi, Umganaam!*' ('Bring water, friend!') was all he said; and each time the request was so quickly answered that I had the guilty feeling of being one in a great conspiracy of silence.

The following afternoon I received an ultimatum. We had just returned from the town when from a group of boys squatting round the fire there stood up one big fellow – a stranger – who raised his hand high above his head in Zulu fashion and gave their salute in the deep bell-like voice that there was no mistaking, '*Inkos! Bayete!*'

He stepped forward, looking me all over and announced with calm and settled conviction, 'I have come to work for you!' I said nothing. Then he rapped a chest like a big drum, and nodding his head with a sort of defiant confidence added in quaint English, 'My naam Makokela! Jim Makokel'! Yes! My catchum lion 'live! Makokela, me!'

He had heard that I wanted a driver, had waited for my return and annexed me as his future 'baas' without a moment's doubt or hesitation.

I looked him over. Big, broad-shouldered, loose-limbed and as straight as an assegai! A neck and head like a bull's; a face like a weather-beaten rock, storm-scarred and furrowed, rugged and ugly, but steadfast, massive and strong.

I nodded and said, 'You can come.'

Once more he raised his head aloft, and, simply and without a trace of surprise or gratification, said:

'Yes, you are my chief, I will work for you.' In his own mind it had been settled already. It had never been in doubt.

*

Jim – when sober – was a splendid worker and the most willing of servants, and, drunk or sober, he was always respectful in an independent, hearty kind of way. His manner was as rough and rugged as his face and character – almost fierce and aggressive. But this was only skin deep. The childlike simplicity of the African native was in him to the full, and rude bursts of titanic laughter came readily – laughter as strong and unrestrained as his bursts of passion.

To the other boys he was what his nature and training had made him – not really a bully, but masterful and over-riding. He gave his orders with the curtness of a drill sergeant and the rude assurance of a savage chief. Walking, he gave way for none of them. At the outspan or on the road or footpath he shouldered them aside as one walks through standing corn – not aggressively, but with superb indifference of right and habit unquestioned. If one, loitering before

him, blocked his way, there was no pause or step aside –
just '*Suka!*' ('Get out!') and a push that sent the offender
staggering; or if he had his sticks, more likely a smart whack
on the stern, and not even the compliment of a glance back
from Jim as he stalked on. He was like the old bull in a
herd – he walked his course; none molested and none dis-
puted; the way opened before him.

When sober Jim spoke Zulu. When drunk, he broke into
the strangest and most laughable medley of kitchen-Kaffir,
bad Dutch and worse English. There was no difficulty in
knowing when Jim would go wrong. He broke out whenever he got a chance, whether at a kraal, at a wayside can-
teen or in a town. Money was fatal – he drank it all out.

But want of money was no security, for he was known to everyone and seemed to have friends everywhere; and if he had not, he made them on the spot – annexed and overwhelmed them.

I had many troubles with Jim and his troubles all came from drink. The exasperation was at times almost unbearable – so great, indeed, that on many ocasions I heartily repented ever having taken him on.

The trouble began as soon as we reached a town, and he had a hundred excuses for going in, and a hundred more for not coming out. He had some one to see, boots to be mended, clothes to buy or medicine to get – the only illness I ever knew him have was 'a pain inside', and the only medicine wanted – grog! Or, someone owed him money – a stock excuse, and the idea of Jim, always penniless and always in debt, posing as a creditor never failed to raise a laugh. Then he had relations in every town! Jim, the sole survivor of his fighting kraal, produced brothers and sisters, fathers and even 'mamas' in profusion, and they died regularly just before we reached the place – and he had to go to the funeral.

My first precaution was to keep him at the wagons and put the towns and canteens 'out of bounds'. The last defence was to banish him entirely until he came back sober – and meanwhile set other boys to do his work, paying them his wages in his presence when he returned fit for duty. There was never a trace of feeling to be detected when these affairs were squared off, but I knew how he hated the treatment, and it helped a little from time to time to keep him right.

Banishing him from the wagons was not a device to save myself trouble. I did it only when it was clear that he could stand the strain no longer. It seemed to me better to let him go – clearly understanding the conditions – than drive him into breaking away, with bad results to him and bad effects on the others of disobeying orders.

It was, as a rule, far indeed from saving me trouble, for after the first bout of drinking he almost invariably found his way back to the wagons. The drink always produced a ravenous craving for meat, and when his money was gone and he had fought his fill, he would come back at any hour of the night, perhaps even two or three times between dark and dawn, to beg for meat. Warnings and orders had no effect whatever. He was unconscious of everything except the overmastering craving for meat.

He would come to my wagon and begin that deadly monotonous recitation, 'Funa 'nyama, Inkos!' There was a kind of hopeless determination in the tone conveying complete indifference to all consequences: meat he must have. He was perfectly respectful. Every order to be quiet or go away or go to bed was received with the formal raising of the hand aloft, and the assenting 'Inkos!' but in the very next breath would come the old monotonous request, 'Funa 'nyama, Inkos.' The persistency was maddening and there was no remedy, for it was not the result of a conscious effort on his part. It was a result of his physical condition, and he could no more have resisted it than have resisted breathing.

When the meat was there I gave it, and he would sit by the fire for hours eating incredible quantities – cutting it off in slabs and devouring it when not much more than warmed. But it was not always possible to satisfy him in that way. Meat was expensive in the towns and often we had none at all at the wagons. Then the night became one long torment. The spells of rest might extend from a quarter of an hour to an hour. Then from the dead sleep of downright weariness I would be roused by the deep far-reaching voice. 'Funa 'nyama, Inkos' wove itself into my dreams, and waking I would find Jim standing beside me remorselessly urging the same request – and interspersing the old, old, hatefully familiar explanation of the difference between 'man's food' and 'piccanins' food', with grandiose declarations that he was 'Makokela – Jim Makokel',' who 'catchum lion 'live'. Sometimes he would expand this into comparisons between himself and the other boys, much to their disadvantage. On these occasions he invariably worked round to his private grievances, and expressed his candid opinions of Sam.

Sam was the boy whom I usually set to do Jim's neglected work. He was a 'mission boy', that is a Christian – very proper in his behaviour, but a weakling and not much good at his work. Jim would enumerate all Sam's shortcomings: how he got his oxen mixed up on dark nights and could not pick them out of the herd – a quite unpardonable offence; how he stuck in the drifts and had to be 'double-spanned' and pulled out by Jim; how he once lost his way in the bush; and how he upset the wagon coming down Devil's Shoot.

Jim had once brought down the Berg from Spitzkop a loaded wagon on which there was a cottage piano packed standing upright. The road was an awful one, and few drivers could have handled so top-heavy a load without capsizing. To him the feat was one without parallel in the history of wagon driving, and when drunk he usually coupled it with his other great achievement of catching a lion alive. His contempt for Sam's misadventure on the Devil's Shoot was therefore great, and to it was added resentment against Sam's repectability and superior education – which the latter was able to rub in by ostentatiously reading his Bible aloud at nights as they sat round the fire. Jim was a heathen and openly affirmed his conviction that a Christian black man was an impostor, a bastard and a hypocrite – a thing not to be trusted under any circumstances whatever.

The end of his morose outburst was always the same. When his detailed indictment of Sam was completed he would wind up with 'My catchum lion 'live. My bling panyanna fon Diskop (I bring piano from Spitzkop). My naam Makokela: Jim Makokel'. Sam no good; Sam leada Bible (Sam reads the Bible). Sam no good!'

The intensity of conviction and the gloomy disgust put into the last reference to Sam are not to be expressed in words.

The Allies

JOCK disliked black men. So did Jim. To Jim there were three
big divisions of the human race – white men, Zulus and
others. Zulu, old or young, was greeted by him as equal,
friend and comrade – but the rest were trash. He cherished
a most particular contempt for the Shangaans and Chopis,
as a lot who were just about good enough for what they
did – that is, work in the mines. They could neither fight nor
handle animals, and the sight of them stirred him to contempt and hostility.

It was not long before Jim discovered this bond of sympathy between him and Jock. It was very important that
Jock should have nothing to do with strange natives, and
should treat them with suspicion and keep them off the
premises. He did it by his own choice and instinct, but this
being so, it needed all the more intelligence and training to
get him to understand just where to draw the line. Jim made
the already difficult task practically impossible by egging
Jock on.

As far as I know the first incident arose out of the intrusion of a strange native at one of the outspans. Jock

objected, and he was forcing the scared boy back step by step – doing the same feinting rushes that he practised with game – until the boy tripped over a camp stool and sat plumb down on the three-legged pot of porridge cooking at the camp fire. I did not see it, for Jock was, as usual, quite silent – a feature which always had a most terrifying effect on his victims. It was a roar like a lion's from Jim that roused me. Jock was standing off with his feet on the move forwards and backwards, his head on one side and his face full of interest, as if he would dearly love another romp in; and the wagon-boys were reeling and rolling about in the grass, helpless with laughter.

That was how it began, and by degrees it developed into the Shangaan gang trick. The natives going to or from the gold-fields travel in small gangs. They walk along in Indian file, and when going across the veld they wind along singly in the footsteps of the leader. What prompted the dog to start this new game I cannot imagine. Certainly no one could have taught it to him. He did it entirely 'off his own bat', without anything to lead up to or suggest it.

One day a gang of about thirty of these Shangaans, each carrying his load of valuables on his head, was coming along a footpath some twenty yards away from the wagons. Jock strolled out and sat himself down in the middle of the path. The leader of the gang was suspicious and shied off wide into the veld. He passed in a semicircle round Jock, a good ten yards away, and came safely back to the path again. The dog with his nose in the air merely eyed him with a look of humorous interest and mild curiosity. The second boy made the loop shorter, and the third shorter still, as they found their alarm and suspicion unjustified. As each came along, the loop was lessened until they passed in safety almost brushing against Jock's nose. And still he never moved – except, as each boy approached, to look up at his face and, slowly turning his head, follow him round with his eyes until he re-entered the path.

There was something extremely funny in the mechanical regularity with which his head swung round. It was so funny that not only the wagon-boys noticed it and laughed; the unsuspecting Shangaans themselves shared the joke. The heavy bundles on their heads made turning round a slow process, so that they were content to enjoy what they saw in front and to know by the laughter from behind that the joke had been repeated all down the line.

The last one walked calmly by. As he did so there came one short muffled bark from Jock as he sprang out and nipped the unsuspecting Shangaan behind. The boy let out a yell that made the whole gang jump and clutch wildly at their toppling bundles, and Jock raced along the foot-path, scattering them this way and that, in a romp of wild enjoyment. The ridiculous rout of the thirty Shangaans in every direction, abandoning their baggage and fleeing from the little red enemy only just visible in the grass, was too much for my principles and far too much for my gravity. To be quite honest, I weakened badly.

But the weakening brought its own punishment and the joke was not far from getting us all into serious trouble. Many times while lying some way off in the shade of a tree or under another wagon I heard Jim, all unconscious of my presence, call in a low, deep voice, 'Jock, Jock. Shangaans!' Jock's head was up in a moment, and a romp of some sort followed unless I intervened.

＊

Jim had his faults, but getting others into mischief while keeping out of it himself was not one of them. If he egged Jock on, he was more than ready to stand by him and to take a hand in the row himself.

There was a day outside Barberton which I remember well. We were to start that evening, and knowing that if Jim got into the town he might not be back and fit to work for days, I made him stay with the wagons. He lay there flat out under his wagon with his chin resting on his arms, as morose and unapproachable as a surly old watch-dog. From the tent of my wagon I saw him raise his head and, following his glance, picked out a row of bundles against the sky-line. Presently a long string of about fifty time-expired mine-boys came in sight. Jim on his hands and knees scrambled over to where Jock lay asleep and shook him – for this incident occurred after Jock had become deaf.

'Shangaans, Jock. Shangaans! Kill them, kill, kill, kill!' said Jim in gusty ferocious whispers. It must have seemed as if Fate had kindly provided an outlet for the rebellious rage and the craving for a fight that were consuming him.

As Jock trotted out to head them off Jim reached up to the buck-rails and pulled down his bundle of sticks and lay down like a leopard on the spring. I had had a lot of trouble with Jim that day, and this annoyed me; but my angry call to stop was unavailing. Jim, pretending not to understand, made no attempt to stop Jock, but contented himself with calling to him to come back. And Jock, stone deaf, trotted evenly along with his head, neck, back and tail, all level – an old trick of Jess's which generally meant trouble for someone.

Slowing down as he neared the Shangaans he walked quietly on until he headed off the leader, and there he stood on the path. It was just the same as before. The boys, finding that he did nothing, merely stepped aside to avoid bumping against him.

They were boys taking back their purchases to their kraals to dazzle the eyes of the ignorant with the wonders of civilization – gaudy blankets, collections of bright tin billies and mugs, tin plates, three-legged pots, clothing, hats and even small tin trunks painted brilliant yellow. The last boy was wearing a pair of Royal Artillery trousers and it was from the seat of these ample bags that Jock took a good mouthful – and it was the boy's frantic jump, rather than Jock's tug, that made the piece come out. The sudden fright and the attempt to face about quickly caused several downfalls. The clatter of these spread the panic, and on top of it all came Jock's charge along the broken line.

Jim had burst into great bellows of laughter and excited shouts of encouragement to Jock, who could not have heard a trumpet at ten yards.

But there came a very unexpected change. One big Shangaan had drawn from his bundle a brand new side-axe. I saw the bright steel head flash, as he held it menacingly aloft by the short handle and marched towards Jock. There was a scrambling bound from under the wagon, and Jim, with face distorted and grey with fury, rushed out. In his right hand he brandished a tough stout fighting stick. In his left I was horrified to see an assegai, and well I knew that, with the fighting fury on him, he would think nothing of using it.

The Shangaan saw him coming, and stopped. Then, still facing Jim, with the axe raised and feinting repeatedly to throw it, he began to back away. Jim never paused for a second. He came straight on with wild leaps and blood-curdling yells in Zulu fighting fashion and ended with a bound that seemed to drop him right on top of the other. The stick came down with a whirr and a crash that crimped every nerve in my body; and the Shangaan dropped like a log.

I had shouted myself hoarse at Jim, but he heard or heeded nothing. Seizing a stick from one of the other boys I was already on the way to stop him, but before I got near him he had wrenched the axe from the kicking boy and, without pause, gone headlong for the next Shangaan he saw. Then everything went wrong. The more I shouted and the harder I ran, the worse the row. The Shangaans seemed to think I had joined in and was directing operations against them. Jim seemed to be inspired to wilder madness by my shouts and gesticulations. And Jock – well, Jock at any rate had not the remotest doubt as to what he should do. When he saw me and Jim in full chase behind him, his

plain duty was to go in for all he was worth – and he did it.

It was half an hour before I got that mad savage back. He was as unmanageable as a runaway horse. He had walloped the majority of the fifty himself; he had broken his own two sticks and used up a number of theirs; on his forehead there was a small cut and a lump like half an orange, and on the back on his head another cut left by the sticks of the enemy.

It was strange how Jim, even in that mood, yielded to the touch of one whom he regarded as his '*Inkos*'. He yielded to the light grip of my hand on his wrist and walked freely along with me. But a fiery bounding vitality possessed him, and with long springy strides he stepped out – looking excitedly about. And all the time there came from him a torrent of excited gabble in pure Zulu, which was punctuated by bursting allusions to 'dogs of Shangaans', 'axes', 'sticks', and 'Jock'.

Near the wagons we passed over the 'battle-field', and a huge guffaw of laughter broke from Jim as we came on the abandoned impedimenta of the defeated enemy. Jim looked on it all as the spoils of war, wanting to stop and gather in his loot there and then, and when I pressed on, he shouted to the other drivers to come out and collect the booty.

But my chief anxiety was to end the wretched escapade as quickly as possible and get the Shangaans on their way again. So I sent Jim back to his place under the wagon, and told the cook-boy to give him the rest of my coffee and half a cup of sugar to provide him with something else to think of and to calm him down.

After a wait of half an hour or so, a head appeared just over the rise, and then another and another, at irregular intervals and at various points. They were scouting very cautiously before venturing back again. I sat in the tent-wagon out of sight and kept quiet, hoping that in a few minutes they would gain confidence, collect their goods and go their way again.

Jim, lying flat under the wagon, was much lower than I was, and – continuing his gabble to the other boys – saw nothing. Unfortunately he looked round just as a scared face peered cautiously over the top of an ant-heap. The temptation was, I suppose, irresistible. He scrambled to his knees with a pretence of starting afresh and let out one ferocious yell that made my hair stand up; and in that second every head bobbed down and the field was deserted once more.

If this went on there could be but one ending: the police would be appealed to, Jim arrested and I should spend days hanging about the courts. So I sallied out as my own herald of peace. But the position was more difficult than it looked. As soon as the Shangaans saw me, they scattered like chaff before the wind, and ran as if they would never stop. They evidently took me for the advance guard in a fresh attack. I stood upon an ant-heap and waved and called, but each shout resulted in a fresh spurt and only made them more suspicious. It seemed a hopeless case, and I gave up.

On the way back to the wagons, however, I thought of Sam. Sam would surely be the right envoy. Even the routed Shangaans would feel that there was nothing to fear there. But Sam was by no means anxious to earn laurels, and it was a poor-looking, weak-kneed and much dejected scarecrow that dragged its way reluctantly out into the veld to hold parley with the enemy that day. Between rough gusts of laughter Jim rained on him crude ridicule and rude comments; and Sam slouched off with head bent, relieving his heart with occasional clicks and low murmurs of disgust.

But to Sam's relief, the Shangaans seemed to view him merely as a decoy, even more dangerous than I was. When he came in sight they looked anxiously around, and then headed off in a long string down the valley towards the river.

Now, no one had ever run away from Sam before, and the exhilarating sight so encouraged him that he marched boldly on after them. Goodness knows when, if ever, they would have stopped, if Sam had not met a couple of other natives whom the Shangaans had passed and induced them to turn back and reassure the fugitives.

An hour later Sam came back in mild triumph, at the head of the Shangaan gang. 'Clothed in a little brief authority', he stood guard and superintended while they collected their scattered goods – all except the axe that caused the trouble. That they failed to find.

At the first outspan from Barberton next day I saw Jim carving his mark on the handle, unabashed, under my very nose.

*

The next time Jim got drunk he added something to his opinion of Sam:

'Sam no good: Sam leada Bible! Shangaan, Sam; Shangaan!'

The Berg

THE last day of each trip in the Bushveld was always a day of trial and hard work for man and beast. For perhaps a week the towering bulwarks of the Highveld were visible as we toiled along – at first only in occasional hazy glimpses, then daily clearer, higher and grander – standing up before us like an impassable barrier. There was no road that the eye could follow. Here and there a broad furrowed streak of red soil straight down some steep grass-covered spur was visible. It looked like a mountain timber-slide or the scour of some tropical storm.

After many hard treks through the broken foothills, with their rocky sideling slopes and boulder-strewn torrent beds, at last the Berg itself was reached. There, on a flat-topped, terrace-like spur where the last outspan was, we took breath, halved our loads, double-spanned, and pulled ourselves together for the last, big climb.

From there the scoured red streaks stood out revealed as road tracks – for made road there was none – but even from there not nearly all the track was visible. The bumpy rumbling and heavy clattering of wagons on the rocky trail, the shouts of drivers and the crack of whips, mixed with confusing echoes from somewhere above. Then in unexpected places other wagons would be seen against the shadowy mountains; creeping up with infinite labour foot by foot; tackling at all sorts of angles; winding by undetected spur and slope and ridge towards the summit – the long spans of oxen and the bulky loads, dwarfed into miniature by the vast background, looking like snails upon a face of rock.

To those who do not know, there is not much difference between spans of oxen, and the driving of them seems merely a matter of brute strength in arm and lung. But it is not so. Heart and training in the cattle, skill and judgement in the driver, are needed, for the Berg is a searching test of man and beast. Patience, understanding, judgement and decision : those are the qualities it calls for.

It was on the Berg that I first saw what a really first-class man can do. There were many wagons facing the pass that day. Portions of loads, dumped off to ease the pull, dotted the roadside; tangles of disordered, maddened spans blocked the way; and fragments of yokes, skeys, strops and reims, and broken disselbooms, told the tale of trouble.

Old Charlie Roberts came along with his two wagons. He was 'old' with us – being nearly fifty; he was also stout and in poor health. He walked slowly up past us, to 'take a squint at things', as he put it, and see if it was possible to get past the stuck wagons. A little later he started, making three loads of his two and going up with single spans of eighteen oxen each – because the other wagons, stuck in various places on the road, did not give him room to work double spans. To us it seemed madness to attempt with eighteen oxen a harder task than we and others were essaying with thirty. We would have waited until the road ahead was clear.

We were halfway up when we saw old Charlie coming along steadily and without any fuss at all. He had no second driver to help him. He did no shouting. He walked along heavily and with difficulty beside the span, playing the long whip lightly about as he gave the word to go or called quietly to individual oxen by name, but he did not touch them; and when he paused to 'blow' them he leaned heavily on his whip-stick to rest himself.

We were completely blocking the road when he caught up. Anyone else would have waited : he pulled out into the rough, sideling track on the slope below, to pass us. Even a good span with a good driver may well come to grief in trying to pass another that is stuck – for the sight and example are demoralizing – but old Charlie did not turn a hair. He went steadily on, giving a brisker call and touching up his oxen here and there with light flicks. They used to say he could kill a fly on a front ox or on the toe of his own boot with the voorslag of his big whip.

The track he took was so steep and rough there that a pull of ten yards between the spells for breath was all one could hope for. At the second pause, as they were passing us, one of his oxen turned, leaning inward against the chain, and looked back. Old Charlie remarked quietly, 'I thought he would chuck it; only bought him last week. He's got no heart.'

He walked along the span up to the shirking animal, which continued to glare back at him in a frightened way, and touched it behind with the butt of his long whip-stick to bring it up to the yoke. The ox started forward into place with a jerk, but eased back again slightly as Charlie went back to his place near the after oxen. Once more the span went on and the shirker got a smart reminder as Charlie gave the call to start. At the next stop it lay back worse than before.

Not one driver in a hundred would have done then what he did. They would have tried other courses first. Charlie dropped his whip quietly and outspanned the ox and its mate, saying to me as I gave him a hand :

'When I strike a rotter, I chuck him out before he spoils the others!' In another ten minutes he and his stalwarts had left us behind.

Old Charlie knew his oxen – each one of them, their

characters and what they could do. I think he loved them too. At any rate, it was his care for them that day – handling them himself instead of leaving it to his boys – that killed him. We buried him at Pilgrim's Rest a week later. The cold, clear air on top of the Berg that night, when he brought the last load up, brought out the fever. It was his last trek.

*

There are many and great differences in the temperaments and characters of oxen, just as there are in other animals or in human beings. I can remember some of them now far better than many of the men known then and since :

Achmoed and Bakir, the big after oxen who carried the disselboom contentedly through the trek and were spared all other work to save them for emergencies; who, at a word, heaved together – their great backs bent like bows and their giant strength thrown in to hoist the wagon from the deepest hole and up the steepest hill; who were the standby in the worst descents, lying back on their haunches to hold the wagon up when brakes could do no more; and inseparable always – even when outspanned the two old comrades walked together.

There was Zole, contented, sociable and short of wind, looking like a fat boy on a hot day, always in distress. There was Bantom, the big red ox with the white band, lazy and selfish, with an enduring evil obstinacy that was simply incredible. There was Rooiland, the light red, with yellow eyeballs and topped horns; a fierce, wild, unapproachable, unappeasable creature, restless and impatient, always strain-

ing to start, always moaning fretfully when delayed; nervous as a young thoroughbred, aloof and unfriendly to man and beast, ever ready to stab or kick even those who handled him daily. He would work with a straining, tearing impatience, ever ready to outpace the rest; and at the outspan stand out alone, hollow flanked and panting, eyes and nostrils wide with fierceness and distress, yet always ready to start again – a miracle of intense vitality!

And then there was old Zwaartland, the coal-black front ox, and the best of all: the sober, steadfast leader of the span, who knew his work by heart and answered with quickened pace to any call of his name; swinging wide at every curve to avoid cutting corners; easing up, yet leading free, at every steep descent, so as neither to rush the incline nor entangle the span; holding his ground, steady as a rock when the big pull came, heedless of how the team swayed and strained – steadfast even when his mate gave in. He stood out from all the rest; the massive horns – like one huge spiral pin passed through his head, eight feet from tip to tip – balancing with easy swing; the clean limbs and small, neat feet moving with the quick precision of a buck's tread; and the large, grave eyes so soft and clear and deep!

The work itself was full of test and teaching. The hard abstemious life had its daily lesson in patience and resource, driven home by every variety of means and incident on that unkindly road. And the dumb cattle – in their plodding toil, in their sufferings from drought and over work, and in their strength and weakness – taught and tested too.

There was a day at Kruger's Post when everything seemed small beside the figure of one black front ox, who held his ground when all others failed. The wagon had sunk to the bed-plank in gluey turf, and, although the whole load had been taken off, three spans linked together failed to move it. For eight hours that day we tried to dig and pull it out, but forty-four oxen on that soft, greasy flat toiled in vain. The long strain of bullocks, desperate from failure and bewilderment, swayed in the middle from side to side to seek escape from the flying whips. The unyielding wagon held them at one end, and the front oxen – with their straining fore-feet scoring the slippery surface as they were dragged backwards – strove to hold them true at the other.

Seven times that day we changed, trying to find a mate who would stand with Zwaartland; but he wore them all down. He broke their hearts and stood it out alone! I looked at the ground afterwards. It was grooved in long parallel lines where the swaying spans had pulled him backwards, with his four feet clawing the ground in an effort to hold them true. But he had never once turned or wavered.

*

There was a day at Sand River, when we saw a different picture. The wagons were empty, yet as we came up out of the stony drift, Bantom the sulky hung lazily back, dragging on his yoke and throwing the span out of line. Jim curled the big whip round him, without any good effect, and when the span stopped for a breather in the deep narrow road, he lay down and refused to budge. There was no reason in the world for it except the animal's obstinate sulky temper. When the whip – the giraffe-hide thong,

doubled into a heavy loop – produced no effect, the boys took the yoke off to see if freedom would tempt the animal to rise! It did. At the first touch of the whip Bantom jumped up and charged them. Seeing that there was nothing at all the matter, the boys inspanned him and made a fresh start – not touching him again for fear of another fit of sulks; but at the first call on the team, down he went again.

Many are the stories of cruelty to oxen, and I had never understood how human beings could be so fiendishly cruel as to do some of the things that one heard of; nor under what circumstances or for what reasons such acts of brutality could be perpetrated. But what I saw that day threw some light on these questions, and, more than anything else, it showed the length to which sulkiness and obstinacy will go.

There were two considerations here which governed the whole case. The first was that as long as the ox lay there it was impossible to move the wagon, and there was no way for the others to pass it. The second, that the ox was free, strong and perfectly well, and all he had to do was to get up and walk.

The drivers from the other wagons came up to lend a hand and clear the way so that they might get on. Sometimes three were at it together with their double whips; and, before they could be stopped, sticks and stones were used to hammer the animal on the head and horns, along the spine, on the hocks and shins, and wherever he was supposed to have feeling. Then he was tied by the horns to the trek-chain, so that the span would drag him bodily; but not once did he make the smallest effort to rise.

The road was merely a gutter scoured out by the floods and it was not possible either to drag the animal up the steep sides or to leave him and go on – the wagon would have to pass over him. And all this time he was outspanned and free to go; but would not stir.

Then they did the native trick – doubled the tail and bit it: very few bullocks will stand that, but Bantom never winced. Then they took their clasp knives and used them as spurs – not stabbing to do real injury, but pricking enough to draw blood in the fleshy parts, where it could be most felt: he twitched to the pricks – but nothing more. Then they made a fire close behind him, and, as the wood blazed up, the heat seemed unendurable. The smell of singed hair was strong, and the flames, not a foot away, seemed to roast the flesh. One of the drivers took a brand and pressed the glowing red coal against the inside of the hams; but beyond a vicious kick at the fire, there was no result. Then they tried to suffocate him, gripping the mouth and nostrils so that he could not breathe. But, when the limit of endurance was reached and even the spectators tightened up with a sense of suffocation, a savage shake of the head always freed it – the brute was too strong for them. Then they raised the head with reims, and with the nose held high poured water down the nostrils, at the same time keeping the mouth firmly closed. But he blew the water all over them and shook himself free again.

For the better part of an hour the struggle went on, but there was not the least sign of yielding on Bantom's part. The string of waiting wagons grew longer, and many others, white men and black, gathered round watching, helping or suggesting.

At last some one brought a bucket of water, and into this Bantom's muzzle was thrust as far as it would go; and reims, passed through the ears of the bucket, were slipped round his horns so that he could not shake himself free at will. We stood back and watched the animal's sides for signs of breathing. For an incredible time he held out. But at last with a sudden plunge he was up. A bubbling muffled bellow came from the bucket; the boys let go the reims; and the terrified animal, ridding himself of the bucket after a frantic struggle, stood with legs apart and eyeballs starting from the sockets, shaking like a reed.

It stood passive, and apparently beaten, while the boys inspanned it again. But at the first call to the team to start, and without a touch to provoke its temper again, it dropped down once more. Not one of those looking on would have believed it possible, but there it was. In the most deliberate manner the challenge was again flung down, and the whole fight begun afresh.

We really felt desperate. One could think of nothing but to repeat the bucket trick, for it was the only one that had succeeded at all. The bucket had been flung aside on the stones as the ox freed itself, and one of the boys picked it up to fetch more water. But no more was needed. The rattle of the bucket brought Bantom to his feet with a terrified jump and flinging his whole weight into the yoke, he gave the wagon a heave that started the whole span, and they went out at a run.

It would have taken a good man to handle Bantom at any time – even in the beginning. But, full grown, and confirmed in his evil ways, only the butcher could make anything out of him.

And only the butcher did!

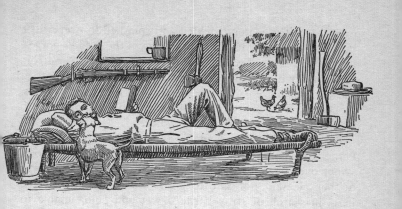

Paradise Camp

THERE is a spot on the edge of the Berg which we made our summer quarters. When September came round and the sun swung higher in the steely blue, blazing down more pitilessly than ever – when the little creeks ran dry, the water-holes became saucers of cracked mud and the whole country smelt of fine impalpable dust – it was a relief to quit the Bushveld, and even the hunting was given up almost without regret.

Paradise Camp perched on the very edge of the Berg. Behind us rolled green slopes to the feet of the higher peaks, and in front of us lay the Bushveld. From the broken battlements of the Berg we looked down three thousand feet, and eastward to the sea a hundred and fifty miles away, across the vast panorama.

Black, densely timbered kloofs broke the edge of the plateau into a long series of projecting turrets, in some places cutting far in – deep crevices into which the bigger waterfalls plunged and were lost. But the top of the Berg itself was bare of trees. The breeze blew cool and fresh for ever there. The waters trickled and splashed in every little break or tumbled with steady roar down the greater gorges. Deep pools, fringed with masses of ferns, smooth as mirrors or flecked with dancing sunlight, were set like brilliants in the silver chain of each little stream; and rocks and pebbles, wonderful in their colours, were magnified and glorified into polished gems by the sparkling water.

But Nature has her moods, and it was not always thus at Paradise Camp. When the cold mist-rains, like wet grey fogs, swept over us and for a week blotted out creation, it was neither pleasant nor safe to grope along the edge of the Berg, in search of stray cattle – wet and cold, unable to see, and checked from time to time by a keener, straighter gust that leapt up over the unseen precipice a few yards off.

And there was still another mood when the summer rains set in and the storms burst over us, and the lightning stabbed viciously in all directions, and the crackling of the thunder seemed as if the very Berg must be split and shattered. Then the rivers rose, the roar of waters was all around us, and Paradise Camp was isolated from the rest by floods which no man would face lightly.

Paradise Camp stood on the edge of the kloof where the nearest timber grew. Tumbling Waters, where stood the thousand grey sandstone sentinels of strange fantastic shapes, was a couple of miles away facing Black Buff – the highest point of all – and The Camel, The Wolf, The Sitting Hen and scores more, rough casts in rock by Nature's hand, stood there. Close below us was the Bathing Pool, with its twenty feet of purest water, its three rock-ledge 'springboards', and its banks of moss and canopies of tree ferns.

Further down, the stream spread in a thousand pools and rapids over a mile of black bedrock, and then poured in one broad sheet over Graskop Falls. And still further down were the Mac Mac Falls, three hundred feet straight drop into the rock-strewn gorge, where the straight walls were draped with staghorn moss, like countless folds of delicate green lace, bespangled by the spray.

We were felling and slipping timber for the gold-fields then, and it was in these surroundings that the work was done.

It was a Sunday morning, and I was lying on my back on a sack-stretcher taking it easy, when Jock gave a growl and trotted out. Presently I heard voices in the next hut and wondered who the visitors were – too lazily content to get up and see. Then a cold nose was poked against my cheek and I looked round to see Jess's little eyes and flickering ears within a few inches of my face. For the moment she did not look cross, but as if a faint smile of welcome were flitting across a soured face; then she trotted back to the other hut where Ted was patting Jock and trying to trace a likeness to The Rat.

It was a long time since mother and son had been together, and if the difference between them was remarkable, the likeness seemed to me more striking still. Jock had grown up by himself and made himself. He was so different from other dogs that I had forgotten how much he owed to good old Jess. But now that they were once more side by side everything he did and had done recalled the likeness and yet showed the difference between them. Many times as we moved about the camp or worked in the woods they walked or stood together, sometimes sniffing along some spoor and sometimes waiting and watching for us to come up – handsome son and ugly mother. Ugly she might be – with her little, fretful, hostile eyes and her uncertain ever-moving ears – and silent, sour and cross. But stubborn fidelity and reckless courage were hers too; and all the good Jock had in him came from Jess.

To see them side by side was enough. Every line in his golden brindle coat had its counterpart in her dull markings. His jaw was hers, every whit as determined but without the savage look. His eyes were hers – brown to black as the moods changed – yet not fretful and cross; serenely observant when quiet, and black, hot and angry, like hers, when roused – yet without the look of relentless cruelty. His ears were hers – and yet how different; not shifting, flickering and ever on the move, but sure in their movements and faithful reflectors of a more balanced temper; and so often cocked – one full and one half – with a look of genuinely friendly interest which, when he put his head on one side, seemed to change in a curiously comical way into an expression of quiet amusement.

The work kept us close to camp and we gave no thought to shooting; yet Jess and Jock had some good sport together. We gave them courses for breathers after oribi in the open, but these fleetest of little antelopes left them out of sight in a very few minutes. Bushbuck too were plentiful enough, but so wily in keeping to the dark woods and deep kloofs that, unless we organized a drive, the only chance one got was to stalk them in the early morning as they fed on the fringes of the bush. I often wondered how the dogs would have fared with those desperate fighters that have injured and killed more dogs and more men than any other buck, save perhaps the sable.

Then the dainty little klipspringers led them many a crazy

dance along the crags and ledges of the mountain face, jumping from rock to rock with the utmost ease and certainty and looking down with calm curiosity at the clumsy scrambling dogs as they vainly tried to follow. The dassies too – watchful, silent and rubber-footed – played hide-and-seek with them in the cracks and crevices; but the dogs had no chance there.

Often there were races after baboons. There were thousands of them along the Berg, but, except when a few were found in the open, we always called the dogs in. Among a troop of baboons the best of dogs would have no show at all. Ugly, savage and treacherous as they are, they have at least one quality which compels admiration – they stand by each other. If one is attacked or wounded the others will often turn back and help, and they will literally tear a dog to pieces. Even against one full-grown male a dog has little or no chance; for they are very powerful, quick as lightning, and fierce fighters. Their enormous jaws and teeth outmatch a dog's, and with four 'hands' to help them the advantage is altogether too great. Their method of fighting

is to hold the dog with all four feet and tear pieces out of him with their teeth.

One day while at work in the woods there came to us a grizzled worn-looking old native, whose head ring of polished black wax attested his dignity as a kehla. He carried an old musket and was attended by two youngsters armed with throwing-sticks and a hunting assegai each. He appeared to be a 'somebody' in a small way, and we knew at a glance that he had not come for nothing.

The old man, passing and ignoring the group of boys, came towards us as we sat in the shade for the midday rest. Slowly he came to a stand a few yards off, leaning on his long flint-lock quietly taking stock of us each in turn, and waiting for us to inspect him. Then, after three or four minutes of this, he proceeded to salute us separately with '*Sakubona, Umlungu!*' delivered with measured deliberation at intervals of about a quarter of a minute. Each salutation was accompanied by the customary upward movement of the head – their respectful equivalent of our nod or bow.

When he had done the round, his two attendants took their turns, when this was over – and another long pause had served to mark his respect – he drew back a few paces to a spot about halfway between us and where the natives sat, and, tucking his loin skins comfortably under him, squatted down. Ten minutes more elapsed before he allowed his eyes to wander absently round towards the boys and finally to settle on them for a repetition of the performance that we had been favoured with. But in this case it was they who led off with the '*Sakubona, Umganaam!*' which he acknowledged with the raising of the head and a soft murmur of contented recognition, '*A-hé*'.

Once more there was silence for a spell, while he waited to be questioned in the customary manner and to give an account of himself, before it would be courteous or proper to introduce the subject of his visit. It was Jim's voice that broke the silence – clear and imperative, as usual, but not uncivil.

'*Velapi, Umganaam?*' (Where do you come from, friend?) he asked, putting the question which is recognized as courteously providing the stranger with an opening to give an account of himself; and he is expected and required to do so before he in turn can ask all about them.

The talk went round in low exchanges until at last the old man moved closer and joined the circle. Then the other voices dropped out, only to be heard once in a while in some brief question, or that briefest of all comments – the native click and 'ow!' It may mean anything, according to the tone, but it was clearly sympathetic on that occasion. The old man's voice went on monotonously in a low-pitched impassive tone; but the boys hung intent on every word to the end. Then one or two questions, briefly answered in the same tone, brought their talk to a close.

The old fellow tapped his carved wood snuff-box with the carefully preserved long yellowish nail of one forefinger, and, pouring some snuff into the palm of his hand, drew it into each nostril in turn with long luxurious sniffs. Then, resting his arms on his knees, he relapsed into complete silence.

We called the boys to start work again, and they came away, as is their custom, without a word or look towards the man whose story had held them for the last half-hour. Nor did he speak or stir, but sat on unmoved, a picture of stoical indifference.

We asked no questions, for we knew it was no accident that had brought the old man our way: he wanted something, and we would learn soon enough what it was. So we waited.

As we gathered round the fallen tree to finish the cleaning and slip it down the track Jim remarked irrelevantly that leopards were 'schelms', and it was his conviction that there were a great many in the kloofs round about. At intervals during the next hour or so he dropped other scraps about leopards and their ways, and how to get at them, winding up with a short account of how two seasons back an English 'Capitaine' had been killed by one only a few miles away.

Jim was no diplomatist : he had leopard on the brain, and showed it. So when I asked him bluntly what the old man had been talking about, the whole story came out.

There was a leopard – it was of course the biggest ever seen – which had been preying on the old chief's kraal for the last six months : dogs, goats and sheep innumerable had disappeared, even fowls were not despised; and only two days ago the climax had been reached when, in the cool of the afternoon and in defiance of the yelling herd-boy, it had slipped into the herd at the drinking place and carried off a calf – a heifer-calf too! The old man was poor. The leopard had nearly ruined him, and he had come up to see if we, 'who were great hunters', would come down and kill the thief, or at least lend him a leopard-trap, as he could not afford to buy one.

In the evening when we returned to camp we found the old fellow there, and heard the story told with the same patient resignation of stoical indifference with which he had told it to the boys. And we decided to go.

The following afternoon we set off with our guns and blankets, a little food for two days, and the leopard-trap; and by nightfall we had reached the foot of the Berg by paths and ways which you might think only a baboon could follow.

It was moonlight, and we moved along through the heavily timbered kloofs in single file behind the shadowy figure of the shrivelled old chief. His years seemed no handicap to him, as with long, easy, soft-footed strides he went on hour after hour. The air was delightfully cool and sweet with the fresh smells of the woods. The damp carpet of moss and dead leaves dulled the sound of our more blundering steps. Now and again through the thick canopy of evergreens we caught glimpses of the moon, and in odd places the light threw stumps or rocks into quaint relief or turned some tall bare trunk into a ghostly sentinel of the forest.

We had crossed the last of the many mountain streams and reached open ground when the old chief stopped. Pointing to the face of a high krans – black and threatening in the shadow, as it seemed to overhang us – he said that somewhere up there was a cave which was the leopard's home; and it was from this safe refuge that he raided the countryside.

The kraal was not far off. From the top of the spur we could look round – as from the pit of some vast coliseum – and see the huge wall of the Berg towering up above and half enclosing us, the whole arena roofed over by the starspattered sky. The brilliant moonlight picked out every ridge and hill, deepening the velvet black of the shadowed valleys, and on the rise before us there was the twinkling light of a small fire; and the sound of voices came to us, borne on the still night air, so clearly that words picked out here and there were repeated by our boys with grunting comments and chuckles of amusement.

We started on again down an easy slope passing through some bush, and at the bottom came on level ground thinly covered with big shady trees and scattered undergrowth. As we walked briskly through the flecked and dappled light and shade, we were startled by the sudden and furious rush of Jess and Jock off the path and away into the scrub on the left; and immediately after there was a grunting noise, a crashing and scrambling, and then one clear sharp yelp of pain from one of the dogs. The old chief ran back behind us, shouting 'Ingwe, ingwe!' (Leopard, leopard!) We slipped our rifles round and stood facing front, unable to see anything and not knowing what to expect. There were sounds of some sort in the bush – something like a faint scratching, and something like smothered sobbing grunts, but so indis-

tinct as to be more ominous and disquieting than absolute
silence.

'He has killed the dogs,' the old chief said in a low voice.

But as he said it there was a rustle in front, and something came out towards us. The guns were up and levelled,
instantly, but dropped again when we saw it was a dog;
and Jess came back limping badly and stopping every few
paces to shake her head and rub her mouth against her fore-
paws. She was in great pain and breathed out faint barely
audible whines from time to time.

We waited for minutes, but Jock did not appear; and as
the curious sounds still came from the bush we moved forward in open order, very slowly and with infinite caution.
As we got closer, scouting each bush and open space, the
sounds grew clearer, and suddenly it came to me that it was
the noise of a body being dragged and the grunting breathing of a dog. I called sharply to Jock and the sound stopped.
Then taking a few paces forward, I saw him in a moonlit
space turning round and round on the pivot of his hind-
legs and swinging or dragging something much bigger than
himself.

Jim gave a yell and shot past me, plunging his assegai
into the object and shouting, 'Porcupine, porcupine,' at
the top of his voice. We were all round it in a couple of
seconds, but I think the porcupine was as good as dead
even before Jim had stabbed it. Jock was still holding on
grimly, tugging with all his might and always with the

same movement of swinging it round him, or of himself circling round it – perhaps that is the fairer description, for the porcupine was much the heavier. He had it by the throat where the flesh is bare of quills, and had kept himself out of reach of the terrible spikes by pulling away all the time, just as he had done with duiker and other buck to avoid their hind-feet.

This encounter with the porcupine gave us a better chance of getting the leopard than we ever expected – too good a chance to be neglected. So we cut the animal up and used

the worthless parts to bait the big leopard-trap – having first dragged them across the veld for a good distance each way to leave a blood spoor which would lead the leopard up to the trap. This, with the quantity of blood spread about in the fight, lying right in the track of his usual prowling ought to attract his attention, we thought. We fastened the trap to a big tree, making an avenue of bushes up to the bait so that he would have to walk right over the trap hidden under the dead leaves, in order to get to the bait. We hoped that, if it failed to hold, it would at least wound him badly enough to enable us to follow him up in the morning.

In the bright light of the fire that night, as Jock lay beside me having his share of the porcupine steaks, I noticed something curious about his chest, and on looking closer found the whole of his white 'shirt front' speckled with dots of blood. He had been pricked in dozens of places, and it was clear that it had been no walk-over for him; he must have had a pretty rough handling before he got the porcupine on the swing. He was none the worse, however, and was the picture of contentment as he lay beside me in the ring facing the fire.

But Jess was a puzzle. From the time that she had come hobbling back to us, one foot in the air, and stopping to rub her mouth on her paws, we had been trying to find out what was the matter. The foot trouble was clear enough, for there was a quill fifteen inches long and as stiff and thick as a lead pencil still piercing the ball of her foot, with the needle-like point sticking out between her toes. Fortunately it had not been driven far through and the hole was small, so that once it was drawn and the foot bandaged she got along fairly well. It was not the foot that was troubling her; all through the evening she kept repeating the movement of her head, either rubbing it on her front legs or wiping her muzzle with the paws, much as a cat does when washing its face. She would not touch food and could not lie still for five minutes; and we could do nothing to help her.

The Leopard and the Baboons

No one had doubted Jess's courage, even when we saw her come back alone. We knew there was something wrong, but in spite of every care and effort we could not find out what it was; and poor old Jess went through the night in suffering, making no sound, but moving from place to place weary and restless, giving long tired quivering sighs, and pawing at her mouth from time to time. In the morning light we again looked her all over carefully, and especially opened her mouth and examined that and her nostrils, but could find nothing to show what was wrong.

The puzzle was solved by accident: Ted was sitting on the ground when she came up to him, looking wistfully into his face again with one of the mute appeals for help.

'What is it, Jess, old girl?' he said, and reached out. He caught her head in both hands and drew her towards him, but with a sharp exclamation he instantly let go again, pricked by something, and a drop of blood oozed from one finger-tip. Under Jess's right ear there was a hard sharp point just showing through the skin. We all felt it, and when the skin was forced back we saw it was the tip of a porcupine quill. There was no pulling it out or moving it, however, nor could we for a long time find where it had entered. At last Ted noticed what looked like a tiny narrow strip of bark adhering to the outside of her lower lip, and this turned out to be the broken end of the quill, snapped off close to the flesh. Not even the end of the quill was visible – only the little strip that had peeled off in the breaking.

Poor old Jess! We had no very grand appliances for surgery, and had to slit her lip down with an ordinary skinning knife. Ted held her between his knees and gripped her head with both hands, while one of us pulled with steel pliers on the broken quill until it came out. The quill had pierced her lower lip, entered the gums beside the front teeth, run all along the jaw and through the flesh behind, coming out just below the ear. It was over seven inches long. She struggled a little under the rough treatment, and there was a protesting whimper when we tugged; but she did not let out one cry under all the pain.

We knew then that Jess had done her share in the fight, and guessed that it was she who in her reckless charge had rolled the porcupine over and given Jock his chance.

The doctoring of Jess had delayed us considerably, and while we were still busy at it the old chief came up to say that his scouts had returned and reported that there was no leopard to be seen, but that they thought the trap had been sprung. They had not liked to go close up, preferring to observe the spot from a tree some way off.

The first question was what to do with Jess. We had no collar or chain, of course, and nothing would induce her to stay behind once Ted started. She would have bitten through ropes and reims in a few minutes, and no native would have faced the job of watching over and checking her. Finally we put her into one of the reed and mud huts, closing the entrance with some raw hides weighted with heavy stones; and off we went.

We found the trap sprung and the bait untouched. The

spoor was a leopard's right enough. We saw where it had circled suspiciously all round before finally entering the little fenced approach which we had built to shepherd it on to the trap. There each footprint was clear, and it appeared that instead of cautiously creeping right up to the bait and stepping on the setting-plate, it had made a pounce at the bait from about ten feet away, releasing the trap by knocking the spring or by touching the plate with the barrel of its body. The leopard had evidently been nipped, but the body was too big for the teeth to close on. No doubt the spring it gave, on feeling the grip underneath, set it free

with nothing worse than a bad scraping and a tremendous fright. There was plenty of hair and some skin on the teeth of the trap, but very little blood there, and none at all to be found round about.

That was almost the worst result we could have had. The leopard was not crippled, nor was it wounded enough to enable us to track it. But it must have been so thoroughly alarmed that it would certainly be extremely nervous and suspicious of everything now, and would probably avoid the neighbourhood for some time to come.

The trap was clearly of no further use, but after coming so far for the leopard we were not disposed to give up the hunt without another effort. The natives told us it was quite useless to follow it up as it was a real 'schelm', and by that time would be miles away in some inaccessible krans. We determined however to go on, and if we failed to get a trace of the leopard, to put in the day hunting bushbuck or wild pig, both of which were fairly plentiful.

We had not gone more than a few hundred yards when an exclamation from one of the boys made us look round, and we saw Jess on the opposite slope coming along full speed after us with her nose to the trail. She had scratched and bitten her way through the reed and mud wall of the hut, scared the wits out of a couple of boys who had tried to head her off, and raced away after us with a pack of kraal mongrels yelping unnoticed at her heels. She really did not seem much the worse for her wounds, and was – for her – quite demonstrative in her delight at finding us again.

In any case there was nothing to be done but to let her come, and we went on once more beating up towards the lair in the black krans with the two dogs in the lead.

The guides led us down into the bed of one of the mountain streams, and following this up we were soon in the woods where the big trees meeting overhead made it dark and cool. It was difficult in that light to see anything clearly at first, and the considerable undergrowth of shrub and creepers and the boulders shed from the Berg added to the difficulty and made progress slow. We moved along as much as possible abreast, five or six yards apart, but were often driven by obstacles into the bed of the stream for short distances in order to make headway at all. Although there did not seem to be much chance of finding the leopard at home, we crept along cautiously and noiselessly, talking – when we had to – only in whispers.

We were bunched together, preparing to crawl along a rock overhanging a little pool, when the boy in front made a sign and pointed with his assegai to the dogs. They had crossed the stream and were walking – very slowly and abreast – near the water's edge. The rawest of beginners would have needed no explanation. The two stood for a few seconds sniffing at a particular spot and then both together looked steadily upstream. There was another pause and they moved very slowly and carefully forward a yard or so and sniffed again with their noses almost touching. As they did this the hair on their backs and shoulders began to rise until, as they reached the head of the pool, they were bristling like hedgehogs and giving little purring growls.

The guide went over to them while we waited, afraid to move lest the noise of our boots on the stones should betray us. After looking round for a bit he pointed to a spot on the bank where he had found the fresh spoor of the leopard, and picking up something there to show to us he came back

to our side. It was a little fragment of whitish skin with white hairs on it. There was no doubt about it then: we were on the fresh spoor of the leopard where it had stopped to drink at the pool and probably to lick the scratches made by the trap; and leaving the bed of the stream it had gone through the thick undergrowth up towards the krans.

We were not more than a hundred yards from the krans then, and the track taken by the leopard was not at all an inviting one. It was at first merely a narrow tunnel in the undergrowth up the steep hillside, through which we crept in single file with the two dogs a few yards in front. They moved on in the same silent deliberate way, so intent and strung up that they started slightly and instantly looked up in front at the least sound. As the ascent became steeper and more rocky, the undergrowth thinned and we were able to spread out into line once more, threading our way through several roughly parallel game tracks or natural openings and stooping low to watch the dogs and take our cue from them.

We were about fifteen yards from the precipitous face of the krans, and had just worked round a huge boulder into a space fairly free of bush but cumbered with many big rocks and loose stones, when the dogs stopped and stood quivering and bristling all over, moving their heads slowly about with noses well raised and sniffing persistently. There was something now that interested them more than the spoor : they winded the leopard itself, but could not tell where. No one stirred. We stood watching the dogs and snatching glances right and left among the boulders and their shady creeper-hidden caves and recesses.

As we stood thus, grouped together in breathless silence, an electrifying snarling roar came from the krans above and the spotted body of the leopard shot like a streak out of the black mouth of a cave and across our front into the bush. There was a series of crashing bounds, as though a stone rolled from the mountain were leaping through the jungle; and then absolute silence.

We explored the den, but there was nothing of interest in it – no remains of food, no old bones or other signs of cubs. It seemed to be the retreat of a male leopard – secluded, quiet and cool. The opening was not visible from any distance, a split-off slab of rock partly hiding it. But when we stood upon the rock platform we found that almost the whole of the horseshoe bay in the Berg into which we had descended was visible. It was with surprise and mortification that the kraal boys found they could see the kraal itself and their goats and cattle grazing on the slopes and in the valley below.

It would have been a waste of time to follow our leopard – he would be on the watch and on the move for hours. So we gave it up at once, and struck across the spurs for another part of the big arena where pig and bushbuck were known to feed in the mornings. It was slow and difficult work, as the bush was very dense and the ground rough. The place was riddled with game tracks, and we saw spoor of kudu and eland several times, and tracks innumerable of wild pig, rietbuck, bushbuck and duiker. But there was more than spoor: a dozen times we heard the crash of startled animals through the reeds or bush only a few yards away without being able to see a thing.

We had nearly reached the kloof we were aiming for when we had the good luck to get a bushbuck in a very unexpected way. We had worked our way out of a particularly dense patch of bush and brambles into a corner of the woods and were resting on the mossy ground in the shade of the big trees, when the sound of clattering stones a good way off made us start up again and grab our rifles. Presently we saw, outlined against the band of light which marked the edge of the timber, a buck charging down towards us. Three of us fired together, and the buck rolled over within a few yards of where we stood.

We were then in a 'dead end' up against the precipitous face of the Berg where there was no road or path other than game tracks, and where no human being ever went except for the purpose of hunting. We knew there was no one else shooting there, and it puzzled us considerably to think what had scared the bushbuck, for the animal had certainly been startled and perhaps chased. The pace, the noise it made, and the blind recklessness of its dash, all showed that. The only explanation we could think of was that the leopard, in making a circuit along the slopes of the Berg to get away from us, must have put the buck up and driven it down on to us in the woods below. If that were so, the reports of our rifles must have made him think that he was never going to get rid of us.

We skinned and cut up the buck and pushed on again. But the roughness of the trail and the various stoppages had delayed us greatly, and we made for the nearest stream in the woods for a feed and a rest before returning to camp. We had failed to get the leopard, it is true, and it would be useless giving more time or further thought to him, for in all probability it would be a week or more before he returned to his old hunting-ground and his old marauding tricks. But on the whole, although disappointed, we were not dissatisfied. In fact, it would have needed an ungrateful spirit indeed to feel discontented in such surroundings.

Big trees of many kinds and shapes united to make a canopy of leaves overhead through which only occasional shafts of sunlight struck. The cold mountain stream tumbling over ledges, swirling among rocks or rippling over pebble-strewn reaches, gurgled, splashed and bubbled with that wonderful medley of sounds that go to make the lullaby of the brook. The floor of the forest was carpeted with a pile of staghorn moss a foot thick; Traveller's Joy covered whole trees with dense creamy bloom and spread fragrance everywhere; wild clematis trailed over stumps and fallen branches; quantities of maidenhair overflowed the banks and dropped to the water all along the course of the stream; while, marshalled on either side, perched on rocks and grouped on overhanging ledges, stood the tree-ferns – as though they had come to drink – their wide-reaching delicate fronds, like giant green ostrich-feathers, waving gently to each breath of air or quivering as the movement of the water shook the trunks.

Long-tailed greeny-grey monkeys with black faces peered down at us, moving lightly on their branch trapezes, and pulled faces or chattered their indignant protest against intrusion. In the tops of the wild fig trees bright green pigeons watched us shyly – great birds of a wonderful green; gorgeous louries, too, flashed their colours and raised their crests – pictures of extreme and comical surprise; golden cuckoos

there were also and beautiful little green-backed, ruby-throated honey-suckers flitted like butterflies among the flowers on the sunlit fringe of the woods.

Now and again guinea-fowl and bush-pheasant craned their necks over some fallen log or stone to peer curiously at us, then stooping low again darted along their well-worn runs into the thick bush. The place was in fact a natural preserve; a 'bay' let into the wall of the Berg, half encircled by cliffs which nothing could climb, a little world where the common enemy – man – seldom intruded.

We stayed until the afternoon sun had passed behind the crest of the Berg above us, and, instead of going back the way we came, skirted along the other arm enclosing the bay to have the cool shade of the mountain with us on our return journey. But the way was rough, the jungle was dense, we were hot and torn and tired, and the shadow of the mountain stretched far out across the foothills by the time the corner was reached. We sat down to rest at last in the open on the long spur on which, a couple of miles away, the slanting sun picked out the red and black cattle, the white goats and the brown huts of the native kraal.

Our route lay along the side of the spur, skirting the rocky backbone and winding between occasional boulders

and clumps of trees and bush. We had moved on only a little way when a loud 'waugh' from a baboon on the mountain behind made us stop to look back. The hoarse shout was repeated several times, and each time more loudly and emphatically. It seemed like the warning call of a sentry who had seen us. Moved by curiosity we turned aside on to the ridge itself, and from the top of a big rock scanned the almost precipitous face opposite.

The spur on which we stood was divided from the Berg itself only by a deep but narrow kloof or ravine, and every detail of the mountain side stood out in the clear evening air. Against the many-coloured rocks the grey figure of a baboon was not easy to find as long as it remained still.

Although from time to time the barking roar was repeated, we were still scanning the opposite hill when one of the boys pointed down the slope immediately below us and called out, 'There, there, Baas!'

The troop of baboons had evidently been quite close to us – hidden from us only by the little line of rocks – and on getting warning from their sentry on the mountain had stolen quietly away and were then disappearing into the timbered depth of the ravine. We sat still to watch them come out on the opposite side a few minutes later and clamber up the rocky face, for they are always worth watching. But while we watched, the stillness was broken by an agonized scream – horribly human in its expression of terror – followed by roars, barks, bellows and screams from scores of voices in every key; and the crackle of breaking sticks and the rattle of stones added to the medley of sounds as the baboons raced out of the wood and up the bare rocky slope.

'What is it? What's the matter?' 'There's something after them.' 'Look, look! there they come,' burst from one and another of us as we watched the extraordinary scene. The cries from below seemed to waken the whole mountain. Great booming 'waughs' came from different places far apart and high up the face of the Berg. Each big roar seemed to act like a trumpet-call and bring forth a multitude of others; and the air rang with bewildering shouts and echoes volleying round the kloofs and faces of the Berg. The strange thing was that the baboons did not continue their terrified scramble up the mountain, but, once out of the bush, they turned and rallied. Forming an irregular semicircle, they faced down hill, thrusting their heads forward with sudden jerks as though to launch their cries with greater vehemence and feinting to charge. They showered loose earth, stones and debris of all sorts down with awkward underhand scrapes of their fore-paws, and gradually but surely descended to within a dozen yards of the bush's edge.

'Baas, Baas, the leopard! Look, the leopard! There, there on the rock below!'

Jim shot the words out in vehement gusts, choky with excitement, and true enough there the leopard was. The long spotted body was crouched on a flat rock just below the baboons. He was broad-side to us, with his fore-quarters slightly raised and his face turned towards the baboons. With wide-opened mouth he snarled savagely at the advancing line, and with right paw raised made threatening dabs in their direction. His left paw pinned down the body of a baboon.

The voices from the mountain boomed louder and nearer

as, clattering and scrambling down the face, came more and more baboons. There must have been hundreds of them. The semicircle grew thicker and blacker, more and more threatening, foot by foot closer. The leopard raised himself a little more and took swift looks from side to side across the advancing front, and then his nerve went, and with one spring he shot from the rock into the bush.

There was an instant forward rush of the half-moon, and the rock was covered with roaring baboons, swarming over their rescued comrade; and a moment later the crowd scrambled up the slope again, taking the leopard's victim with them. In the seething rabble, I could pick out nothing, but all the natives maintained they could see the mauled one dragged along by its arms by two others, much as a child might be helped uphill.

We were still looking excitedly about – trying to make out what the baboons were doing, watching the others still coming down the Berg, and peering anxiously for a sight of the leopard – when once more Jim's voice gave us a shock.

'Where are the dogs?' he asked, and the question turned us cold. If they had gone after the baboons they were as good as dead already – nothing could save them. Calling was useless. Nothing could be heard in the roar and din that the enraged animals still kept up. We watched the other side of the ravine with something more than anxiety, and when Jock's reddish-looking form broke through the bracken near to the leopard's rock, I felt like shutting my eyes till all was over. We saw him move close under the rock and then disappear. We watched for some seconds – it may have been a minute, but it seemed an eternity – and then, feeling the utter futility of waiting there, jumped off the rock and ran down the slope in the hope that the dogs would hear us call from there.

From where the slope was steepest we looked down into the bed of the stream at the bottom of the ravine, and the two dogs were there. They were moving cautiously down the wide stony watercourse just as we had seen them move in the morning, their noses thrown up and heads turning slowly from side to side. We knew what was coming. There was no time to reach them through the bush below, the cries of the baboons made calling useless, and the three of us sat down with rifles levelled ready to fire at the first sight.

With gun gripped and breath held hard, watching intently every bush and tree and rock, every spot of light and shade, we sat – not daring to move. Then, over the edge of a big rock overlooking the two dogs, appeared something round; and, smoothly yet swiftly and with a snake-like movement, the long spotted body followed the head and, flattened against the rock, crept stealthily forward until the leopard looked straight down upon Jess and Jock.

Three rifles cracked like one, and with a howl of rage and pain the leopard shot out over the dogs' heads, raced along the stony bed, and suddenly plunging its nose into the ground, pitched over – dead.

It was shot through the heart, and down the ribs on each side were the scraped marks of the trap.

Buffalo, Bushfire and Wild Dogs

THE summer slipped away and among the massed ever-greens of the woods there stood out here and there bright spots of colour, yellow and brown, orange and crimson, all vividly distinct, yet all in perfect harmony. The rivers ran full but clear; the days were bright; the nights were cold; the grass was rank and seeding; and it was time to go.

Once more the Bushveld beckoned us away.

We picked a spot where grass and water were good, and waited for the rivers to fall, and it was while loitering there that a small party from the gold-fields making for the Sabi came across us and camped for the night. In the morning two of our party joined them for a few days to try for something big.

It was too early in the season for really good sport. The rank tropical grass – six to eight feet high in most places, twelve to fourteen in some – and the stout stems and heavy seed heads made walking as difficult as in a field of tangled sugar cane. For long stretches it was not possible to see five yards, and the dew in the early mornings was so heavy that after a hundred yards of such going one was drenched to the skin.

On the third day two of us started out to try a new quarter in the hilly country towards the Berg. My companion, Francis, was an experienced hunter and his idea was that we should find the big game, not on the hot humid flats or the stony rises, but still higher up on the breezy hilltops or in the cool shady kloofs running towards the mountains. We passed a quantity of smaller game that morning, and several times heard the stampede of big animals – wildebeeste and waterbuck as we found by the spoor – but it was absolutely impossible to see them.

Jock fared better than we did, finding openings and game tracks at his own level, which were of no use to us. He also knew better than we did what was going on ahead. It was tantalizing in the extreme to see him slow down and stand with his nose thrown up, giving quick soft sniffs and ranging his head from side to side, when he knew there was something quite close; and knew, too, that a few more toiling steps in that rank grass would be followed by a rush of something which we would never see.

After two hours of this we struck a stream, and there we made somewhat better pace and less noise, often taking to the bed of the creek for easier going. There, too, we found plenty of drinking places and plenty of fresh spoor of the bigger game, and, as the hills began to rise in view above the bush and trees, we found what Francis was looking for. Something caught his eye on the far side of the stream, and he waded in. I followed and, when halfway through, saw the contented look on his face and caught the words: 'Buffalo! I thought so!'

We sat down then to think it out. The spoor told of a troop of a dozen to sixteen animals – bulls, cows and calves – and it was that morning's spoor. Even in the soft, moist ground at the stream's edge the water had not yet oozed into most of the prints. Fortunately there was a light breeze from the hills, and, as it seemed probable that they would make that way for the hot part of the day, we decided to follow for some distance on the track and then make for the likeliest poort in the hills.

The buffalo had come up from the low country in the night, striking the creek at the drinking place. Their departing spoor confirmed the idea that, after their night's feed in the rich grass lower down, they were making for the hills again in the morning and had touched at the stream to drink.

Jock seemed to gather from our whispered conversations and silent movements that there was work to hand, and his eyes moved from one place to the other as we talked, much as a child watches the faces in a conversation it cannot quite follow. When we got up and began to move along the trail, he gave one of his little sideways bounds, and then with several approving waggings of his tail settled down at once to business.

Jock went in front. It was best so, and quite safe, for, while certain to spot anything long before we could, there was not the least risk of his rushing it or making any noise. The slightest whisper of a 'hst' from me would have brought him to a breathless standstill at any moment; but even this was not likely to be needed, for he kept as close a watch on my face as I did on him.

There was, of course, no difficulty whatever in following the spoor. The animals were as big as cattle, and their trail through the rank grass was as plain as a road. Our difficulty was to get near enough to see them without being heard. Under the down-trodden grass there were plenty of dry sticks to step on, any of which would have been as fatal to our chances as a pistol shot, and even the unavoidable rustle of the grass might betray us while the buffalo themselves remained hidden. Thus our progress was very slow, a particularly troublesome impediment being the grass stems thrown down across the trail by the animals crossing and recrossing each other's spoor. The tambookie grass in these parts has a stem thicker than a lead pencil, more like young bamboo than grass; and these stems thrown crossways by storms or game make an entanglement through which the foot cannot be forced. It means high stepping all the time.

Jock moved steadily along the trodden track, sliding easily through the grass or jumping softly and noiselessly over impediments, and we followed, looking ahead as far as the winding course of the trail permitted.

To the right and left of us stood the screen of tall grass, bush and trees. Once Jock stopped, throwing up his nose, and stood for some seconds while we held our breath. But having satisfied himself that there was nothing of immediate consequence, he moved on again – rather more slowly, as it appeared to us – and the feeling of expectation grew stronger and stronger until it amounted to absolute certainty. Then Jock stopped – stopped in mid-stride, not with his nose up ranging for scent, but with head erect, ears cocked and tail poised – dead still : he was looking at something.

We had reached the end of the grass where the bush and trees of the mountain slope had choked it out, and before us there was fairly thick bush mottled with black shadows and patches of bright sunlight in which it was most difficult to see anything. There we stood like statues, the dog in front with the two men abreast behind him, and all peering intently. Twice Jock slowly turned his head and looked into my eyes, and I felt keenly the sense of hopeless inferiority. 'There it is, what are you going to do?' was what the first look seemed to say; and the second: 'Well, what are you waiting for?'.

How long we stood thus it is not possible to say. Time is no measure of such things, and to me it seemed unending suspense; but we stood our ground scarcely breathing,

knowing that something was there, because he saw it and told us so, and knowing that as soon as we moved it would be gone. Then close to the ground there was a movement – something swung – and the full picture flashed upon us. It was a buffalo calf standing in the shade of a big bush with its back towards us, and it was the swishing of the tail that had betrayed it. We dared not breathe a word or pass a look – a face turned might have caught some glint of light and shown us up. So we stood like statues each knowing that the other was looking for the herd and would fire when he got a chance at one of the full-grown animals.

My eyes were strained and burning from the intensity of

the effort to see; but except the calf I could not make out a living thing. The glare of the yellow grass in which we stood, and the sun-splotched darkness beyond it beat me.

At last, in the corner of my eye, I saw Francis's rifle slowly rise. There was a long pause, and then came the shot and wild snorts of alarm and rage. A dozen huge black forms started into life for a second and as quickly vanished – scattering and crashing through the jungle.

The first clear impression was that of Jock, who after one swift run forward for a few yards stood ready to spring off in pursuit, looking back at me and waiting for the word to go. But at the sign of my raised hand, opened with palm towards him, he subsided slowly and lay down flat with his head resting on his paws.

*

A few yards from where the buffalo had stood we picked up the blood spoor. There was not very much of it, but we saw from the marks on the bushes here and there, and more distinctly on some grass further on, that the wound was pretty high up and on the right side. Crossing a small stretch of more open bush we reached the dense growth along the banks of the stream, and as this continued up into the kloof it was clear we had a tough job before us.

After a couple of hundred yards of that sort of going, we took to the creek again, making occasional cross-cuts to the trail, to be sure he was still ahead. After the fourth cross-cut it was certain that the buffalo was following the herd and making for the poort, so we made what pace we could along the creek to reach the narrow gorge where we reckoned to pick up the spoor again.

There are, however, few short-cuts in hunting. When we reached the poort there was no trace to be found of the wounded buffalo. The rest of the herd had passed in, but we failed to find blood or other trace of the wounded one.

We had overshot the mark and there was nothing for it

but to hark back to the last blood spoor, and, by following it up, find out what had happened. This took over an hour, for we spoored him then with the utmost caution, being convinced that the buffalo, if not dead, was badly wounded and lying in wait for us.

A wounded buffalo in thick bush is considered to be about as nasty a customer as anyone may desire to tackle. Its vindictive, indomitable courage and extraordinary cunning are a very formidable combination – as a long list of fatalities bears witness.

We came on his 'stand' in a well-chosen spot, where the game path took a sharp turn round some heavy bushes. The buffalo had stood, not where one would naturally expect it – in the dense cover which seemed just suited for this purpose – but among lighter bush on the *opposite* side. There was no room for doubt about his hostile intentions. His selection of more open ground on the other side seemed so fiendishly clever that it made one feel cold and creepy.

The marks showed us he was badly hit, but there was no limb broken, and no doubt he was good for some hours yet. We followed along the spoor, more cautiously than ever. When we reached the sharp turn beyond the thick bush we found that on our way up the bed of the creek we had passed within twenty yards of where the buffalo was waiting for us. No doubt he had heard us then as we walked past, and had winded us later on when we got ahead of him into the poort.

Had he followed up to attack us? Was he waiting somewhere near? Or had he broken away into the bush on finding himself headed off? These were some of the questions we asked ourselves as we crept along.

On reaching the poort again we found his spoor, freshly made since we had been there. He had walked right along through the gorge without stopping again, and gone into the kloof beyond.

*

A breeze had risen since morning, and as we approached the hills it grew stronger. In the poort itself it was far too strong for our purpose – the wind coming through the narrow opening like a forced draught. The herd would not stand there, and it was not probable that the wounded animal would stop until he joined the others or reached a more sheltered place. We were keen on the chase, and as he had about an hour's start of us and it was already midday, there was no time to waste.

Inside the poort the kloof opened out into a big valley away to our left, but to the right the formation was quite different and rather peculiar. The stream – known to the natives as Hlamba-Nyati, or Buffalo's Bathing Place – had, in the course of time, eaten into the left bank, leaving a high, and in most places, inaccessible terrace above it on the left side. This terrace was bounded on one side by the steep bank of the stream and walled in on the other side by the precipitous kranses of the mountains. At the top end it opened out like a fan into numberless small kloofs and spurs fringing the amphitheatre of the hills. No doubt the haunts of the buffalo were away in these spurs, and we worked steadily along the spoor in that direction.

Game paths were numerous and very irregular, and the place was a perfect jungle of trees, bush, bramble and the tallest, rankest grass. It was desperately hard work, but we did want to get the buffalo; and although the place was full of game – we put up kudu, wildebeeste, rietbuck, bushbuck and duiker – we held to the wounded buffalo's spoor, neglecting all else.

Just before ascending the terrace we had heard the curious far-travelling sound of natives calling to each other from a distance, but, except for a passing comment, paid no heed to it and passed on. Later we heard it again and again, and at last – when we happened to pause in a more open portion of the bush after we had gone halfway along the terrace – the calling became so frequent and came from so many quarters that we stopped to take note. Francis who spoke Zulu like one of themselves, at last made out a word or two which gave the clue.

'They're after the wounded buffalo!' he said. 'Come on, man, before they get their dogs, or we'll never see him again.'

Knowing then that the buffalo was a long way ahead, we scrambled on as fast as we could while holding to his track. But it was very hot and rough and, to add to our troubles, smoke from a grass fire came driving into our faces.

Natives habitually fire the grass in patches during the summer and autumn, as soon as it is dry enough to burn, in order to get young grass for the winter or the early spring, and although the smoke worried us there did not seem to be anything unusual about the fire. But ten minutes later we stopped again. The smoke was perceptibly thicker; birds were flying past us down wind, with numbers of locusts and other insects; two or three times we heard buck and other animals break back; and all were going the same way. Then the same thought struck us both : this was no ordinary mountain grass fire; it was the bush.

Francis was a quiet fellow, one of the sort it is well not to rouse. The blood rose slowly to his face, until it was bricky red, and he looked an ugly customer as he said : 'The brutes have fired the valley to burn him out. Come on quick. We must get out of this on to the slopes!'

We did not know that there were no slopes – only a precipitous face of rock with dense jungle to the foot of it; and after we had spent a quarter of an hour in that effort, we found our way blocked by the krans and a tangle of undergrowth much worse than that in the middle of the terrace. The noise made by the wind in the trees and our struggling through the grass and bush had prevented our hearing the fire at first, but now its ever-growing roar drowned all sounds. Ordinarily, there would have been no real difficulty in avoiding a bush fire; but, pinned in between the river and the precipice and with miles of dense bush behind us, it was not at all pleasant.

Had we turned back even then and made for the poort it is possible we might have travelled faster than the fire, but it would have been rough work indeed. Moreover, that would have been going back – and we did want to get the buffalo – so we decided to make one more try, towards the river this time. It was not much of a try, however, and we had gone no further than the middle of the terrace again when it became alarmingly clear that this fire meant business.

The wind increased greatly, as it always does once a bush fire gets a start; the air was thick with smoke, and full of flying things; in the bush and grass about us there was a constant scurrying; the terror of stampede was in the very atmosphere. A few words of consultation decided us, and we started to burn a patch for standing room and protection.

The hot sun and strong wind had long evaporated all the dew and moisture from the grass, but the sap was still up, and the fire – our fire – seemed cruelly long in catching on. With bunches of dry grass for brands we started burns in twenty places over a length of a hundred yards, and each little flame licked up, spread a little, and then hesitated or died out. It seemed as if ours would never take, while the other came on with roars and leaps, sweeping clouds of sparks and ash over us in the dense rolling mass of smoke.

At last a fierce rush of wind struck down on us, and in a few seconds each little flame became a living demon of destruction; another minute and the stretch before us was a field of swaying flame. There was a sudden roar and crackle, as of musketry, and the whole mass seemed lifted into the air in one blazing sheet: it simply leaped into life and swept everything before it.

When we opened our scorched eyes the ground in front of us was all black, with only here and there odd lights and torches dotted about; and on ahead, beyond the trellis work of bare scorched trees, the wall of flame swept on.

Then down on the wings of the wind came the other fire, and before it fled every living thing. Heaven only knows what passed us in those few minutes when a broken stream of terrified creatures dashed by, hardly swerving to avoid us. There is no coherent picture left of that scene – just a medley of impressions linked up by flashes of unforgettable vividness. A herd of kudu came crashing by. I know there was a herd, but only the first and last will come to mind – the space between seemed blurred. The clear impressions are of the kudu bull in front, with nose out-thrust, eyes shut

against the bush, and great horns laid back upon the withers, as he swept along opening the way for his herd; and then, as they vanished, the big ears, U-neck and tilting hind-quarters of the last cow – between them nothing but a mass of moving grey!

The wildebeeste went by in Indian file, uniform in shape, colour and horns; and strangely uniform in their mechanical action, lowered heads and fiercely determined rush.

A rietbuck ram stopped close to us, looked back wide-eyed and anxious, and whistled shrilly, and then cantered on with head erect and white tail flapping; but its mate neither answered nor came by. A terrified hare with its ears laid flat scuttled past within a yard of Francis and did not seem to see him. Above us scared birds swept or fluttered down wind; while others again came up swirling and swinging

about, darting boldly through the smoke to catch the insects driven before the fire.

But what comes back with the suggestion of infinitely pathetic helplessness is the picture of a beetle. We stood on the edge of our burn, waiting for the ground to cool, and at my feet a pair of tock-tockie beetles, hump-backed and bandy-legged, came toiling slowly and earnestly along; they reached the edge of our burn, touched the warm ash and turned patiently aside – to walk round it!

A school of chattering monkeys raced out on to the

blackened flat, and screamed shrilly with terror as the hot earth and cinders burnt their feet.

Porcupine, antbear, meerkat! They are vague, so vague that nothing is left but the shadow of their passing; but there is one other thing – seen in a flash as brief as the others, for a second or two only, but never to be forgotten! Out of the yellow grass, high up in the waving tops, came sailing down on us the swaying head and glittering eyes of a black mamba – swiftest, most vicious, most deadly of snakes. Francis and I were not five yards apart and it passed between us, giving a quick, chilly, beady look at each – pitiless, and hateful – and one hiss as the slithering tongue shot out: that was all, and it sailed past with strange effortless movement. How much of the body was on the ground propelling it, I cannot even guess; but we had to look upwards to see the head as the snake passed between us.

The scorching breath of the fire drove us before it on to the baked ground, inches deep in ashes and glowing cinders, where we kept marking time to ease our blistering feet; our hats were pulled down to screen our necks as we stood with our backs to the coming flames; our flannel shirts were so hot that we kept shifting our shoulders for relief. Jock, who had no screen and whose feet had no protection, was in my arms; and we strove to shield ourselves from the furnace-blast with the branches we had used to beat out the fire round the big tree which was our main shelter.

The heat was awful! Live brands were flying past all the time, and some struck us; myriads of sparks fell round and on us, burning numberless small holes in our clothing, and dotting blisters on our backs; great sheets of flame leaped out from the driving glare, and, detached by many yards from their source, were visible for quite a space in front of us. Then, just at its maddest and fiercest there came a gasp and sob, and the fire devil died behind us as it reached the black, bare ground. Our burn divided it as an island splits the flood, and it swept along our flanks in two great walls of living, leaping, roaring flame.

Two hundred yards away there was a bare, yellow place in a world of inky black, and to that haven we ran. It was strange to look about and see the naked country all round us, where but a few minutes earlier the tall grass had shut us in; but the big, bare ant-heap was untouched, and there we flung ourselves down, utterly done.

Faint from heat and exhaustion – scorched and blistered, face and arms, back and feet; weary and footsore, and with boots burnt through – we reached camp long after dark, glad to be alive.

We had forgotten the wounded buffalo; he seemed part of another life!

There was no more hunting for us; our feet had 'gone in', and we were well content to sleep and rest. The burnt stubbly ends of the grass had pierced the baked leather of our boots many times; and Jock, too, had suffered badly and could hardly bear to set foot to the ground next day. The best we could hope for was to be sound enough to return to our wagons in two or three days' time.

The camp was under a very large wild fig tree, whose dense canopy gave us shade all through the day. We had burnt the grass for some twenty or thirty yards round as a protection against bush fires; and as the trees and scrub were not thick just there it was possible to see in various directions rather further than one usually can in the Bushveld. The big tree was a fair landmark by day, and at night we made a good fire which, owing to the position of the camp,

one could see from a considerable distance. These precautions were for the benefit of strayed or belated members of the party, but I mention them because the position of the camp and the fire brought us a strange visitor.

It was between eight and nine o'clock on the last day of our stay. Francis and I were fit again, and Jock's feet, thanks to care and washing and plenty of castor oil, no longer troubled him. We were examining our boots – resoled now with raw-hide in the rough but effective veld fashion; Teddy – old Teddy Blacklow of Ballarat, one of the old alluvial diggers, a warm-hearted, impulsive, ever-young old boy – was holding forth about the day's chase; and the natives round their own fire were keeping up the simultaneous gabble characteristic of hunting boys after a good day and with plenty of meat in camp.

I was sitting on a small camp stool critically examining a boot and wondering if the dried hide would grip well enough to permit the top lacing being removed. Jock was lying in front of me carefully licking the last sore spot on one fore-paw, when I saw his head switch up suddenly and his whole body set hard in a study of intense listening. Then he got up and trotted briskly off some ten or fifteen yards, and stood – a bright spot picked out by the glare of the camp-fire – with his back towards me and his uneven ears topping him off.

I walked out to him, and silence fell on the camp. All watched and listened. At first we heard nothing, but soon the call of a wild dog explained Jock's movements. The sound, however, did not come from the direction in which he was looking, but a good deal to the right; and as he instantly looked to this new quarter I concluded that this was not the dog he had previously heard, or else it must have moved rapidly. There was another wait, and then there followed calls from other quarters.

There was nothing unusual in the presence of wild dogs: hyenas, jackals, wild dogs and all the smaller beasts of prey were heard nightly. What attracted attention in this case was the regular calling from different points. The boys said the wild dogs were hunting something and calling to each other to indicate the direction of the hunt, so that those in front might turn the buck and by keeping it in a circle enable fresh or rested dogs to jump in from time to time – and so, eventually, wear the poor hunted creature down. This, according to the natives, is the system of the wild pack.

The hunt went on round us, sometimes near enough to hear the dogs' eager cries quite clearly, sometimes so far away that for a while nothing could be heard; and Jock moved from point to point in the outermost circle of the camp-fire's light nearest to the chase.

When at last hunters and hunted completed their wide circuit round the camp, and passed again the point where we had first heard them, the end seemed near, for there were no longer single calls widely separated, but the voices of the pack in hot close chase. They seemed to be passing

193

half a mile away from us, but in the stillness of the night sound travels far, and one can only guess. Again a little while and the cries sounded nearer and as if coming from one quarter – not moving round us as before; a few minutes more, and it was certain they were still nearer and coming straight towards us. We took our guns then, and I called Jock back to where we stood under the tree with our backs to the fire.

The growing sounds came on out of the night where all was hidden with the weird crescendo effect of a coming flood. We could pick them out then – the louder harsher cries; the crashing through bush; the rush in grass; the sobbing gasps in front; and the hungry panting after. The hunt came at us like a cyclone out of the stillness, and in the forefront of it there burst into the circle of light an impala ewe with open mouth and haunting, hunted, despairing eyes and wide spread ears. The last staggering strides brought her in among us, tumbling at our feet.

A native jumped out with assegai aloft; but Teddy, with the spring of a leopard and a yell of rage, swung his rifle round and down on the assegai arm; and the fiery, soft-hearted old boy was down on to his knees in a second, panting with anger and excitement, and threw his arms about the buck.

The foremost of the pack followed hot foot close behind the buck – oblivious of fire and men, seeing nothing but the quarry – and at a distance of five yards a mixed volley of bullets and assegais tumbled it over. Another followed, and again another: both fell where they had stopped, a dozen yards away; and still more and more came on, but, warned by the unexpected check in front, they stopped at the clearing's edge, until over twenty pairs of eyes reflecting the fire's light shone out at us in a rough semicircle. The shot-guns came in better then, and more than half the pack went under that night before the others cleared off. Perhaps they did not realize that the shots and flashes were not part of the camp-fire from which they seemed to come. Perhaps their system of never relinquishing a chase had not been tried against the white man before.

One of the wild dogs, wounded by a shot, seemed to go mad with agony and raced straight into the clearing towards the fire, uttering the strangest maniac-like yaps. Jock had all along been straining to go for them from where I had jammed him between my feet as I sat and fired, and the charge of this dog was more than he could bear. He shot out like a rocket, and the collision sent the two flying apart, but he was on to the wild dog again and had it by the throat before it could recover.

Instantly the row of lights went out, as if switched off – they were no longer looking at us. There was a rustle and a sound of padded feet, and dim grey-looking forms gathered at the edge of the clearing nearest where Jock and the wounded dog fought. I shouted to Jock to come back, and several of us ran out to help, just as another of the pack made a dash in. It seemed certain that Jock, gripping and worrying his enemy's throat, had neither time nor thought for anything else; yet as the fresh dog came at him he let go his grip of the other, and jumped to meet the new-comer. In mid-spring Jock caught the other by the ear and the two spun completely round – their positions being reversed; then, with another wrench as he landed, he flung the attacker behind him and jumped back at the wounded one which had already turned to go.

It looked like the clean and easy movement of a finished gymnast. It was an affair of a few seconds only, for of course the instant we got a chance at the dogs, without the risk to Jock, both were shot; and he, struggling to get at the others, was hauled back to the tree.

While this was going on the impala stood with widespread legs, dazed and helpless, between Teddy's feet, just as he had placed it. Its breath came in broken choking sobs; the look of terror and despair had not yet faded from the staring eyes; the head swayed from side to side; the mouth hung open and the tongue lolled out; all told beyond the power of words the tale of desperate struggle and exhaustion. It drank greedily from the dish that Teddy held for it – emptied it, and five minutes later drank it again and then lay down.

For half an hour it lay there, slowly recovering. Sometimes for spells of a few minutes it appeared to breathe normally once more, then the heavy open-mouthed panting would return again. All the time Teddy kept on stroking or patting it gently and talking to it as if he were comforting a child.

At last it rose briskly, and standing between his knees looked about, taking no notice of Teddy's hands laid on either side and gently patting it. No one moved or spoke. Jock, at my feet, appeared most interested of all, but I am afraid his views differed considerably from ours on that occasion, and he must have been greatly puzzled. He remained watching intently with his head laid on his paws, his ears cocked, and his brown eyes fixed unblinkingly. At each movement on the buck's part something stirred in him, drawing every muscle tense and ready for the spring – internal grips which were reflected in the twitching and stiffening of his neck and back; but each time as I laid a hand on him he slackened out again and subsided.

We sat like statues as the impala walked out from its stall between Teddy's knees and stood looking about wonderingly at the faces white and black, at the strange figures, and at the fire. It stepped out quite quietly, much as it might have moved about here and there in any peaceful morning in its usual haunts; the head swung about briskly, but unalarmed; and ears and eyes were turned this way and that in easy confidence and mild curiosity.

With a few more steps it threaded its way close to one sitting figure and round a bucket, and stepped daintily over Teddy's rifle.

It seemed to us like a scene in fairyland in which some spell held us while the beautiful wild thing strolled about unfrightened.

A few yards away it stopped for perhaps a couple of minutes. Its back was towards us and the fire. The silence was absolute, and it stood thus with eyes and ears for the bush alone. There was a warning whisk of the white tail and it started off again – this time at a brisk trot – and we thought it had gone; but at the edge of the clearing it once more stood and listened. Now and again the ears flickered and the head turned slightly one way or another, but no sound came from the bush. The out-thrust nose was raised with gentle tosses, but no taint reached it on the gentle breeze.

All was well!

It looked slowly round, giving one long full gaze back at us which seemed to be 'Good-bye, and – thank you!' and cantered out into the dark.

Snowball and Tsetse

SNOWBALL was an 'old soldier' – he had been through the wars and seen the ups and downs of life. Tsetse was also an old soldier, but he was what you might call a gentleman old soldier, with a sense of duty. Snowball was no gentleman: he was selfish and unscrupulous, a confirmed shirker, often absent without leave, and upon occasions a rank deserter.

Tsetse belonged to my friend Hall; but Snowball was mine! For Snowball and Tsetse were horses.

Tsetse had his peculiarities and prejudices: for instance, he would not under any circumstances permit mounting on the wrong side. On the mountains it often happened that the path was too narrow and the slope too steep to permit one to mount on the left side, whereas the rise of the ground made it very easy on the right. But Tsetse made no allowance for this, and if the attempt were made he would stand quite still until the rider was off the ground but not yet in the saddle, and then buck continuously until the offender shot overhead and went skidding down the slope. To one encumbered with a rifle in hand, and a kettle or perhaps a couple of legs of buck slung on the saddle, Tsetse's protest was usually irresistible.

Snowball had no unpractical prejudices: he objected to work – that was all. He was a pure white horse, goodness knows how old, with enormously long teeth, and his eyes had an aged and resigned look. The reproach of this venerable look nearly put me off taking him – it seemed such a shame to make the dear old fellow work. But I hardened my heart and, feeling rather a brute, bought him because he was 'salted' and would live in the Bushveld. Beside that all other considerations were trivial.

Hunting horses live almost entirely by grazing, as it is seldom possible to carry grain or other foods for them and never possible to carry enough. Salted horses have therefore a particular value in that they can be turned out to graze at night or in the morning and evening dews when animals not immunized will contract horse-sickness. Thus they feed during the hours when hunting is not possible and keep their condition when an unsalted horse would fall away from sheer want of food.

Snowball had one disfigurement, consisting of a large black swelling as big as a small orange behind his left eye, which must have annoyed him greatly. It could easily have been removed, and many suggestions were made on the subject but all of them were firmly declined. Without that lump I should have had no chance against him: it was the weak spot in his defence. It was the only cover under which it was possible to stalk him when he made one of his determined attempts to dodge or desert; for he could see nothing that came up behind him on the left side without turning his head completely round. Hence one part of the country was always hidden from him, and of course it was from this quarter that we invariably made our approaches to attack.

It was not as a rule at the outspan – where many hands

were available – that Snowball gave trouble, but out hunting when I was alone or with only one companion. A trained shooting horse should stop as soon as his rider lays hand on mane to dismount, and should remain where he is left for any length of time until his master returns. Some horses require the reins to be dropped over their heads to remind them of their duty, but many can safely be left to themselves and will be found grazing quietly where left.

Snowball knew well what to do, but he pleased himself about doing it. Sometimes he would stand; sometimes move off a little way, and keep moving – just out of reach; sometimes, with a troop of buck moving on ahead or perhaps a wounded one to follow, this old sinner would right-about-face and simply walk off – with occasional liftings of his hindquarters to let me know what to expect, and his right eye on me all the while – and if I ran to head him off, he would break into a trot and leave me a little worse off than before; and sometimes, in familiar country, he would make straight away for the wagons without more ado.

It is demoralizing in the extreme to be expecting a jerk when in the act of aiming – and it is little better, while creeping forward for a shot, to hear your horse strolling off behind and realize that you will have to hunt for him and perhaps walk many miles back to camp without means of carrying anything you may shoot. The result of experience was that I had to choose between two alternatives: either to hook him up to a tree or bush, or hobble him with his reins – and so lose many good chances of quick shots when coming unexpectedly on game; or to slip an arm through the reins and take chance of being plucked off my aim or jerked violently backwards as I fired. Although hobbling is dangerous in a country so full of holes, stumps and all sorts of grass-hidden obstacles, there were times when consideration for Snowball seemed mighty like pure foolishness, and it would have been no grief to me if he had broken his neck!

To the credit of Snowball stand certain things, however. There were times when for days, and even weeks, at a stretch he would behave admirably. Moreover he had qualities which were not to be despised: he was as sound as a bell, very clever on his feet, never lost his condition, and, although not fast, could last for ever at his own pace. It is due to him to say that during one hard season a camp of wagons with their complement of men had to be kept in meat, and it was Snowball who carried – for short and long

distances, through dry rough country, at all times of day or night, hot, thirsty and tired, and without a breakdown or a day's sickness – a bag that totalled many thousands of pounds in weight, and the man who made the bag.

*

On one long horseback journey through Swaziland to the coast, where few white men and no horses had yet been seen, we learned to know Snowball and Tsetse well, and found out what a horse can do when put to it.

It was a curious experience on that trip to see whole villages flee in terror at the first sight of the new strange animals – one brown and one white. Once, when we came unexpectedly upon a party of naked urchins playing on the bank of a stream, the whole pack set off full cry for the water and, jumping in like a school of alarmed frogs, disappeared. Infinitely amused by the stampede we rode up to see what had become of them, but the silence was absolute, and for a while they seemed to have vanished altogether; then a tell-tale ripple gave the clue, and under the banks among the ferns and exposed roots we picked out little black faces half submerged and pairs of frightened eyes staring at us from all sides.

It is in the rivers that a man feels the importance of a good horse with a stout heart, and his dependence on it. There were no roads, and not even known tracks there and when it came to crossing the Crocodile River we chose the widest spot in the hope that it would be shallow and free of rocks. We fired some shots into the river to scare the crocodiles, and started to cross; but to our surprise Tsetse, the strong-nerved and reliable, who always had the post of honour in front, absolutely refused to enter.

The water of the Crocodile is at its best of amber clearness and we could not see the bottom, but the sloping grassy bank promised well enough and no hint reached us of what the horses knew quite well. All we had was on our horses – food, blankets, billy, rifles and ammunition. We were off on a long trip and, to vary or supplement the game diet, carried a small packet of tea, a little sugar, flour and salt, and some beads with which to trade for native fowls and thick milk. The guns had to do the rest. Thus there were certain things we could not afford to wet, and these we used to wrap up in a mackintosh and carry high when it came to swimming, but this crossing looked so easy that it seemed sufficient to raise the packs instead of carrying part of them.

When Hall, astonished at Tsetse's unexpected obstinacy, gave him both heels, the old horse considerately swung round away from the river, and with a couple of neatly executed bucks shot his encumbered rider off the raised pack, yards away on to the soft grass – water-bottle, rifle, bandolier and man landing in a lovely tangle.

I then put old Snowball at it, fully expecting trouble, but the old soldier was quite at home. He walked quietly to the edge, sat down comfortably, and slid into the water – launching himself with scarce a ripple just like an old hippo. That gave us the explanation of Tsetse's tantrum: the water came up to the seat of my saddle and walking was only just possible. I stopped at once, waiting for Tsetse to

follow; and Hall, prepared for another refusal, sat back and again used his spurs.

No doubt Tsetse, once he knew the depth, was quite satisfied and meant to go in quietly, and the prick of the spur must have been unexpected, for he gave a plunge forward and Hall shot out overhead, landing half across old Snowball's back. There was a moment of ludicrous but agonized suspense! Hall's legs were firmly gripping Tsetse behind the ears while he sprawled on his stomach on Snowball's crupper, with the reins still in one hand and the rifle in the other. Doubled up with suppressed laughter I grabbed a fist full of shirt and held on, every moment expecting Tsetse to hoist his head or pull back and complete the disaster, while Hall was spluttering out directions, entreaties and imprecations. But good old Tsetse never moved, and Hall, handing me the rifle, managed to swarm backwards on to Tsetse's withers and scramble on to the pack again.

Then, saddle-deep in the river – duckings and crocodiles forgotten – we sat looking at each other and laughed till we ached.

The river was about three hundred yards wide there with a good sandy bottom and of uniform depth; but, to our disappointment, we found that the other bank which had appeared to slope gently to the water edge was, in fact, a sheer wall standing up several feet above the river level. The beautiful slope which we had seen consisted of water grass and reed tops, the bank itself was of firm moist clay, and the river bottom close under it was soft mud. We tried a little way up and down, but found deeper water, more mud and reeds, and no break in the bank. There seemed to be nothing for it but to go back and try somewhere else.

When Hall looked at the bank and said, 'We'll have a shot at this,' I thought at first he was joking. Later, to my remark that, 'No horse ever born would face that,' he answered: 'Anyway we could try; it would be just as good as hunting for more places of the same sort!'

Tsetse was ranged up beside the bank, and Hall standing in the saddle threw his rifle and bandolier up and scrambled out himself. I then loosened Tsetse's girths from my seat on Snowball, and handed up the packed saddle – Hall lying down on the bank to take it from me. We did the same with Snowball's load, including my own clothes, for, as it was already sundown, a ducking was not desirable. I loosened one side of Tsetse's reins, and, after attaching one of mine in order to give the necessary length to them, threw the end up to Hall; and he cut and handed me a long supple rod for a whip to stir Tsetse to his best endeavours. The water there was rather more than half saddle-flap high. I know that because it just left me a good expanse of hind-quarters to aim at when the moment came.

'Now!' yelled Hall. 'Up, Tsetse! Up!' and whack went the stick. Tsetse reared up, right on end. He could not reach the top but struck his fore-feet into the moist bank near the top, and with a might plunge that soused Snowball and me, went out. The tug on the leading rein, on which Hall had thrown all his weight when Tsetse used it to lever himself

up, had jerked Hall flat on his face; but he was up in a minute, and, releasing Tsetse, threw back the rein to get Snowball to face it while the example was fresh.

Then for the first time we thought of crocodiles – and the river was full of them. But Snowball, without some one behind him with a stick, would never face that jump. There was nothing for it but to fire some scaring shots, and slip into the water and get the job over as quickly as possible.

Snarleyow was with us -- I had left Jock at the wagons fearing that we would get into fly country on the Umbeluzi

– and the bank was too high and too steep for him. He huddled up against it half supported by reeds, and whined plaintively.

To our relief Snowball faced the jump quite readily; indeed, the old sinner did it with much less effort and splash than the bigger Tsetse. But then came an extremely unpleasant spell. Snowball got a scare, because Hall in his anxiety to get me out rushed up to him on the warty side to get the reins off; and the old ruffian waltzed around, dragging Hall through the thorn, while Snarleyow and I waited in the water for help.

At that moment I had a poorer opinion of Snowball and Snarley than at any other I can remember. I wished Snarley dead twenty times in twenty seconds. Crocodiles love dogs, and it seemed to me a million to one that a pair of green eyes and a black snout must slide out of the water any moment, drawn to us by those advertising whines! And the worst of it was, I was outside Snarley with my white legs gleaming in the open water, while his cringing form was tucked away half hidden by the reeds.

What an age it seemed! How each reed shaken by the river breeze caught the eye, giving me goose-flesh and sending waves of cold shudders creeping over me! How the cold smooth touch of a reed stem against my leg made me want to jump and to get out with one huge plunge as the horses had done! And even when I had passed the struggling, yowling Snarley up, the few remaining seconds seemed painfully long. Hall had to lie flat and reach his furthest to grip my hand; and I nearly pulled him in, scrambling up that bank like a chased cat up a tree.

When one comes to think it out, the bank must have been nine feet high. It was mighty unpleasant, but it taught us what a horse can do when he puts his back into it!

Jock's Mistake

HALFWAY between the Crocodile and Komati rivers, a few miles south of the old road, there are half a dozen or more small kopjes between which lie broad, richly grassed depressions, too wide and flat to be called valleys. There is no running water there in winter, but there are a few big pools – long, narrow, irregularly shaped bits of water – with shady trees around them.

I came upon the place by accident one day, and thereafter we kept it dark as our own preserve; for it was full of game, and a most delightful spot.

Apart from the discovery of this preserve, the day was memorable for it was my first experience of a big mixed herd; and I learned that day how difficult the work may be when several kinds of game run together.

After a dry and warm morning the sight of the big pool had prompted an offsaddle. Snowball was tethered in a patch of good grass, and Jock and I were lying in the shade. When Jock began to sniff and walk up wind I took the rifle and followed; and only a little way off we came into dry vlei ground where there were few trees and the grass stood about waist high. Some two hundred yards away where the ground rose slightly and the bush became thicker there was a fair sized troop of impala, perhaps a hundred or more, and just behind, and mostly to one side of them, were between twenty and thirty tsessebe. We saw them clearly and in time to avoid exposing ourselves. They were neither feeding nor resting, but simply standing about, and individual animals were moving unconcernedly from time to time with an air of idle loitering. I tried to pick out a good tsessebe ram, but the impala were in the way, and it was necessary to crawl for some distance to reach certain cover away on the right.

Crawling is hard work and very rough on both hands and knees in the Bushveld, frequent rests being necessary; and in one of the pauses I heard a curious sound of soft padded feet jumping behind me, and looking quickly about caught Jock in the act of taking his observations. The grass was too high for him to see over, even when he stood up on his hind-legs, and he was giving jumps of slowly increasing strength to get the height which would enable him to see what was going on.

I shall never forget that first view of Jock's ballooning observations. It became a regular practice afterwards, but it is that first view that remains a picture. I turned at the instant when he was at the top of his jump. His legs were all bunched up, his eyes staring eagerly and his ears had flapped out, giving him a look of comic astonishment. It was a most surprisingly unreal sight: he looked like a caricature of Jock shot into the air by a galvanic shock. A sign with my hand brought him flat on the ground, looking distinctly guilty, and we moved along again; but I was shaking with silent laughter.

At the next stop I looked back to see how he was behaving, and to my surprise, although he was following carefully close behind me, he was looking steadily away to our immediate right. I subsided gently on to my left side to see what it was that interested him, and to my delight saw a troop of twenty to twenty-five blue wildebeeste. They too, were 'standing any way', and evidently had not seen us.

I worked myself cautiously round to face them so as to be able to pick my shot and take it kneeling, thus clearing the tops of the grass; but while doing this another surprising development took place. Looking hard and carefully at the wildebeeste two hundred yards away, I became conscious of something else in between us, and only half the distance off, looking at me. It had the effect of a shock: the disagreeable effect of having a book or picture suddenly thrust close to the face; the feeling of wanting to get further away from it to re-focus one's sight.

What I saw was simply a dozen zebra, all exactly alike, all standing full face to me, their fore-feet together, their ears cocked and their heads quite motionless – all gazing steadily at me, alive with interest and curiosity. There was something quite ludicrous in it, and something perplexing also: when I looked at the zebra the wildebeeste seemed to get out of focus and were lost to me; when I looked at the wildebeeste the zebra 'blurred' and faded out of sight. The difference in distance, perhaps as much as the very marked difference in the distinctive colourings, threw me out; and the effect of being watched also told. Of course I wanted to get a wildebeest, but I was conscious of the watching zebra all the time, and could not help constantly looking at them to see if they were going to start off and stampede the others.

While trying to pick out the best of the wildebeeste a movement away on the left made me look that way. The impala jumped off like one animal, scaring the tsessebe into a scattering rout; the zebra switched round and thundered off like a stampede of horses; and the wildebeeste simply vanished. One signal in one troop had sent the whole lot off. Jock and I were left alone, still crouching, looking from side to side, staring at the slowly drifting dust and listening to the distant dying sound of galloping feet.

It was a great disappointment, but the conviction that we had found a really good spot made some amends, and Snowball was left undisturbed to feed and rest for another two hours.

We made for the wagons along another route taking in some of the newly discovered country in the home sweep, and the promise of the morning was fulfilled. We had not been more than a few minutes on the way when a fine rietbuck ram jumped up within a dozen yards of Snowball's nose, and fell to the first shot. He was a fine, big fellow, and as Snowball put on airs and pretended to be nervous when it came to packing the meat, I had to blindfold him; and after hoisting the buck up to a horizontal branch lowered it on to his back.

Snowball was villainously slow and bad to lead. He knew that while being led neither whip nor spur could touch him, and when loaded up with meat he dragged along at a miserable walk: one had to haul him. Once – but only once – I had tried driving him before me, trusting to about 400 lb. weight of kudu meat to keep him steady. But no sooner had I stepped behind with a switch than he went off with a cumbrous plunge and bucked like a frantic mule until he rid himself of his load, saddle and all. The fact is one person could not manage him on foot. It needed one at each end of him, and he knew it. Thus it worked out at a compromise: he carried my load, and I went at his pace!

We were labouring along in this fashion when we came on the wildebeeste again. A white man on foot seems to be recognized as an enemy; but if accompanied by animals – either on horseback, driving a vehicle, leading a horse or walking among cattle – he may pass unnoticed for a long while.

The wildebeeste had allowed me to get close up, and I picked out the big bull and took the shot kneeling, with my toe hooked in the reins to secure Snowball – taking chance of being jerked off my aim rather than let him go. But he behaved like an angel, and once more that day a single shot was enough.

It was a long and tedious job skinning the big fellow, cutting him up, hauling the heavy limbs and the rest of the meat up into a suitable tree, and making all safe against the robbers of the earth and the air. Most troublesome of all was packing the head and skin on Snowball, who showed the profoundest mistrust of this dark, ferocious-looking monster.

*

I started off early next morning with the boys to bring in the meat, and went on foot, giving Snowball a rest, more or less deserved. There was very little wanton shooting with us, for when we had more fresh meat than was required, it was dried as 'biltong' for the days of shortage which were sure to come.

By nine o'clock the boys were on their way back, and leaving them to take the direct route I struck away eastwards along the line of the pools, not expecting much and least of all dreaming that fate had one of the worst days in store for us.

We passed the second pool, loitering a few minutes in the cool shade of the evergreens to watch the green pigeons feeding on the wild figs and peering down cautiously at us; then moved briskly into more open ground. It is not wise to step too suddenly out of the dark shade into strong glare and it may have been that act of carelessness that enabled the kudu to get off before I saw them. They cantered away in a string with the cows in the rear, between me and two full-grown bulls. It was a running shot – end on – and the last of the troop, a big cow, gave a stumble; but catching herself up again she cantered off slowly. Her body was all bunched up and she was pitching greatly, and her hind legs kept flying out in irregular kicks, much as you may see a horse kick out when a blind fly is biting him.

There was no time for a second shot and we started off in hot pursuit; and fifty yards further on where there was a clear view I saw that the kudu was going no faster than an easy canter and Jock was close behind.

Whether he was misled by the curious action, and believed there was a broken leg to grip, or was simply over bold, it is impossible to know. Whatever the reason, he jumped for one of the hind legs, and at the same moment the kudu lashed out viciously. One foot struck him under the jaw close to the throat, 'whipped' his head and neck back like a bent switch and hurled him somersaulting backwards.

I have the impression – as one sees oneself in a nightmare

– of a person throwing up his arms and calling the name of his child as a train passed over it.

Jock lay limp and motionless, with the blood oozing from mouth, nose and eyes. I recollect feeling for his heart-beat and breath, and shaking him roughly and calling him by name. Then, remembering the pool near by, I left him in the shade of a tree, filled my hat with water, ran back again and poured it over him into his mouth, shaking him again to rouse him, and several times pressing his sides – bellows fashion – in a ridiculous effort to restore breathing.

The old hat was leaky and I had to grip the rough-cut ventilations to make it hold any water at all. I was returning with a second supply when with a great big heart-jump, I saw Jock heel over from his side, and with his forelegs flat on the ground raise himself to a resting position, his head wagging groggily and his eyes blinking in a very dazed way.

He took no notice when I called his name, but at the touch of my hand his ears moved up and the stumpy tail scraped feebly in the dead leaves. He was stone deaf; but I did not know it then. He lapped a little of the water, sneezed the blood away and licked his chops, and then, with evident effort, stood up.

But this is the picture which it is impossible to forget. The dog was still so dazed and shaken that he reeled slightly, steadying himself by spreading his legs well apart and there followed a few seconds' pause in which he stood thus. Then he began to walk forward with the uncertain staggery walk of a toddling child. His jaws were set close, his eyes were beady black, and he looked 'fight' all over. He took no notice of me; and I, never dreaming that he was after the kudu, watched the walk quicken to a laboured trot before I moved or called. But he paid no heed to the call. For the first time in his life there was rank open defiance of orders, and he trotted slowly along with his nose to the ground. Thinking he was maddened by the kick and not quite responsible for himself and admiring his pluck far too much to be angry, I ran to bring him back. But at a turn in his course he saw me coming, and this time he obeyed the call and signal instantly, and with a limp air of disappointment followed quietly back to the tree.

The reason for Jock's persistent disobedience that day was not even suspected then. Nevertheless it was puzzling that at times he should ignore me in positively contemptuous fashion, and at others obey with all his old readiness. I neither knew he was deaf, nor realized that the habit of using certain signs and gestures when I spoke to him – and even of using them in place of orders when silence was imperative – had made him almost independent of the word of mouth. From that day he depended wholly upon signs; for he never heard another sound.

Jock came back with me and lay down, but he was not content. Presently he rose again and remained standing with his back to me, looking steadily in the direction taken by the kudu. It was fine to see the indomitable spirit, but I did not mean to let him try again. The kudu was as good as dead no doubt, yet a hundred kudu would not have tempted me to risk taking him out: to rest him and get him back to camp was the only thought. I was feeling very soft about the dog then.

While I sat thus watching him and waiting for him to rest and recover, once more and almost within reach of me he started off again. But it was not as he had done before. This time he went with a spring and a rush, and with head lowered and meaning business. In vain I called and followed. He outpaced me and left me in a few strides.

I ran back for the rifle and followed, and he had already disappeared down the steep bank of the donga when, through the trees on the opposite side, I saw a kudu cow moving along at a slow cramped walk. The donga was a deep one with perpendicular sides, and in places even over-hanging crumbling banks. I reached it as Jock, slipping and struggling, worked his way up the other wall, writhing and climbing through the tree roots exposed by the floods. As he rushed out the kudu saw him and turned. There was just a chance before he got in the line of fire; and I took it.

One hind leg gave way, and in the short sidelong stagger that followed Jock jumped at the kudu's throat and they went down together.

It took me several minutes to get through the donga, and by that time the kudu was dead and Jock was standing wide-mouthed and panting, on guard at its head.

*

There was no hunting for several days after the affair with the kudu cow. Jock looked worse the following day than he had done since recovering consciousness. His head and neck swelled up so that chewing was impossible and he could only lap a little soup or milk, and could hardly bend his neck at all.

On the morning of the second day Jim Makokel' came up with his hostile-looking swagger and a cross, worried look on his face, and in a half-angry and wholly disgusted tone jerked out at me, 'The dog is deaf. I say so! Me! Makokela! Jock is deaf. He does not hear when you speak. Deaf! Yes, deaf!'

Jim's tone grew fiercer as he warmed up. He seemed to hold me responsible. The moment the boy spoke I knew it was true – it was the only possible explanation of many little things. Nevertheless I jumped up hurriedly to try him in a dozen ways, hoping to find that he could hear something. Jim was right. He was really stone deaf. It was pathetic to find how each little subterfuge that drew his eyes from me left him out of reach: it seemed as if a link had broken between us and I had lost my hold.

That was wrong, however! In a few days he began to realize the loss of hearing; and after that, feeling so much greater dependence on sight, his watchfulness increased so that nothing escaped him. None of those who saw him in that year, when he was at his very best, could bring themselves to believe that he was deaf. With me it made differences both ways: something lost, and something gained. If he could hear nothing, he saw more; the language of signs developed; and taking it all round I believe the sense of mutual dependence for success and of mutual understanding was greater than ever.

Jantje

THERE was another spot between the Komati and Crocodile rivers, on the north side of the road, where the white man seldom passed and nature was undisturbed. Few knew of water there. It was too well concealed between deep banks and the dense growth of thorns and large trees.

The spot always had great attractions for me apart from the big game to be found there. I used to steal along the banks of this lone water and watch the smaller life of the bush.

There were plenty of birds – guinea-fowl, pheasant, partridge, korhaan and bush pou. Jock accompanied me of course when I took the fowling-piece, but merely for companionship; for there was no need for him on these occasions. I shot birds to get a change of food and trusted to walking them up along the river banks and near the drinking pools.

There were numbers of little squirrel-like creatures there too. They were little fellows like meerkats, with bushy tails ringed in brown, black and white, of which the wagon boys made decorations for their slouch hats.

Along the water's edge one came on the lagavaan – huge

repulsive water-lizards three to four feet long, like crocodiles in miniature – sunning themselves in some favourite
spot in the margin of reeds or on the edge of the bank.
They gave one the jumps by the suddenness of their rush
through the reeds and plunge into deep water.

There were otters too – big, black-brown, fierce fellows,
to be seen swimming close under the banks – and cane rats,
considered by some most excellent and delicate of meats,
as big and tender as small sucking-pigs. The cane rat was one
of the stock surprises and the subject of jokes and tricks

upon the unsuspecting. The hardened ones enjoyed setting
this treat before the hungry and, after a hearty meal, an-
nouncing – 'That was roast rat : good isn't it?'

The water tortoises in the silent pools, grotesque muddy
fellows, were full of interest to the quiet watcher, and better
that way than as the 'turtle soup' which once or twice we
ventured on and tried to think was good!

There were certain hours of the day when it was more
pleasant and profitable to lie in the shade and rest. It is the
time of rest for the Bushveld – that spell about middle-day
– and yet if one remains quiet, there is generally something
to see and something worth watching.

There were the insects on the ground about one which
would not otherwise be seen at all. There were caterpillars
clad in spiky armour made of tiny fragments of grass – fair
defence no doubt against some enemies and a most marvellous disguise; other caterpillars clad in bark, impossible
to detect until they moved. There were grasshoppers like
leaves, and irregularly shaped stick insects, with legs as
bulky as the body, and all jointed by knots like irregular
twigs – wonderful mimetic creatures.

Jock often found these things for me. Something would move and interest him; and when I saw him stand up and examine a thing at his feet, turning it over with his nose or giving it a scrape with his paw, it was usually worth joining in the inspection. The Hottentot-gods always attracted him as they reared up and 'prayed' before him: quaint things, with tiny heads and thin necks and enormous eyes,

that sat up with forelegs raised to pray, as a pet dog sits up and begs.

One day I was watching the ants as they travelled along their route – sometimes stopping to hobnob with those they met, sometimes hurrying past, and sometimes turning as though sent back on a message or reminded of something forgotten – when a little dry brown bean lying in a spot of sunlight gave a jump of an inch or two. At first it seemed that I must have unknowingly moved some twig or grass stem that flicked it; but as I watched it there was another vigorous jump. I took it up and examined it but there was nothing unusual about it, it was just a common, light brown bean with no peculiarities or marks. It was a real puzzle, a most surprising and ridiculous one.

I found half a dozen more in the same place; but it was some days before we discovered the secret. Domiciled in each of them was a very small but very energetic worm, with a trap-door or stopper on his one end, so artfully contrived that it was almost impossible with the naked eye to locate the spot where the hole was. The worm objected to too much heat and if the beans were placed in the sun or near the fire the weird astonishing jumping would commence.

The beans were good for jumping for several months, and once in Delagoa, one of our party put some on a plate in the sun beside a fellow who had become a perfect nuisance to us and we could not get rid of him. He had a mouthful of bread, and a mug of coffee on the way to help it down, when the first bean jumped. He gave a sort of peck, blinked several times to clear his eyes, and then with his left hand pulled slightly at his collar, as though to ease it. Then came another jump, and his mouth opened slowly and his eyes got big. The plate being hollow and glazed the jumpers

could not escape, and in about half a minute eight or ten beans were having a rough and tumble.

With a white, scared face our guest slowly lowered his mug, and after fighting down the mouthful of bread, got up and walked off without a word.

We tried to smother our laughter, but someone's choking made him look back and he saw the whole lot of us in various stages of convulsions. He made one rude remark and went on; but everyone he met that day made some allusion to beans, and he took the Durban steamer next morning.

The insect life was prodigious in its numbers and variety. Round the camp fire at nights it was no uncommon thing to see someone jump up and let out with whatever was handiest at some poisonous intruder. There was always plenty of dead wood about and we piled on big branches and logs freely, and as the ends burnt to ashes in the heart of the fire we kept pushing the logs further in. Of course, dead trees are the home of all sorts of 'creepy-crawly' things. As the log warmed up and the fire ate into the decayed heart and drove thick hot smoke through the cracks and corridors and secret places in the logs, the occupants would come scuttling out at the butt ends. Small snakes were common – the big ones usually clearing when the log was first disturbed – and they slipped away into the darkness giving hard, quick glances about them. But scorpions, centipedes and all sorts of spiders were by far the most numerous.

Occasionally in the mornings we found snakes under our blankets, where they had worked in during the night for the warmth of the human body. But no one was bitten, and one made a practice of getting up at once, and with one

movement, so that unwelcome visitors should not be warned or provoked by any preliminary rolling. The scorpions, centipedes and tarantulas seemed to be more objectionable; but they were quite as anxious to get away as we were, and it is wonderful how little damage was done.

*

I had an old, cross-bred, Hottentot–Bushman boy once who

was full of the folklore stories and superstitions of his strange and dying race, which he half humorously and half seriously blended with his own knowledge and hunting experiences.

Jantje had the ugly, wrinkled, dry-leather face of his breed, with hollow cheeks, high cheek-bones and little pinched eyes, so small and so deeply set that no one ever saw the colour of them. The peppercorns of tight, wiry wool that did duty for hair were sparsely scattered over his head like the stunted bushes in the desert; and his face and head were seamed with scars too numerous to count, the souvenirs of his drunken brawls. He resembled a tame monkey rather than a human creature, being without the moral qualities of human nature which go to mark the distinction between man and monkey. He was normally most cheery and obliging; but it meant nothing, for in a moment the monkey would peep out, vicious, treacherous and unrestrained. Honesty, sobriety, gratitude, truth, fidelity and humanity were impossible to him, and he differed in character and nature from the Zulu as much as he did from the white man.

I put Jantje on to wash clothes the day he turned up at the wagons to look for work, and as he knelt on the rocks stripped to the waist I noticed a very curious knotted line running up his right side from the lowest rib into the armpit. The line was whiter than his yellow skin; over each rib there was a knot or widening in the line; and under the arm there was a big splotchy star – all markings of some curious wound.

He laughed almost hysterically, his eyes disappearing altogether and every tooth showing, as I lifted his arm to investigate; and then in high-pitched falsetto tones he shouted in a sort of ecstasy of delight, 'Die ouw buffels, Baas! Die buffels bull, Baas!'

'Buffalo! Did he toss you?' I asked.

Jantje seemed to think it the best joke in the world and

with constant squeals of laughter and graphic gestures gabbled off his account.

His master, it appears, had shot at and slightly wounded the buffalo, and Jantje had been placed at one exit from the bush to prevent the herd from breaking away. As they came towards him he fired at the foremost one; but before he could reload the wounded bull made for him and he ran for dear life to the only tree near – one of the flat-topped thorns. He heard the thundering hoofs and the snorting breath behind, but raced on hoping to reach the tree and dodge behind it. A few yards short, however, the bull caught him, in spite of a jump aside, and flung him with one toss right on top of the thorn tree.

When he recovered consciousness he was lying face upwards in the sun, with nothing to rest his head on and only sticks and thorns around him. He did not know where he was or what had happened. He tried to move, but one arm was useless and the effort made him slip and sag, and he thought he was falling through the earth. Presently he heard regular tramping underneath him and the breath of a big animal – and the whole incident came back to him. By feeling about cautiously he at last located the biggest branch under him, and getting a grip on this he managed to turn over and ease his right side.

He could then see the buffalo. It had tramped a circle round the tree and was doing sentry over him. Now and again the huge creature stopped to sniff, snort and stamp, and then resumed the round, perhaps the reverse way. The buffalo could not see him and never once looked up, but glared about at its own accustomed level; and, relying entirely on its sense of smell, it kept up the relentless vengeful watch for hours, always stopping in the same place, to leeward, to satisfy itself that the enemy had not escaped.

Late in the afternoon the buffalo, for the first time, suddenly came to a stand on the windward side of the tree, and after a good minute's silence turned its tail on Jantje

and with angry sniffs and tosses stepped swiftly and reso-
lutely forward some paces. There was nothing to be seen;
but Jantje judged the position and yelled out a warning to
his master whom he guessed to be coming through the
bush to look for him; and at the same time he made what
noise he could in the tree top to make the buffalo think he
was coming down.

For many minutes there was dead silence. No answer
came to Jantje's call, and the bull stood its ground glaring
and sniffing towards the bush. At last there was a heavy
thud below, instantly followed by the report of the rifle –
the bullet came faster than sound. The buffalo gave a
heavy plunge and with a grunting sob slid forward on its
chest.

Round the camp fire at night Jantje used to tell tales in
which fact, fancy and superstition were curiously mingled;
and Jantje when not out of humour was free with his
stories. The boys, for whose benefit they were told, listened
open-mouthed; and I often stood outside the ring of gaping
boys at their fire, an interested listener.

The tale of his experiences with the honey-bird was the
first I heard him tell. Who could say how much was fact,
how much fancy and how much the superstitions of his
race? Not even Jantje knew that! He believed it all.

The honey-bird met him one day with a cheery cheep-
cheep, and as he whistled in reply it led him to an old tree
where the beehive was. It was a small hive, and Jantje was
hungry – so he ate it all. All the time he was eating, the
bird kept fluttering about, calling anxiously and expecting
some honey or fat young bees to be thrown out for it; and
when he had finished, the bird came down and searched in
vain for its share. As he walked away the guilty Jantje
noticed that the indignant bird followed him with angry
cries and threats.

All day long he failed to find game. Whenever there

seemed to be a chance an angry honey-bird would appear ahead of him and cry a warning to the game; and that night as he came back, empty-handed and hungry, all the portents of bad luck came to him in turn. An owl screeched three times over his head; a goat-sucker with its long, wavy wings and tail flitted before him in swoops and rings in most ghostly silence – and there is nothing more ghostly than that flappy, wavy, soundless flitting of the goat-sucker; a jackal trotted persistently in front looking back at him; and a striped hyena, humpbacked, savage and solitary, stalked by in silence.

At night as he lay unable to sleep the bats came and made faces at him; a night adder rose up before his face and slithered out its forked tongue – the two black beady eyes glinting the firelight back; and whichever way he looked there was a honey-bird, silent and angry, yet with a look of satisfaction, as it watched. So it went all night : no sleep for him; no rest!

In the morning he rose early and taking his gun and chopper set out in search of hives. He would give all to the honey-bird he had cheated, and thus make amends.

He had not gone far before, to his great delight, there came a welcome chattering in answer to his low whistle, and the busy little fellow flew up to show himself and promptly led the way, going ahead ten to twenty yards at a flight. Jantje followed eagerly until they came to a small donga with a sandy bottom, and then the honey-bird, calling briskly, fluttered from tree to tree on either bank, leading him on.

Jantje, thinking the hive must be near by, was walking slowly along the sandy bed and looking upwards in the trees, when something on the ground caught his eye and he sprang back just as the head of a big puff-adder struck where his bare foot had been a moment before. With one swing of his chopper he killed it. He took the skin off for an ornament, the poison-glands for medicine and the fangs for charms, and then whistled and looked about for the honey-bird; but it had gone.

A little later on, however, he came upon another, and it led him to a big and shady wild fig tree. The honey-bird flew to the trunk itself and cheeped and chattered there, and Jantje put down his gun and looked about for an easy place to climb. As he peered through the foliage he met a pair of large green eyes looking full into his: on a big limb of the tree lay a leopard, still as death, with its head resting on its paws, watching him with a cat-like eagerness for its prey. Jantje hooked his toe in the reim sling of his old gun and slowly gathered it up without moving his eyes from the leopard's and backing away slowly, foot by foot, he got out into the sunshine and made off as fast as he could.

It was the honey-bird's revenge: he knew it then!

He sat down on some bare ground to think what next to do; for he knew he must die if he did not find honey and make good a hundred times what he had cheated.

All day long he kept meeting honey-birds and following them; but he could no longer follow them into the bad places, for he could not tell whether they were new birds or the one he had robbed! Once he had nearly been caught. The bird had perched on an old ant-heap, and Jantje, thinking there was a ground hive there, walked boldly forward. A small misshapen tree grew out of the ant-heap, and one of the twisted branches caught his eye because of the thick ring around it. It was the coil of a long green mamba; and far below that, half hidden by the leaves, hung the snake's head with the neck gathered in half-loop coils ready to strike at him.

After that Jantje kept in the open, searching for himself among rocks and in all the old dead trees for the tell-tale stains that mark the hive's entrance. But he had no luck, and when he reached the river in the early afternoon he was glad of a cool drink and a place to rest.

For a couple of hours he had seen no honey-birds, and it

seemed that at last his pursuer had given him up, for that day at least. As he sat in the shade of the high bank, however, with the river only a few yards from his feet he heard again a faint chattering. It came from the riverside beyond a turn in the bank; and it was too far away for the bird to have seen Jantje from where it called, so he had no doubt about this being a new bird. It seemed to him a glorious piece of luck that he should find honey by the aid of a strange bird, and be able to take half of it back to the hive he had emptied the day before and leave it there for the cheated bird.

There was a beach of pebbles and rocks between the high bank and the river, and as Jantje walked along it on the keen look-out for the bird, he spotted it sitting on a root half-way down the bank some twenty yards ahead. Close to where the chattering bird perched there was a break in the pebbly beach, and there shallow water extended up to the perpendicular bank. In the middle of this little stretch of water, and conveniently placed as a stepping-stone, there was a black rock and the bare-footed Jantje stepped noiselessly from stone to stone towards it.

An alarmed cane-rat, cut off by Jantje from the river, ran along the foot of the bank to avoid him. But when it reached the little patch of shallow water it suddenly doubled back in fright and raced under the boy's feet into the river.

Jantje stopped! He did not know why; but there seemed to be something wrong. Something had frightened the cane-rat back to him, and he stared hard at the bank and the stretch of beach ahead of him. Then the rock he meant to step on to gave a heave, and a long blackish thing curved towards him. He sprang into the air as high as he could and the crocodile's tail swept under his feet!

Jantje fled back like a buck – the rattle on the stones behind him and crash of reeds putting yards into every bound.

For four days he stayed in camp waiting for someone to

find a hive and give him honey enough to make his peace; and then, for an old snuff-box and a little powder, he bought a huge basket full of comb from a native woman at one of the kraals some miles away, and put it all at the foot of the tree he had cleaned out.

Then he had peace.

The boys believed every word of that story. So, I am sure, did Jantje himself. The buffalo story was obviously true, and Jantje thought nothing of it; the honey-bird story was not, yet he gloried in it. It touched his superstitious nature, and it was impossible for him to tell the truth or to separate fact from fancy and superstition.

How much of fact there may have been in it I cannot say. Honey-birds gave me many a wild-goose chase, but when they led to anything at all it was to hives, and not to snakes, leopards and crocodiles. Perhaps it is right to own up that I never cheated a honey-bird! We pretended to laugh at the superstition, but we left some honey all the same – just for luck! After all, as we used to say, the bird earned its share and deserved encouragement.

Monkeys and Wildebeeste

MUNGO was a long, strong, low-built, half-bred Basuto pony, well trained and without guile; he was not a perfect mount, but he was a great improvement on Snowball who had gone onto the retired list. He had a wretched walk and led almost as badly as his predecessor; but this did not matter so much because he could be driven like a pack donkey and relied on not to play pranks. In a gallop after game he was much faster than Snowball, having a wonderfully long stride for so low a pony.

A horse made a good deal of difference in the hunting in many ways, not the least of which was that some sort of excursion was possible on most days. One could go further in the time available and, even if delayed, still be pretty sure of catching up to the wagons without much difficulty.

Sometimes, after a long night's trekking, I would start off after breakfast for some 'likely' spot, off-saddle there in a shady place, sleep during the heat of the day and after a billy of tea start hunting towards the wagons in the afternoon.

It was in such a spot on the Komati River, a couple of

hundred yards from the bank, that on one occasion I settled down to sleep. With Mungo knee-haltered in good grass and Jock beside me, I lay flat on my back with hat covering my eyes and was soon comfortably asleep.

The sleep had lasted a couple of hours when I began to dream that it was raining and woke up in the belief that a hailstorm was just breaking over me. I started up to find all just as it had been, and the sunlight beyond the big tree so glaring as to make the eyes ache. Through half-closed lids I saw Mungo lying down asleep and made out Jock standing some yards away quietly watching me.

With a yawn and stretch I lay back again. Sleep was over but a good lazy rest was welcome. In the doze that followed I was surprised to feel quite distinctly something like a drop of rain strike my leg and then another on my hat.

'Hang it all, it is raining,' I said, sitting up again and quite wide awake this time. There was Jock still looking at me, but only for the moment of moving; for, a minute later, he looked up into the tree above me with ears cocked, head on one side and tail lazily on the horizontal and moving slowly from time to time.

It was his look of interested amusement.

A couple of leaves fluttered down, and then the half-eaten pip of a 'wooden orange' struck me in the face as I lay back again to see what was going on above. The pip gave me the line, and away up among the thick, dark foliage I saw a little old face looking down at me. The quick restless eyes were watchfully on the move, and the mouth partly opened in the shape of an O – a vivid expression of surprise and indignation combined with breathless interest.

As my eyes fairly met those above me, the monkey ducked its head forward and promptly 'made a face' at me without uttering a sound. Then others showed up in different places, and whole figures became visible now as the monkeys stole softly along the branches to get a better look at Jock and me.

They are the liveliest, most restless and most inquisitive of creatures; ludicrously nervous and excitable; quick to chattering anger and bursts of hysterical passion, which are intensely comical. They are creatures whose method of progress betrays them by the swaying of a branch or quivering of leaves, yet they can steal about and melt away at will, like small, grey ghosts, silent as the grave.

I had often tried to trap them, but never succeeded. Jantje caught them, as he caught everything, with great cunning; pitfalls, nooses, whip-traps, fall-traps, foot-snares, drags, slip-knots of all kinds, were in his repertory; but he

disliked showing his traps, and when told to explain he would half sulkily show one of the common kind.

The day he caught the monkey he was well pleased, and may possibly have told the truth. The trap he used was an old calabash or gourd with a round hole in it about an inch in diameter. A few pumpkin seeds and mealies and a hard crust of bread, just small enough to get into the calabash, formed the bait.

After fastening the gourd by a cord to a small stump, he left it lying on its side on the ground where he had been sitting. A few crumbs and seeds were dropped near it and the rest placed in the gourd, with one or two showing in the mouth. Then he walked off on the side where he would be longest in view – knowing that they were watching his every movement, but knowing also that their intense curiosity would draw them to it the moment it seemed safe. When well out of sight he sped round in a circuit to a previously selected spot where he could get close up again and watch.

The foremost monkey was already on the ground when he got back and others were hanging from low branches or clinging to the stems, ready to drop or retreat. Then began the grunts and careful timid approaches; the squatting and waiting, making pretences of not being particularly interested, while their quick eyes watched everything; then the deft picking up of one thing – instantly dropped again, as one picks up a roasted chestnut and drops it in the same movement, in case it should be hot; and finally the greedy scramble and chatter.

Jantje waited until the tugs at the gourd became serious, and then, knowing that the smaller things had been taken out or shaken out and eaten, and that some enterprising monkey had put his arm into the hole and grabbed the crust, he ran out.

A monkey rarely lets go any food it has grabbed, and when the hand is jammed in a narrow neck, the letting go cannot easily be done. So Jantje caught his monkey, and flinging his ragged coat over the captive sat down to make it safe. By pushing the monkey's arm deeper into the gourd the crust became released and the hand freed; he then gradually shifted the monkey about until he got it into the sleeve of the loose, old coat, with the head appearing at the cuff-opening and the body jammed in like a bulging, over-stuffed sausage. The monkey struggled, screamed, chattered, made faces and cried like a child; but Jantje, gripping it between his knees, worked away unmoved.

He next took the cord from the calabash and tied one end securely round the monkey's neck and the other end to a stout bush stick about seven or eight feet long; and then slipped monkey, cord and stick back through the sleeve and had his captive safe. The cord prevented it from getting away, and the stick from getting too close and biting him.

The grimacing little imps invariably tempt one to tease

or chase them, just to see their antics and methods. When I rose – openly watching them and stepping about for a better view – they bounded freely from branch to branch, always ducking behind something if I pointed the gun or a stick or even my arm at them, and getting into paroxysms of rage and leaning over to slang and cheek me whenever it seemed safe.

Jock was full of excitement, thoroughly warmed up and anxious to be at them, running about from place to place

to watch them, tacking and turning and jumping for better views, and now and then running to the trunk and scraping at it. The idea of playing a trick on them struck me and I caught Jock up and put him in the fork of a big main branch about six feet from the ground. The effect was magical: the whole of the top of the tree seemed to whip and rustle at once, and in two seconds there was not a monkey left.

Then a wave in the top of a small tree some distance off betrayed them and we gave chase – a useless romping schoolboy chase. They were in the small trees away from the river and it was easy to see and follow them; and to add to the fun and excitement I threw stones at the branches behind them. Their excitement and alarm then became hysterical and, as we darted about to head them off, they were several times obliged to scamper a few yards along the ground to avoid me and gain other trees.

It was then that Jock enjoyed himself most; he ran at them and made flying leaps and snaps as they sprang up the trees out of reach. They got away into the big trees once more, to Jock's disappointment but greatly to my relief; for I was quite pumped from the romp and laughter.

The river at this point was broken into several sluices by islands formed of piles of rocks on which there were a few stunted trees and dense growth of tall reeds; and here and there little spits of white sand were visible. There was plenty of small game in that part, and it was a great place for crocodiles. As we were then about half a mile below where Mungo had been left I strolled along the bank on the lookout for a shot, frequently stopping to examine suspicious-looking rocks on the sand spits or at the borders of the reed fringes on the little islands.

The shooting of crocodiles was an act of war. It was enmity and not sport that prompted it, and, when it did not interfere with other chances, we never missed a shot at these fellows. I picked out several suspicious-looking 'rocks', and twice, while I was trying to make them out, they slid silently into the water before there was time to fire.

However, further on there came a better chance. There was something so peculiar about the look of this 'rock' that I picked a good spot and sat down to watch it. Presently the part nearest me turned slightly, just enough to show that it was a crocodile lying on the flat sand with his nose towards me and his tail hidden in the reeds. It was fifty yards away, and from where I sat there was not much to aim at, as a Martini bullet would glance from almost any part of that polished, hard case if it struck at such an angle.

I was sitting on the bank above the shelving beach of the river on which a dense mass of reeds grew, and the waving feathery tops partly obscured the sight. I know the bullet hit him somewhere, because he bounded with astonishing strength and activity several feet in the air and his tail slashed through the reeds like a mighty scythe. The huge jaws opened and he gave a horrible angry bellow – something between a roar and a snarl – as he plunged into the river, sending masses of spray and water flying every way. He made straight across, apparently at me, swimming on top of the water at amazing speed and throwing up a wave on either side and a white whirl of foam from the propelling tail.

It was certainly a most surprising and unheard-of proceeding, and as he reached my side of the stream, and because hidden from me by the screen of reeds at my feet, I turned and bolted. It may be that he came at me with murderous intent; or it may be that, blinded by rage or pain, he came towards me simply because he happened to be facing that way; but, whatever the reason, it was painfully clear that if he meant business he would be on to me before it was possible to see him in the reeds. That was enough for me. It had never occurred to me that there was going to be any fun in this for the crocodile.

With twenty yards of open ground between us I turned and waited. But no crocodile appeared, nor was there a sound to be heard in the reeds; and not being disposed to go into the reeds to look for something which I did not want, but might want me, I returned to Mungo.

Half an hour's jogging along the bank having failed to propose anything, I struck away from the river taking a line through the bush towards camp, and eventually came across a small herd of blue wildebeeste. Mungo's pricked ears and raised head warned me; but the grass being high it was not easy to see enough of them from the ground to place an effective shot, and before a chance offered they moved off. I walked after them, leading Mungo and trying to get a fair opening on slightly higher ground.

Presently half a dozen blackish things appeared above the tall grass. They were the heads of the wildebeeste – all turned one way, and all looking at us with ears wide spread. Only the upper halves of the heads were visible through the thinner tops of the grass, and even an ordinary standing shot was not possible. I had to go to a tree for support in order to tip-toe for the shot, and while in the act of raising my rifle the heads disappeared. But I took a chance and fired just below where the last one had shown up.

The wildebeeste were out of sight, hidden by grass six feet high, but a branch of the tree beside me served as a horizontal bar and hoisting myself chin high I was able to see them again. In front of us there was a dry vlei quite free of bush, some two hundred yards across and four hundred yards long. The wildebeeste had gone away to the right and were skirting the vlei, apparently meaning to get round to the opposite side, avoiding the direct cut across the vlei for reasons of their own. It occurred to me that there must be a deep donga or perhaps a mudhole in front which they were avoiding; but that it might be possible for me to get across, or even halfway across, in time to have another shot at them the next time they stopped to look back – as they were almost certain to do. So I ran straight on.

Stooping slightly to prevent my bobbing hat from showing up in the grass tops, and holding the rifle obliquely before me as a sort of snowplough to clear the grass from my eyes, I made as good pace as the ground would allow.

No doubt the rifle held in front of me made it difficult to notice anything on the ground; but the concentrated stare across the vlei in the direction of the galloping wildebeeste was quite as much the cause of what followed. Going fast and stooping low, with all my weight thrown forward, I ran right into a wildebeest cow. My shot had wounded her through the kidneys, completely paralysing the hind-quarters, and she had instantly dropped out of sight in the grass. The only warning I got was a furious snort, and the black-looking monster with great, blazing, blood-shot eyes rose up on its front legs as I ran into it.

To charge into a wounded wildebeest ready to go for you, just when your whole attention is concentrated upon others two hundred yards beyond, is nearly as unpleasant as it is unexpected. It becomes a question of what will happen to you, rather than of what you will do. The rifle, if it had hindered me, also helped : held out at arm's length it struck the wildebeest across the forehead and the collision saved my chest from the horns. There was an angry toss of the big head and the rifle was twirled out of my hand, as one might flip a match away.

I do not know exactly what happened. The impression is of a breathless second's whirl and scramble, and then finding myself standing untouched five yards away, with the half-paralysed wildebeest squatting like a dog and struggling to drag the useless hind-quarters along in its furious efforts to get at Jock, who had already intervened to help me.

The rifle lay within the circle of the big hooked horns; and the squatting animal, making a pivot of its hind-quarters, slewed round and round, making savage lunges at Jock and great heaves at me each time I tried to get the rifle. I tried to hook the gun out with a stick but the wildebeest swung round and faced me at once, snapping the sticks and twirling them out of my hands with surprising ease and quickness.

It often happens that shots touching the kidneys produce a paralysis, temporarily severe, which passes off to a great extent after some minutes and leaves the wounded animal well able to charge. So I then tried another game, and by making feint attacks from the other side at last got the animal gradually worked away from my gun – and the next attempt at raking was successful.

When the excitement was over and there was a chance of taking stock of the position, I found that Jock had a

pretty good 'gravel rash' on one hip and a nasty cut down one leg. He had caught the wildebeest by the nose the instant I ran into it, and it had 'wiped the floor' with him and flung him aside.

I found my bandolier with a broken buckle lying on the grass; one shirt sleeve was ripped open; the back of the right hand cut across; hands and knees were well grated; and there were lumps and bruises about the legs for which there was no satisfactory explanation. I must have scrambled out like an unwilling participant in a dog fight.

It was a long job skinning, cutting up and packing the wildebeest, and when we reached the outspan the wagons had already started and we had a long tramp before us to catch them.

I drove Mungo before me, keeping him at an easy jog. We had been going for possibly an hour and it was quite dark, except for the stars and the young moon low down on our right. The road was soft and Mungo's jogging paces sounded like floppy pats; there was no other sound at all, not even a distant rumble from the wagons to cheer us. Mungo must have been sick of it and one might have thought him jogging in his sleep but for the occasional pricking of his ears – a trick that always makes me wonder how much more do horses see in the dark than we do. I walked like a machine, with rifle on shoulder and glad to be rid of the broken bandolier, then transferred to Mungo; and Jock trotted at my heels.

This tired monotonous progress was disturbed by Mungo: his ears pricked; his head went up; and he stopped, looking hard at a big low bush on our left. I gave him a tap with the switch, and without an instant's hesitation he dashed off to the right making a half circle through the veld and coming into the road again fifty yards ahead and galloped away leaving a rising column of dust behind him.

I stood and faced the bush that Mungo had shied at, and the first thing that occurred to me was that my bandolier and cartridges were with the pony. Then Jock growled low and moved a few steps forward and slightly to the right, also sheering off from that bush. I felt that he was bristling all over, but there was neither time nor light to watch him. I stepped slowly sideways after him gripping the rifle and looking hard at the bush.

Our line was much the same as Mungo's and would take us some seven or eight paces off the road – more than that was not possible owing to the barrier of thorns on that side. When we got abreast of the bush two large spots of pale light appeared in the middle of it, apparently waist high from the ground.

It is impossible to forget the tense creepy feeling caused by the dead stillness, the soft light and the pale expressionless glow of those eyes – the haunting mystery of eyes and nothing more!

It is not unusual to see eyes in the night; but this was a 'nervy' occasion, and there is no other that comes back with all the vividness and reality of the experience itself, as this one does. And I was not the only nervous one. Mungo incontinently bolted – probably what he saw warranted it. Jock as ever faced it; but when my foot touched his hind leg as we sidled away he flew round with a convulsive jump. He too was strung to concert pitch.

As we moved on and passed the reflecting angle of the moon, the light of the eyes went out as suddenly and silently as it had appeared. There was nothing then to show me where danger lay; but Jock knew, and I kept watch on him. He jogged beside me, lagging slightly as if to cover our retreat, always looking back. A couple of times he stopped entirely and stood in the road, facing straight back and growling; and I followed suit. He was in command; he knew!

There was nothing more. Gradually Jock's subdued purring growl died down and the glances back became fewer. I found Mungo a long way on, brought to a standstill by the slipping of his load; and we caught up to the wagons at the next outspan.

The Old Crocodile

WE reached the Crocodile river drift on a Sunday morning, after a particularly dry and dusty night trek. 'Wanting a wash' did not on such occasions mean a mild inclination for a luxury : it meant that washing was badly needed. The dust lay inches deep on the one worn veld road, and the long strings of oxen toiling along kicked up suffocating clouds of fine dust which there was seldom any breeze to carry off. It powdered white men and black to an equal level of yellowy red. The wagons were a couple of hundred yards from the river; and, taking a complete change, I went off for a real clean up.

We generally managed to get in a couple of bathes at the rivers – real swims – but that was only done in the regular drifts and when there were people about or wagons crossing. In such conditions crocodiles rarely appeared; they prefer solitude and silence.

Being alone that day I had no intention of having a swim or of going into the open river, and I took a little trouble to pick a suitable pool with a rock on which to stand and dress. The water was clear and I could see the bottom of the pool. It was quite shallow – three feet deep at most – and divided from the main stream by a narrow spit of sand. At

241

the top end of the sand spit was a flat rock – my dressing table.

After a dip in the pool I stood on to the sand spit to scrub off the brown dust, keeping one unsoaped eye roving round for intrusive crocodiles, and the loaded rifle lying beside me. The brutes slide out so silently and unexpectedly that in that exposed position, with water all round, one could not afford to turn one's back on any quarter for long. There is something laughable – it seemed faintly humorous even then – in the idea of a naked man hastily washing soap out of his eyes and squeezing away the water to take a hurried look behind him; and then, after careful survey, doing an 'altogether' douse just as hastily – blowing and spluttering all the time like a boy after his first dive.

The bath was successful and ended without incident – not a sign of a crocodile the whole time! Breakfast was ready when I reached the wagons, and feeling very fit and clean in a fresh flannel shirt and white moleskins, I sat down to it. Jim Makokel' brought the kettle of coffee from the fire and was in the act of pouring some into a big mug when he stopped with a grunt of surprise and, looking towards the river, called out sharply, 'What is it?'

One of the herd boys was coming at a trot towards us, and the drivers, thinking something had happened to the oxen, called a question to him. He did not answer until he reached them and even then spoke in so quiet a tone that I could not catch what he said. But Jim, putting down the kettle, ran to his wagon and grabbing his sticks and assegais called to me in a husky shouting whisper: '*Ingwenye, Inkos! Ingwenye Umkulu!* Big Clocodile! *Groot Krokodil, Baas!*'

Then, abandoning his excited polyglot, he gabbled off in pure Zulu and at incredible speed a long account of the big crocodile. It had carried off four boys going to the gold-fields that year; it had taken a woman and a baby from the kraals near by, but a white man had beaten it off with a bucket; it had taken all the dogs, and even calves and goats, at the drinking place; and goodness knows how much more. How Jim got his news, and when he made his friends, were puzzles never solved.

Hunting stories, like travellers' tales, are proverbially dangerous to reputations, however literally true they may be. There are two crocodile incidents which, even in the day of their happening, divided men into believers and un-believers. The one was of 'Mad' Owen riding through the Komati Drift one moonlight night alone and unarmed, who found his horse brought to a stop, plunging, kicking and struggling on the sand bank in mid-stream where the water was not waist deep. Owen looking back saw that a crocodile had his horse by the leg. All he had was a leaded hunting-crop, but jumping into the water he laid on so vigorously that the crocodile made off, and Owen remounted and rode out.

I crossed that same drift one evening and on riding up the bank to Furley's store saw a horse standing in a dejected attitude, with one hind leg clothed in 'trousers' made of sacking and held up by a suspender ingeniously fastened across his back.

During the evening I asked a question and Furley's ans-wer was, 'One night, a week ago, Owen turned up here dripping wet, and after having a drink told us the yarn. He had the leaded hunting-crop in his hand – and that's the horse he was riding!'

I have no doubt about the incident. Owen did not invent: he had no need to.

The other incident concerns 'Lying Tom' – brave, merry-faced, blue-eyed Tom; bubbling with good humour; over-flowing with kindness; and full of the wildest yarns, so steep that they made the most case-hardened draw in a long breath.

Tom was a prospector who 'came in' occasionally for supplies or licences; and there came a day when Barberton was convulsed by Lying Tom's latest.

He had been walking along the bank of the Crocodile river, and on hearing screams ran down just in time to see a native woman with a child on her back dragged off through the shallow water by a crocodile. Tom ran in to help – 'I kicked the dashed thing on the head and in the eyes,' he said, 'and pinched its ribs and then grabbed the bucket that the woman had in her hand and hammered the blamed thing over the head till it let go.'

Of course this story went the rounds as Tom's latest and best. But one day we turned up in Barberton to deliver our loads, and that evening a whisper went about: 'Tom's crocodile story is true!'

For our party, shooting guinea-fowl in the native lands along the river, came upon a kraal where there sat a woman with an arm so scarred and marked that we could not but ask what had caused it. There was no difference in the stories, except that the natives added that the white man had also kicked and beaten with the bucket the two men who were there, saying that they were not men but dogs, who would not go in and help the woman.

That was what Jim referred to when he called me to kill the murderer of women and children. It pleased him and others to say that this was the same crocodile; and I believe it was. The locality was the same, and the kraal boys said that it was in the old place from which all its murderous raids had been made.

*

I took the rifle and went with the herd boy. Jim followed close behind, walking on his toes with the waltzy, springy movements of an ostrich, eager to get ahead and repeatedly silenced and driven back by me in the few hundred yards' walk to the river.

A queer premonitory feeling came over me as I saw we were making straight for the bathing pool. But before reaching the bank the herd boy squatted down, indicating that somewhere in front and below us the enemy would be found. An easy crawl brought me to the river bank and, sure enough, on the very spot where I had stood to wash, only fifty yards from us, there was an enormous crocodile.

He was lying along the sand spit with his full length exposed to me. Such a shot would have been a moral certainty, but as I brought the rifle slowly up it may have glinted in the sun, or perhaps the crocodile had been watching us all the time, for with one easy turn and no splash at all he slid into the river and was gone.

It was very disgusting and I pitched into Jim and the other boys behind for having made a noise and shown themselves; but they were still squatting when I reached them and vowed they had neither moved nor spoken. We had already turned to go when there came a distant call from beyond the river. To me it was merely a native's voice and a sound quite meaningless – but to the boys' trained ears it spoke clearly. Jim pressed me downwards and we all squatted again.

'He is coming out on another sandbank,' Jim explained.

Again I crawled to the bank and lay flat, with the rifle ready. There was another sand streak a hundred yards out in the stream with two out-croppings of black rock at the upper end of it – they were rocks right enough, for I had examined them carefully when bathing. This was the only other sand bank in sight. It was higher than it appeared to be from a distance and the crocodile, while hidden from us, was visible to the natives on the opposite bank as it lay in the shallow water and emerged inch by inch to resume its morning sun bath.

The crocodile was so slow in showing up that I quite thought it had been scared off again, and I turned to examine other objects and spots up and down the stream. But presently, glancing back at the bank again, I saw what appeared to be a third rock, no bigger than a loaf of bread. This object I watched until my eyes ached and swam. It was the only possible crocodile – yet it was so small, so motionless, so permanent-looking, it seemed absurd to doubt that it really was a stone which had passed unnoticed before.

As I watched unblinkingly it seemed to grow bigger and again contract with regular swing, as if it swelled and shrank with breathing; and knowing that this must be merely an optical delusion caused by staring too long, I shut my eyes for a minute. The effect was excellent: the rock was much bigger; and after that it was easy to lie still and wait for the cunning old reptile to show himself.

It took half an hour of this cautious manoeuvring and edging on the part of the crocodile before he was comfortably settled on the sand with the sun warming all his back. In the meantime the wagon boys behind me had not stirred. On the opposite side of the river natives from the neighbouring kraal had gathered to the number of thirty or forty, men, women and children, and they stood loosely grouped, instinctively still and silent and watchful, like a little scattered herd of deer. All on both sides were watching me and waiting for the shot.

It seemed useless to delay longer. The whole length of the body was showing, but it looked so wanting in thickness, so shallow in fact, that it was evident the crocodile was lying, not on the top, but on the other slope of the sand spit; and probably not more than six or eight inches – in depth – of body was visible.

It was little enough to aim at, and the bullet seemed to strike the top of the bank first, sending up a column of sand; and then, probably knocked all out of shape, ploughed into the body with a tremendous thump.

The crocodile threw a back somersault – that is, it seemed to rear up on its tail and spring backwards. The jaws divided into a huge fork as, for a second, it stood up on end; and it let out an enraged roar, seemingly aimed at the heavens. It was a very sudden and dramatic effect, following on the long silence.

Then the whole world seemed to burst into indescribable turmoil. Shouts and yells burst out on all sides. The natives rushed down to the banks – the men armed with sticks and assegais, and the women and children with nothing more formidable than their voices. The crocodile was alive – very much alive – and in the water. The wagon boys, headed by Jim, were all round me and all yelling out together what should or should not be done, and what would happen if we did or did not do it.

With the first plunge the crocodile disappeared, but it came up again ten yards away thrashing the water into foam and going up stream like a paddle-boat gone reeling, roaring mad. I had another shot at him the instant he reappeared, but one could neither see nor hear where it struck; and again and again I fired whenever he showed up for a second. He appeared to be shot through the lungs; at any rate the natives on the other bank, who were then quite close enough to see, said that it was so. The wagon boys had run down the bank out on to the first sand spit and I followed them, shouting to the natives opposite to get out of the line of fire, as I could no longer shoot without risk of hitting them.

The crocodile after his first straight dash up stream had tacked about in all directions during the next few minutes, disappearing for short spells and plunging out again in unexpected places. One of these sudden reappearances brought him once more abreast, and quite near to us, and Jim with a fierce yell and with his assegai held high in his right hand dashed into the water, going through the shallows in wild leaps. I called to him to come back, but against his yells and the excited shouts of the ever-increasing crowd my voice could not live; and Jim, mad with excitement, went on. Twenty yards out, where increasing depth steadied him, he turned for a moment, and seeing himself alone in the water called to me with eager confidence, 'Come on, Baas.'

It had never occurred to me that anyone would be such an idiot as to go into water after a wounded crocodile. There was no need to finish off this one, for it was bound to die, and no one wanted the meat or skin. Who, then, would be so mad as to think of such a thing? But there was a world of unconscious irony in Jim's choice of words 'Come on!' and 'Baas!'

The boy giving the lead to his master was too much for me; and in I went!

*

I cannot say that there was much enjoyment in it for the first few moments – not until the excitement took hold and all else was forgotten. The first thing that struck me was that in the water my rifle was worth no more than a walking-stick, and not nearly as useful as an assegai. But what drove this and many other thoughts from my mind in a second was the appearance of Jock on the stage and his sudden jump into the leading place.

In the first confusion he had passed unnoticed, probably at my heels as usual, but the instant I answered Jim's challenge by jumping into the water, he gave one whimpering yelp of excitement and plunged in too; and in a few seconds he had outdistanced us all and was leading straight for the crocodile. I shouted to him, of course in vain – he heard nothing; and Jim and I plunged and struggled along to head the dog off.

As the crocodile came up Jock went straight for him – his eyes gleaming, his shoulders up, his nose out, his neck stretched to the utmost in his eagerness – and he ploughed along straining every muscle to catch up. When the crocodile went under he slackened and looked anxiously about, but each fresh rise was greeted by the whimpering yelps of intense suppressed excitement as he fairly hoisted himself out of the water with the vigour of his swimming.

The water was now breast high for us, and we were far out in the stream, beyond the sand spit where the crocodile had lain, when the natives on the bank got their first chance and a flight of assegais went at the enemy as he rose. Several struck and two remained in him. He rose again a few yards from Jim, and that sportsman let fly one that struck well home. Jock, who had been toiling close behind for some time and gaining slowly, was not five yards off then. The floundering and lashing of the crocodile were bewildering, but on he went as grimly and eagerly as ever. I fired again – not more than eight yards away – but the water was then up to my arms, and it was impossible to pick a vital part. The brain and neck were the only spots to finish him, but one could see nothing beyond a great upheaval of water and clouds of spray and bloodstained foam.

The crocodile turned from the shot and dived up stream, heading straight for Jock. The din of yelling voices stopped instantly as the huge open-mouthed thing plunged towards the dog; and for one sick, horrified moment I stood and watched – helpless.

Had the crocodile risen in front of Jock that would have been the end – one snap would have done it. But it passed clear underneath, and, coming up just beyond him, the great lashing tail sent the dog up with the column of water a couple of feet in the air. He did as he had done when the kudu bull tossed him : his head was round straining to get at the crocodile before he was able to turn his body in the water; and the silence was broken by a yell of wild delight and approval from the bank.

Before us the water was too deep and the stream too strong to stand in. Jim in his eagerness had gone in shoulder high, and my rifle when aimed only just cleared the water. The crocodile was the mark for more assegais from the bank as it charged up stream again, with Jock tailing behind, and it was then easy enough to follow its movements by the shafts that were never all submerged. The struggles became perceptibly weaker and, as it turned again to go with the stream, every effort was concentrated on killing and landing it before it reached the rocks and rapids.

I moved back for higher ground and, finding that the bed shelved up rapidly down stream, made for a position where there would be enough elevation to put in a brain shot. The water was not more than waist high then and, as the crocodile came rolling and thrashing down, I waited for his head to show up clearly. My right foot touched a sloping rock which rose almost to the surface of the water close above the rapids, and anxious to get the best possible position for a last shot, I took my stand there.

The rock was uptilted at an easy angle and cut off sheer on the exposed side, and the wave in the current would have shown this to anyone not wholly occupied with other things. But I had eyes for nothing except the crocodile which was then less than a dozen yards off, and in my anxiety to secure a firm footing for the shot I moved the right foot again a few inches – over the edge of the rock. The result was as complete a spill as if one unthinkingly stepped backwards off a diving board: I disappeared in deep water, with the knowledge that the crocodile would join me there in a few seconds.

One never knows how these things are done or how long they take. I was back on the rock – without the rifle – and had the water out of my eyes in time to see the crocodile roll helplessly by, six feet away, with Jock behind making excited but ridiculously futile attempts to get hold of the tail. Jim – swimming, plunging and blowing like a maddened hippo – formed the tail of the procession, which was headed by my water-logged hat floating heavily a yard or so in front of the crocodile.

While a crowd of yelling natives under the generalship of Jim were landing the crocodile, I had time to do some diving, and managed to fish out my rifle.

My Sunday change was wasted. But we got the old crocodile, and that was something, after all.

The Fighting Baboon

On the way to Lydenburg, not many treks from Paradise Camp, we were outspanned for the day. Those were the settled parts. On the hills and in the valleys about us were the widely scattered workings of the gold diggers or the white tents of occasional prospectors.

The place was a well-known and much-frequented public outspan, and a fair-sized wayside store marked its importance. After breakfast we went to the store to 'swap' news with the men on the spot and a couple of horsemen who had offsaddled there.

There were several other houses of sorts. They were rough wattle and daub erections and one of these belonged to Seedling, the Field Cornet and only official in the district. He was the petty local Justice who was supposed to administer minor laws, collect certain revenues and taxes, and issue passes.

He was neither popular nor trusted. Many tales of great harshness and injustice to the natives, and of corruption and favouritism in dealing with the whites – added to habitual drunkenness and uncertain temper – made a formidable tally in the account against him. He was also a bully and a coward, and all knew it – but unfortunately he was the law!

We all knew him personally. He was effusively friendly; and we suffered him and – paid for the drinks. That was in his public capacity. In his private capacity he was the owner of the fighting baboon of evil and cruel repute.

We had been sitting on the little store-counter and talking for over an hour – a group of half a dozen, swapping off the news of the gold-fields and the big world against that from Delagoa and the Bushveld. Seedling had joined us early and, as usual, began the morning with drinks. We were not used to that on the road or out hunting; indeed, we rarely took any drink, and most of us never touched a drop except in the towns. The transport rider had opportunities which might easily become temptations – the load often consisting of liquor, easy to broach and only to be paid for at the end of the trip. Apart from this, however, we did not take liquor because we could not work as well or last as long, run as fast or shoot as straight, if we did. And that was reason enough!

We had one round of drinks which was 'called' by one of the horsemen, and then, to return the compliment, another round called by one of us. A few minutes later Seedling announced effusively that it was his 'shout'. But it was only ten in the morning, and those who had taken spirits had had enough; indeed, several had only taken a sip of the second round in order to comply with a stupid and vicious custom. I would not and could not attack another bottle of sour gingerbeer; and thus Seedling's round was reduced to himself and the proprietor.

A quarter of an hour passed, and Seedling, who had said nothing since his 'shout' was declined, turned away and strolled out, with hands thrust deep in the pockets of his riding breeches and a long heavy sjambok dangling from one wrist. There was silence as he moved through the door-way, and, when the square patch of sunlight on the earth floor was again unbroken, the man behind the counter remarked:

'Too long between drinks for him! Gone for a pull at the private bottle. He reckoned you'd all shout your turns and drinks'd come regular; but he sees you're not on. He'll be wrong all day today. I know him!'

*

We had forgotten Seedling, and were hearing all about the new finds reported from Barberton district, when one of the wagon boys came running into the store calling to me and shouting excitedly, 'Baas, Baas! come quickly! The baboon has got Jock: it will kill him!'

I had known all about the vicious brute, and had often heard of Seedling's fiendish delight in arranging fights or enticing dogs up to attack it for the pleasure of seeing the beast kill the over-matched dogs. The dog had no chance at all, for the baboon remained out of reach in his house on the pole as long as it chose, and made its rush when it would tell best. But apart from this the baboon was an exceptionally big and powerful one, and it is very doubtful if any dog could have tackled it successfully in an open field.

The creature was as clever as even they can be. Its enormous jaws and teeth were quite equal to the biggest dog's, and it had the advantage of four 'hands'. Its tactics in a fight were quite simple and most effective: with its front-feet it caught the dog by the ears or neck, holding the head so that there was no risk of being bitten; and then, gripping the body lower down with the hind feet, it tore lumps out of the throat, breast and stomach – pushing with all four feet and tearing with the terrible teeth. The poor dogs were hopelessly outmatched.

I did not see the beginning of Jock's encounter, but the boys' stories pieced together told everything. It appears that when Seedling left the store he went into his own hut and remained there some little time. On coming out again he strolled over to the baboon's pole about halfway between the two houses and began teasing it; throwing pebbles at it to see it dodge and duck behind the pole; and then flicking at it with the sjambok, amused by its frightened and angry protests. While he was doing this, Jock, who had followed me to the store, strolled out again making his way towards the wagons. He was not interested in our talk. He had twice been accidentally trodden on by men stepping back as he lay stretched out on the floor behind them; and doubtless he felt that it was no place for him. His deafness prevented him from hearing movements, except such as caused vibration in the ground, and, poor old fellow, he was always at a disadvantage in houses and towns.

The baboon had then taken refuge in its box on top of the pole to escape the sjambok, and when Seedling saw Jock come out he commenced whistling and calling softly to him. Jock, of course, heard nothing. He may have responded mildly to the friendly overtures conveyed by the extended hand and patting of legs, or more probably simply took the nearest way to the wagon where he might sleep in peace, since there was nothing else to do.

What the boys agreed on is that as Jock passed the pole Seedling patted and held him, at the same time calling the baboon, and then gave the dog a push which did not quite roll him over but upset his balance; and Jock, recovering himself, naturally jumped round and faced Seedling, standing almost directly between him and the baboon. He could not hear the rattle of the chain on the box and pole, and saw nothing of the charging brute, and it was the purest accident that the dog stood a few inches out of reach. The baboon – chained by the neck instead of the waist, because it used to bite through all loin straps – made its rush, but the chain brought it up before its hands could reach Jock and threw the hind quarters round with such force against him that he was sent rolling yards away.

I can well believe that the second attack from a different and wholly unexpected quarter thoroughly aroused him, and can picture how he turned to face it.

It was at this moment that Jim first noticed what was going on. The other boys had not expected anything when Seedling called the dog, and they were taken completely by surprise by what followed. Jim would have known what to expect. His kraal was in the neighbourhood; he knew Seedling well, and had already suffered in fines and confiscations at his hands. He also knew about the baboon; but he was ignorant, just as I was, of the fact that Seedling had left his old place across the river and come to live in the new hut, bringing his pet with him.

It was the hoarse, threatening shout of the baboon as it jumped at Jock, as much as the exclamations of the boys, that roused Jim. He knew instantly what was on, and grab-

bing a stick made a dash to save the dog, with the other boys following.

When Jock was sent spinning in the dust the baboon recovered itself first, and standing up on its hind legs reached out its long ungainly arms towards him, and let out a shout of defiance. Jock regaining his feet dashed in, jumped aside, feinted again and again, as he had learnt to do when big horns swished at him; and he kept out of reach just as he had done ever since the duiker taught him the use of its hoofs. He knew what to do, just as he had known how to swing the porcupine. The dog – for all the fighting fury that possessed him – took the measure of the chain and kept outside it. Round and round he flew, darting in, jumping back, snapping and dodging, but never getting right home.

The baboon was as clever as he was: at times it jumped several feet in the air, straight up, in the hope that Jock would run underneath; at others, it would make a sudden lunge with the long arms, or a more surprising reach out with the hind legs to grab him. Then the baboon began gradually to reduce its circle, leaving behind it slack chain enough for a spring; but Jock was not to be drawn. In cleverness they were well matched – neither scored in attack; neither made or lost a point.

When Jim rushed up to save Jock, it was with eager anxious shouts of the dog's name that warned Seedling and made him turn; and as the boy ran forward the white man stepped out to stop him.

'Leave the dog alone!' he shouted, pale with anger.

'Baas, Baas, the dog will be killed,' Jim called excitedly as he tried to get round; but the white man made a jump towards him, and with a back-hand slash of the sjambok struck him across the face, shouting at him again:

'Leave him, I tell you.'

Jim jumped back, thrusting out his stick to guard another vicious cut; and so it went on with alternate slash and guard, and the big Zulu danced round with nimble bounds, guarding, dodging or bearing the sjambok cuts, to save the dog. Seedling was mad with rage; but Jim would not give way. He kept trying to get in front of Jock, to head him off the fight, and all the while shouting to the other boys to call me. But Seedling was the Field Cornet, and not one of them dared to move against him.

At last the baboon, finding that Jock would not come on, tried other tactics. It made a sudden retreat and, rushing for the pole, hid behind it as for protection. Jock made a jump and the baboon leaped out to meet him, but the dog stopped at the chain's limit, and the baboon – just as in the first dash of all – overshot the mark. It was brought up by the jerk of the collar, and for one second sprawled on its back. That was the first chance for Jock and he took it. With one spring he was in. His head shot between the baboon's hind legs, and with his teeth buried in the soft stomach he lay back and pulled – pulled for dear life, as he had pulled and dragged on the legs of wounded game; tugged as he had tugged at the porcupine; held on, as he had held when the kudu bull wrenched and strained every bone and muscle in his body.

Then came the sudden turn! As Jock fastened on to the baboon, dragging the chain taut while the screaming brute struggled on its back, Seedling stood for a second irresolute, and then with a stride forward raised his sjambok to strike the dog. That was too much for Jim. He made a spring in and grasping the raised sjambok with his left hand held Seedling powerless, while in his right the boy raised his stick on guard.

'Let him fight, Baas! You said it! Let the dog fight!' he panted, hoarse with excitement.

The white man, livid with fury, struggled and kicked, but the wrist loop of his sjambok held him prisoner and he could do nothing.

That was the moment when a panic-stricken boy plucked up courage enough to call me; and that was the scene we saw as we ran out of the little shop. Jim would not strike the white man; but his face was muddy grey, and it was written there that he would rather die than give up the dog.

Before I reached them it was clear to us all what had happened. Jim was protesting to Seedling and at the same time calling to me; it was a jumble, but a jumble eloquent enough for us, and all intelligible. Jim's excited gabble was addressed with reckless incoherence to Seedling, to me and to Jock!

'You threw him in; you tried to kill him. He did it. It was not the dog. Kill him, Jock, kill him. Leave him, let him fight. You said it – Let him fight! Kill him, Jock! Kill! Kill! Kill!'

Then Seedling did the worst thing possible; he turned on me with:

'Call off your dog, I tell you, or I'll shoot him and your — nigger too!'

'We'll see about that! They can fight it out now,' and I took the sjambok from Jim's hand and cut it from the white man's wrist.

'Now! Stand back!'

And he stood back.

The baboon was quite helpless. Powerful as the brute was, and formidable as were the arms and gripping feet, it had no chance while Jock could keep his feet and had strength to drag and hold the chain tight. The collar was choking it, and the grip on the stomach – the baboon's own favourite and most successful device – was fatal.

I set my teeth, and thought of the poor helpless dogs that had been decoyed in and treated the same way. Jim danced about, the white seam of froth on his lips, hoarse gusts of encouragement bursting from him as he leant over Jock, and his whole body vibrating like an over-heated boiler. And

Jock hung on in grim earnest, the silence on his side broken only by grunting efforts as the deadly tug – tug – tug went on. Each pull caused his feet to slip a little on the smooth worn ground; but each time he set them back again and the grunting tugs went on.

It was not justice to call Jock off; but I did it. The cruel brute deserved killing, but the human look and cries and behaviour of the baboon were too sickening; and Seedling went into his hut without even a look at his stricken champion.

Jock stood off, with his mouth open from ear to ear and his red tongue dangling, blood-stained and panting, but with eager feet ever on the move shifting from spot to spot, ears going back and forward, and eyes – now on the baboon and now on me – pleading for the sign to go in again.

Before evening the baboon was dead.

*

The day's excitement was too much for Jim. After singing and dancing himself into a frenzy round Jock; after shouting the whole story of the fight in violent and incessant gabble over and over again; after making every ear ring and every head swim with his mad din; he grabbed his sticks once more and made off for one of the kraals – there to find drink for which he thirsted body and soul.

In the afternoon the sudden scattering of the inhabitants of a small kraal on the hillside opposite, and some lusty shouting, drew attention that way. At distances of from two to five hundred yards from the huts there stood figures, singly or grouped in twos and threes, up to the highest slopes. They formed a sort of crescent above the kraal; and on the lower side of it, hiding under the bank of the river, were a dozen or more whose heads only were visible. They were all looking towards the kraal like a startled herd of buck. Now and then a burly figure would dart out from the huts with wild bounds and blood-curdling yells, and the watchers on that side would scatter like chaff and flee for dear life up the mountainside or duck instantly and disappear in the river. Then he would stalk back again and disappear, to repeat the performance on another side a little later on.

It was all painfully clear to me. Jim had broken out.

We were loaded for Lydenberg – another week's trekking through and over the mountains – and as we intended coming back the same way a fortnight later I decided at once to leave Jim at his kraal, which was only a little further on, and pick him up on the return journey.

Jim was a splendid worker and as true as steel; so that in spite of all the awful worry I had a soft spot for him and had taken a good deal of trouble on his account. He had good wages, and for many months at a time would draw no money; he got his pay at the end of the trip or the season, but not in cash. It was invested for him – greatly to his disgust at the time, I am bound to say – in livestock, so that he would not be able to squander it in drink or be robbed of it while incapable.

Jim's gloomy dignity was colossal when it came to squaring up. To be treated like an irresponsible child; to be met by the laughter of the other boys, for whom he had the most profound contempt, to see the respectable Sam counting out with gleaming eyes the good red gold, while he, Makokela the Zulu, was treated like a picannin – Ugh! It was horrible! Intolerable!

Jim would hold aloof in injured gloomy silence, not once looking at me, but standing sideways and staring stonily past me into the far distance; and not relaxing for a second the expression of profound displeasure on his weatherbeaten face.

We had the same fight over and over again, but I always won in the end. When it was all over Jim recovered rapidly, and at parting time there was the broadest of grins and a stentorian shout of 'Hlala Kahle! Inkos!'

261

This time Jim was too fully wound up to be dealt with as before, and I simply turned him off, telling him to come to the camp in a fortnight's time.

*

I was a day behind the wagons returning, and riding up to the camp towards midday found Jim waiting for me. He looked ill and shrunken, wrapped in an old coat and squatting against the wall of the little hut. As I passed he rose slowly and gave his 'Sakubona! Inkos!' with that curious controlled air by which the native manages to suggest a kind of fatalist resignation or indifference touched with disgust. There was something wrong.

It was a bad story, almost as bad as one would think possible where civilized beings are concerned.

Several days after our departure Jim went down to the store again and raised some liquor. He was not fighting, but he was noisy, and was the centre of a small knot of shouting,

arguing boys near the store when Seedling returned after a two days' absence. No doubt it was unfortunate that the very first thing he saw on his return was the boy who had defied him and who was the cause of his humiliation; and that that boy should, by his behaviour, give an excuse for interference was unlucky. Seedling's mind was made up from the moment he set eyes on Jim.

Throwing the reins over his horse's head he walked into the excited gabbling knot, and laid about with the sjambok, scattering and silencing them instantly. He then took Jim by the wrist saying, 'I want you.' He called to one of his own boys to bring a reim, and leading Jim over to the side of the store tied him up to the horse rail with arms at full stretch. Taking out his knife he cut the boy's clothing down the back so that it fell away in two halves in front of him; then he took off his own coat and flogged the boy with his sjambok.

I would like to tell all that happened for one reason : it would explain the murderous man-hunting feeling that possessed us when we heard it! But it was too cruel : let it be! Only one thing to show the spirit : twice during the flogging Seedling stopped to go into the store for a drink.

Jim crawled home to find his kraal ransacked and deserted, and his wives and children driven off in panic. In addition to the flogging Seedling had imposed fines far beyond the boy's means in cash, so as to provide an excuse for seizing what he wanted. The police boys had raided the kraal; and the cattle and goats – his only property – were gone.

He told it all in a dull monotone. For the first time the life and fire were gone out of him; but he was not cowed, not broken. There was a curl of contempt on his mouth and in his tone that whipped the white skin on my own back and made it all a disgrace unbearable. That this should be the reward for his courageous defence of Jock seemed too awful.

We went inside to talk it over and make our plans. The wagons should go on next day as if nothing had happened, Jim remaining in one of the half tents or elsewhere out of sight of passers-by. I was to ride to Lydenburg and lodge information – for in such a case the authorities would surely act.

There was no difficulty about the warrant, for there were many counts in the indictment against Seedling. But even so worthless a brute as that seemed to have one friend, or perhaps an accomplice, to give him warning; and before we reached his quarters with the police he had cleared on horse-back for Portuguese territory, taking with him a led horse.

We got most of Jim's cattle back for him – which he seemed to consider the main thing – but we were sorely disgusted at the man's escape.

That was the year of the 'rush'. Thusands of newcomers poured into the country on the strength of the gold discoveries. Materials and provisions of all kinds were almost unprocurable and stood at famine prices; and consequently we – the transport riders – reaped a golden harvest.

Thus the days lost in the attempt to catch Seedling were valuable days. The season was limited, and, as early rains might cut us off, a few days thrown away might mean the loss of a whole trip. We hurried down, therefore, for the Bay, doing little hunting that time.

Near the Crocodile on our way down we heard from men coming up that Seedling had been there some days before, but – hearing we were on the way down and had sworn to shoot him – he had ridden on to Komati, leaving one horse behind bad with horse-sickness. The report about shooting him was, of course, ridiculous, but it was some comfort to know that he was in such a state of terror that his own fancies were hunting him down.

At Komati we learned that he had stayed three days at the store of that Goanese murderer, Antonio. Suspecting something wrong about a white man who dawdled aimlessly three days at Komati Drift, going indoors whenever a stranger appeared, Antonio wormed the secret out with liquor and sympathy; and when he had got most of Seedling's money out of him – by pretence of bribing the Portuguese officials – made a bold bid for the rest by saying that a warrant was out for him in Delagoa and he must on no account go on. The evil-looking half-caste no doubt hoped to get the horse, saddle and bridle, as well as the cash; and was quite prepared to drug Seedling when the time came, and slip him quietly into the Komati at night where the crocodiles would take care of the evidence.

Antonio, however, overshot the mark. Seedling took fright, saddled up and bolted up the river meaning to make for the Lebombo, near the Tembe Drift, where Bob McNab and his merry comrades ran free of governments and were a law unto themselves. It was no place for a nervous man, but Seedling had no choice, and he went on. He had liquor in his saddle bags and food for several days; but he was not used to the bush, and at the end of the first day he had lost his way and was beyond the river district where the natives lived.

So much is believed, though not positively known. At any rate he left the last kraal in those parts about noon, and was next heard of two days later at a kraal under the Lebombo. There he learnt that the Black Umbeluzi, which it would be necessary to swim – as Snowball and Tsetse had done – lay before him, and that it was yet a great distance to Sebougwaans, and even then he would be only halfway to Bob's. Seedling could not face it alone, and turned back for the nearest store.

The natives said that before leaving the kraal he bought beer from them, but did not want food; for he looked sick. He was red and swollen in the face, and his eyes were wild. The horse was weak and also looked sick, being very thin and empty. They showed him the foot-path over the hills which would take him to Tom's — a white man's store on the road to Delagoa — and he left them! That was Tom Barnett's at Piscene, where we always stopped; for Tom was a good friend of ours.

That was how we came to meet Seedling again. He had made a loop of a hundred and fifty miles in four days in his efforts to avoid us; but he was waiting for us when we arrived at Tom Barnett's.

Tom stood in the doorway of his store as we walked up, with his hands resting idly on his hips and a queer smile on his face as he nodded welcome.

'Did a white man come here on horseback during the last few days from the Drift?'

'No!'

'On foot?'

'No, not the whole way.'

'Is he here now?'

Tom nodded.

'You know about him, Tom?'

'Seedling! the chap you're after, isn't it?'

'Yes,' we answered, lowering our voices.

Tom looked from one to the other with the same queer smile, and then making a move to let us into the store said quietly : 'He's dead!'

Some natives coming along the foot-path from the 'Bombo had found the horse dead of horse-sickness half a day away, and further on — only a mile or so from the store — the rider lying on his back in the sun, dying of thirst. He died before they got him in.

He was buried under a big fig tree where another and more honoured grave was made later on.

*

Jim sat by himself the whole evening and never spoke a word.

The Last Trek

It was Pettigrew's Road that brought home to me the wisdom of the old transport riders' maxim : 'Take no risks'.

We all knew that there were 'fly' belts on the old main road but we rushed these at night, for we knew enough of the tsetse fly to avoid it. However, the discovery of the new road to Barberton – a short cut with plenty of water and grass, which offered the chance of working an extra trip into the short Delagoa season – tempted me, among others, to take a risk. We had seen no 'fly' when riding through to spy out the land, and again on the trip down with empty wagons all had seemed to be well; but I had good reason afterwards to recall that hurried trip down and the night spent at Low's Creek.

It was a lovely moonlight night, cool and still, and the grass was splendid; after many weeks of poor feeding and drought the cattle revelled in the land of plenty. We had timed our treks so as to get through the suspected parts of the road at night, believing that the fly did not trouble after dark; and thus we were that night outspanned in the worst spot of all – a tropical garden of clear streams, tree ferns, foliage plants, mosses, maidenhair and sweet grass! I moved among the cattle myself, watching them feed greedily and waiting to see them satisfied before inspanning again to trek through the night to some higher and more open ground.

I noticed then that their tails were rather busy. At first it seemed the usual accompaniment of a good feed, an expression of satisfaction; after a while, however, the swishing became too vigorous for this, and when heads began to swing round and legs also were made use of, it seemed clear that something was worrying them. The older hands were so positive that at night cattle were safe from fly, that it did not even then occur to me to suspect anything seriously wrong. Weeks passed by, and although the cattle became poorer, it was reasonable enough to put it down to the exceptional drought.

It was late in the season when we loaded up for the last time in Delagoa and ploughed our way through the Matolla swamp and the heavy sands at Piscene; but late as it was there was no sign of rain, and the rain that we usually wanted to avoid would have been very welcome then. The roads were all blistering stones or powdery dust, and it was cruel work for man and beast. The heat was intense, and there was no breeze; the dust moved along slowly apace with us in a dense cloud – men, wagons and animals, all toned to the same hue; and the poor oxen toiling slowly along drew in the finely powdered stuff at every breath. At the outspan they stood about exhausted and panting, with rings and lines of brown marking where the moisture from nostrils, eyes and mouths had caught the dust and turned it into mud.

At Matolla Poort, where the Lebombo Range runs low, where the polished black rocks shone like anvils, where the stones and baked earth scorched the feet of man and beast to aching, the world was like an oven. The heat came from above, below, around – a thousand glistening surfaces dashing back with intensity the sun's fierce rays. And there, at Matolla Poort, the big pool had given out!

Our stand-by was gone! There, in the deep cleft in the rocks where the feeding spring, cool and constant, had trickled down a smooth black rock beneath another over-hanging slab, and where ferns and mosses had clustered in one little spot in all the miles of blistering rocks, there was nothing left but mud and slime. The water was as green and thick as pea-soup; filth of all kinds lay in it and on it; half a dozen carcases stuck in the mud round the one small, wet spot where the pool had been – just where they fell and died; the coat had dropped away from some, and mats of hair, black, brown and white, helped to thicken the green water. But we drank it. Sinking a handkerchief where the water looked thinnest and making a little well into which the moisture slowly filtered we drank it greedily.

The next water on the road was Komati River, but the cattle were too weak to reach it in one trek, and remembering another pool off the road – a small lagoon found by accident when out hunting the year before – we moved on that night out on to the flats and made through the bush for several miles to look for water and grass.

We found the place just after dawn. There was a string of half a dozen pools ringed with yellow-plumed reeds – like a bracelet of sapphires set in gold – deep deep pools of beautiful water in the midst of acres and acres of rich buffalo grass. It was too incredibly good!

I was trekking alone that trip, the only white man there and – tired out by the all-night's work, the long ride, and the searching in the bush for the lagoon – I had gone to sleep after seeing the cattle to the water and grass. Before midday I was back among them again. Some odd movements struck a chord of memory, and the night at Low's Creek flashed back. Tails were swishing freely, and the bullock nearest me kicked up sharply at its side and swung its head round to brush something away. I moved closer up to see what was causing the trouble: in a few minutes I heard a thin sing of wings, different from a mosquito's, and there settled on my shirt a grey fly, very like and not much larger than a common house-fly, whose wings folded over like a pair of scissors. That was the 'mark of the beast'. I knew then why this oasis had been left by transport-rider and trekker, as nature made it, untrodden and untouched.

Not a moment was lost in getting away from the 'fly'. But the mischief was already done. The cattle must have been bitten at Low's Creek weeks before, and again that morning during the time that I slept; and it was clear that, not drought and poverty, but 'fly' was the cause of their weakness. After the first rains they would begin to die, and the right thing to do was to press on as fast as possible and deliver the loads. Barberton was booming and short of supplies and the rates were the highest ever paid. Even if all the cattle became unfit for use or died, the loads would pay for everything; delay would mean losing both cattle and loads – all I had in the world – and starting again penniless with the years of hard work thrown away.

So the last, hard struggle began. And it was work and puzzle day and night, without peace or rest; trying to nurse the cattle in their daily failing strength, and yet to push them for all they could do; watching the sky cloud over every afternoon, promising rain that never came, and not knowing whether to call it promise or threat; for although rain would bring grass and water to save the cattle, it also meant death to the fly-bitten.

*

We crossed the Komati with three spans – forty-four oxen – to a wagon, for the drift was deep in two places and the weakened cattle could not keep their feet. It was a hard day, and by nightfall it was easy to pick out the oxen who would not last out a week. That night Zole lay down and did not get up again—Zole the little, fat schoolboy, always out of breath, always good-tempered and quiet, as tame as a pet dog.

He was only the first to go; day by day others followed. Some were only cattle: others were old friends and comrades on many a trek. The two big after-oxen Achmoed and Bakir went down early; the Komati Drift had overtired them, and the weight and jolting of the heavy disselboom on the bad roads finished them off. These were the two inseparables who worked and grazed, walked and slept, side by side – never more than a few yards apart day or night since the

day they became yoke-fellows. They died on consecutive days.

But the living wonder of that last trek was still old Zwaartland the front ox! With his steady sober air, perfect understanding of his work, and firm, clean, buck-like tread, he still led the front span. Before we reached the Crocodile his mate gave in – worn to death by the ebbing of his own strength and by the steady indomitable courage of his comrade. Old Zwaartland pulled on; but my heart sank as I looked at him and noted the slightly 'staring' coat, the falling flanks, the tread less sure and brisk, and a look in his eyes that made me think he knew what was coming but would do his best.

The gallant-hearted old fellow held on. One after another we tried with him in the lead, half a dozen or more; but he wore them all down. In the dongas and spruits, where the crossings were often very bad and steep, the wagons would stick for hours, and the wear and strain on the exhausted cattle was killing: it was bad enough for the man who drove them. To see old Zwaartland then holding his ground, never for one moment turning or wavering while the others backed, jibbed and swayed and dragged him staggering backwards, made one's heart ache. The end was sure: flesh and blood will not last for ever; the stoutest heart can be broken.

The worst of it was that with all the work and strain we accomplished less than we used to do before in a quarter of the time. Distances formerly covered in one trek took three, four and even five now. Water, never too plentiful in certain parts, was sadly diminished by the drought, and it sometimes took us three or even four treks to get from water to water. Thus we had at times to drive the oxen back to the last place or on to the next one for their drinks, and by the time the poor beasts got back to the wagons to begin their trek they had done nearly as much as they were able to do.

And trouble begot trouble, as usual! Sam the respectable, who had drawn all his pay in Delagoa, gave up after one hard day and deserted me. He said that the hand of the Lord had smitten me and mine, and great misfortune would come to all; so he left in the dark at Crocodile Drift, taking one of the leaders with him, and joined some wagons making for Lydenburg. The work was too hard for him; it was late in the season; he feared the rains and fever; and he had no pluck or loyalty, and cared for no one but himself.

I was left with three leaders and two drivers to manage four wagons. It was Jim who told me of Sam's desertion. He had the cross, defiant, pre-occupied look of old; but there was also something of satisfaction in his air as he jerked the words out at me speaking in Zulu:

'Sam has deserted you and taken his voorlooper.'

I said nothing. It was just about Sam's form. It annoyed

but did not surprise me. Jim favoured me with a hard, searching look, a subdued grunt, and a click expressive of things he could not put into words; and without another word he turned and walked back to his wagon. But halfway to it he broke silence. Facing me once more, he thumped his chest and hurled at me in mixed Zulu and English: 'I said so! Sam lead a bible. Sam no good. Umph! M'Shangaan! I said so! I always said so!'

When Jim helped me to inspan Sam's wagon, he did it to an accompaniment of Zulu imprecations which only a Zulu could properly appreciate. They were quite 'above my head', but every now and then I caught one sentence repeated like the responses in a litany: 'I'll kill that Shangaan when I see him again!'

*

At Lion Spruit there was more bad luck. Lions had been troublesome there in former years, but for a couple of seasons nothing had been seen of them. Their return was probably due to the fact that, because of the drought and consequent failure of other waters, the game on which they preyed had moved down towards the river. At any rate, they returned unexpectedly and we had one bad night when the cattle were unmanageable, and their nerves all on edge.

The herd boys had seen spoor in the afternoon; at dusk we heard the distant roaring, and later on, the nearer and more ominous grunting. I fastened Jock up in the tent-wagon lest the sight of him should prove too tempting. He was bristling like a hedgehog and constantly working out beyond the cattle, glaring and growling incessantly towards the bush. We had four big fires at the four corners of the outspan, and no doubt this saved a bad stampede, for in the morning we found a circle of spoor where the lions had walked round and round the outspan. There were scores of footprints – the tracks of at least four or five animals.

In the Bushveld the oxen were invariably tied up at night, picketed to the trek-chain, each pair at its yoke ready to be inspanned for the early morning trek. Ordinarily the weight of the chain and yokes was sufficient to keep them in place, but when there were lions about, and the cattle liable to be scared and all to sway off together in the same direction, we took the extra precaution of pegging down the chain and anchoring the front yoke to a tree or stake.

We had a lot of trouble that night, as one of the lions persistently took his stand to windward of the cattle to scare them with his scent. We knew well enough when he was there, although unable to see anything, as all the oxen would face up-wind, staring with bulging eyeballs in that direction and braced up tense with excitement. If one of them made a sudden move, the whole lot jumped in response and swayed off down wind away from the danger, dragging the gear with them and straining until the heavy wagons yielded to the tug. We had to run out and then drive them up again to stay the stampede. It is a favourite device of lions, when tackling camps and outspans, for one of them to go to windward so that the terrified animals on winding him may stampede in the opposite direction where the other lions are lying in wait.

Two oxen broke away that night and were never seen again. Once I saw a low, light-coloured form steal across the road, and took a shot at it; but rifle-shooting at night is a gamble, and there was no sign of a hit.

I was too short-handed and too pressed for time to make a real try for the lions next day, and after a morning spent in fruitless search for the lost bullocks we went on again.

Instead of fifteen to eighteen miles a day, as we should have done, we were then making between four and eight – and sometimes not one. The heat and the drought were awful; but at last we reached the Crocodile and struck up the right bank for the short cut – Pettigrew's Road – to Barberton, and there we had good water and some pickings of grass and young reeds along the river bank.

The clouds piled up every afternoon; the air grew still and sultry; the thunder growled and rumbled; a few drops of rain pitted the dusty road and pattered on the dry leaves; and that was all. Anything seemed preferable to the intolerable heat and dust and drought, and each day I hoped the rain would come, cost what it might to the fly-bitten cattle; but the days dragged on, and still the rain held off.

Then came one black day as we crawled slowly along

the river bank, which is not to be forgotten. In one of the cross-spruits cutting sharply down to the river the second wagon stuck: the poor, tired-out cattle were too weak and dispirited to pull it out. Being short of drivers and leaders it was necessary to do the work in turns, that is, after getting one wagon through a bad place, to go back for another. We had to double-span this wagon, taking the span from the front wagon back to hook on in front of the other; and on this occasion I led the span while Jim drove.

We were all tired out by the work and heat, and I lay down in the dusty road in front of the oxen to rest while the chains were being coupled up. I looked up into old Zwaartland's eyes, deep, placid, constant, dark grey eyes – the ox-eyes of which so many speak and write and so few really know. There was trouble in them; he looked anxious and hunted; and it made me heart-sick to see it.

When the pull came, the back span, already disheartened and out of hand, swayed and turned every way, straining the front oxen to the utmost; yet Zwaartland took the strain and pulled. For a few moments both front oxen stood firm; then his mate cut it and turned; the team swung away with a rush, and the old fellow was jerked backwards and rolled over on his side. He struggled gamely, but it was some minutes before he could rise; and then his eyes looked wilder and more despairing; his legs were planted apart to balance him, and his flanks were quivering.

Jim straightened up the double span again. Zwaartland leaned forward once more, and the others followed his lead; the wagon moved a little and they managed to pull it out. But I, walking in front, felt the brave old fellow stagger, and saw him, with head lowered, plod blindly like one stricken to death.

We outspanned on the rise, and I told Jim to leave the reim on Zwaartland's head. Many a good turn from him deserved one more from me – the last. I sent Jim for the rifle, and led the old front ox to the edge of the donga where a bleached tree lay across it ... He dropped into the donga under the dead tree; and I packed the dry branches over him and set fire to the pile. It looks absurd now; but to leave him to the wolf and the jackal seemed like going back on a friend; and the queer looks of the boys, and what they would think of me, were easier to bear. Jim watched, but said nothing; with a single grunt and a shrug of his shoulders he stalked back to the wagons.

The talk that night at the boys' fire went on in low-pitched tones – not a single word audible to me; but I knew what it was about. As Jim stood up to get his blanket off the wagon, he stretched himself and closed off the evening's talk with his Zulu click, and the remark that 'All white men are mad, in some way.'

So we crawled on until we reached the turn where the

road turned between the mountain range and the river. There we outspanned one day when the heat became so great that it was no longer possible to go on. For weeks the storm-clouds had gathered, threatened and dispersed; thunder had come half-heartedly, little spots of rain enough to pock-mark the dust; but there had been no break in the drought.

It was past noon that day when everything grew still; the birds and insects hushed their sound; the dry leaves did not give a whisper. There was the warning in the air that one knows but cannot explain; and it struck me and the boys together that it was time to spread and tie down the bucksails which we had not unfolded for months.

While we were busy at this there came an unheralded flash and crash; then a few drops as big as florins; and then the flood-gates were opened and the reservoir of the long months of drought was turned loose on us. Crouching under the wagon where I had crept to lash down the sail, I looked out at the deluge, hesitating whether to make a dash for my tent-wagon or remain there.

All along the surface of the earth there lay for a minute or so a two-feet screen of mingled dust and splash: long spikes of rain drove down and dashed into spray, each bursting its little column of dust from the powdery earth. There was an indescribable and unforgettable progression in sounds and smells and sights, rapid yet steady, inevitable, breathless, overwhelming!

The sounds that began with the sudden crash of thunder; the dead silence that followed it; the first great drops that fell with such pats on the dust; then more and faster — yet still so big and separate as to make one look round to see where they fell; the sound on the wagon-sail — at first as of bouncing marbles, then the 'devil's tattoo', and then the roar!

And outside there was the muffled puff and patter in the dust; the rustle as the drops struck dead leaves and grass and sticks; the blend of many notes that made one great sound, always growing, changing and moving on – full of weird significance – until there came the steady swish and hiss of water upon water, when the earth had ceased to stand up against the rain and was swamped. But even that did not last; for then the fallen rain raised its voice against the rest, and little sounds of trickling, scurrying waters came to tone the ceaseless hiss, and grew and grew until from every side the chorus of rushing, tumbling waters filled the air with the steady roar of the flood.

And the smells! The smell of the baked, drought-bound earth; the faint clearing and purifying by the first few drops; the mingled dust and damp; the rinsed air; the clean sense of water, water everywhere; and in the end the bracing sensation in nostrils and head, of, not wind exactly, but of swirling air thrust out to make room for the falling rain; and, when all was over, the sense of glorious clarified air and scoured earth – the smell of a new-washed world!

And the things that one saw went with the rest, marking the stages of the storm's short, vivid life. The first puffs of dust, where drops struck like bullets; the cloud that rose to meet them; the drops themselves that streaked slanting down like a flight of steel ramrods; the dust dissolved in a dado of splash. I had seen the yellow-brown ground change colour; in a few seconds it was damp; then mud; then all asheen. A minute more, and busy little trickles started everywhere – tiny things a few inches long; and while one watched them they joined and merged, hurrying on with twist and turn, but ever onward to a given point – to meet like the veins in a leaf. Each tuft of grass became a fountain-head; each space between, a little rivulet: swelling rapidly, racing away with its burden of leaf and twig and dust and foam until in a few minutes all were lost in one sheet of moving water.

Crouching under the wagon I watched it and saw the little streamlets, dirty and debris-laden, steal slowly on like sluggard snakes down to my feet, and winding round me, meet beyond and hasten on. Soon the grass-tufts and higher spots were wet; and as the water rose on my boots and the splash beat up to my knees, it seemed worthwhile making for the tent of the wagon. But in there the roar was deafening; the rain beat down with such force that it drove through the canvas-covered wagon-tent and greased buck-sail in fine mist. In there it was black dark, the tarpaulin covering all, and I slipped out again back to my place under the wagon to watch the storm.

We were on high ground which fell gently away on three sides – a long spur running down to the river between two of the numberless small water-courses scoring the flanks of the hills. Mere gutters they were, easy corrugations in the slope from the range to the river, insignificant drains in which no water ever ran except during the heavy rains. One would never notice their existence. Yet, when the half-hour's storm was over and it was possible to get out and look round, they were rushing, boiling torrents, twenty to thirty feet across and six to ten feet deep, foaming and plunging towards the river, red with the soil of the stripped earth, and laden with leaves, grass, sticks and branches – water-furies, wild and ungovernable, against which neither man nor beast could stand for a moment.

When the rain ceased the air was full of the roar of waters, growing louder and nearer all the time. I walked down the long, low spur to look at the river, expecting much, and was grievously disappointed. It was no fuller and not much changed. On either side of me the once dry dongas emptied their soil-stained and debris-laden contents in foaming cataracts, each deepening the yellowy-red of the river at its banks; but out in mid-stream the river was undisturbed, and its normal colour – the clear yellow of amber – was unchanged. How small the great storm seemed then! How puny the flooded creeks and dongas!

There are few things more deceptive than the tropical storm. To one caught in it, all the world seems deluged and overwhelmed; yet a mile away it may be all peace and sunshine. I looked at the river and laughed – at myself! The revelation seemed complete; it was humiliating; one felt so small. Still, the drought was broken; the rains had come; and in spite of disappointment I stayed to watch, drawn by the scores of little things caught up and carried by.

A quarter of an hour or more may have been spent thus, when amid all the chorus of the rushing waters there stole in a duller murmur. Murmur it was at first, but it grew steadily into a low-toned, monotoned, distant roar; and it caught and held one like the roar of coming hail or hurricane. It was the river coming down.

The sun was out again, and in the straight reach above the bend there was every chance to watch the flood from the bank where I stood. It seemed strangely long in coming, but come it did at last, in waves like the half-spent breakers on a sandy beach – a slope of foam and broken waters in the van, an ugly wall with spray-tipped feathered crest behind, and tier on tier to follow. Heavens what a scene! The force of waters, and the utter hopeless puniness of man! The racing waves, each dashing for the foremost place; the tall reeds caught waist high and then laid low, their silvery tops dipped, hidden and drowned in the flood; the trees yielding, and the branches snapping like matches and twirling like feathers down the stream; the rumbling thunder of big boulders loosed and tumbled, rolled like marbles on the rocks below; whole trees brought down, and turning helplessly in the flood – drowned giants with their branches swinging slowly over like nerveless arms. It was tremendous; and one had to stay and watch.

Then the waves ceased; and behind the opposite bank another stream began to make its way, winding like a huge snake, spreading wider as it went across the flats beyond, until the two rejoined and the river became one again. The roar of waters gradually lessened; the two cataracts beside me were silent; and looking down I saw that the fall was gone and that water ran to water – swift as ever, but voiceless now – and lost in the river itself. Inch by inch the water rose towards my feet; tufts of grass trembled, wavered and went down; little wavelets flipped and licked like tongues against the remaining bank of soft earth below me; piece after piece of it leant gently forward, and toppled headlong in the eager, creeping tide; deltas of yellow, scum-flecked water worked silently up the dongas, reaching out with stealthy feelers to enclose the place where I was standing; and then it was time to go.

*

The cattle had turned their tails to the storm, and stood it out. They too were washed clean and looked fresher and brighter; but there was nothing in that! Two of them had been seen by the boys moving slowly, foot by foot, before the driving rain down the slope from the outspan, stung by the heavy drops and yielding in their weakness to the easy gradient. Only fifty yards away they should have stopped in the hollow – the shallow, dry donga of the morning; but they were gone! Unwilling to turn back and face the rain, they had no doubt been caught in the rush of storm-water and swirled away, and their bodies were bobbing in the Crocodile many miles below by the time we missed them.

In a couple of hours the water had run off; the flooded dongas were almost dry again; and we moved on.

It was then that the real 'rot' set in. Next morning there were half a dozen oxen unable to stand up; and so again the following day. It was no longer possible to take the four wagons. All the spare cattle had been used up and it was better to face the worst at once. So I distributed the best of the load on the other three wagons and abandoned the rest of it with the fourth wagon in the bush. But day by day the oxen dropped out, and when we reached the Junction and branched up the Kaap, there were not enough left for three wagons.

This time it meant abandoning both wagon and load; and I gave the cattle a day's rest then, hoping that they would pick up strength on good grass to face the eight drifts that lay between us and Barberton.

Our Last Hunt

WE had not touched fresh meat for many days, as there had been no time for shooting; but I knew that game was plentiful across the river in the rough country between the Kaap and Crocodile, and I started off to make the best of the day's delay, little dreaming that it was to be the last time Jock and I would hunt together.

Weeks had passed without a hunt, and Jock must have thought there was a sad falling away on the part of his master. He no longer expected anything. The rifle was never taken down now except for an odd shot from the outspan or to put some poor animal out of its misery. Since the night with the lions, when he had been ignominiously cooped up, there had been nothing to stir his blood and make life worth living; and this morning as he saw me rise from breakfast and proceed to potter about the wagons, he looked on indifferently for a few minutes and then stretched out full length in the sun and went to sleep.

I could not take him with me across the river, as the 'fly' was said to be bad there, and it was no place to risk horse or dog. The best of prospects would not have tempted me to take a chance with him, but I hated ordering him to stay behind, as it hurt his dignity and sense of comradeship; so it seemed a happy accident that he was asleep and I could slip away unseen.

The country was rough on the other side of the river, and the old grass was high and dense, for no one went there in those days, and the grass stood unburnt from season to season. Climbing over rocks and stony ground, crunching dry sticks underfoot, and driving a path through the rank tambookie grass, it seemed well-nigh hopeless to look for a shot. Several times I heard buck start up and dash off only a few yards away, and it began to look as if the wiser course would be to turn back.

At last I got out of the valley into more level and more open ground, and came out upon a ledge or plateau a hundred yards or more wide, with a low ridge of rocks and some thorns on the far side – quite a likely spot. I searched the open ground for my cover, and seeing nothing there crossed over to the rocks, threading my way silently between them and expecting to find another clear space beyond.

The snort of a buck brought me to a standstill among the rocks, and as I listened it was followed by another and another from the same quarter, delivered at irregular intervals; and each snort was accompanied by the sound of trampling feet, sometimes like stamps of anger and at other times seemingly a hasty movement.

I had on several occasions interrupted fights between angry rivals: once two splendid kudu bulls were at it; a second time it was two sables, and the vicious and incredibly swift sweep of the scimitar horns still lives in memory; and another time they were blue wildbeeste. But some interruption had occurred each time, and I had no more than a glimpse of what might have been a rare scene to witness.

I was determined not to spoil it this time. No doubt it was a fight and probably they were fencing and circling for an opening, as there was no bump of heads or clash of horns to indicate the real struggle. I crept on through the rocks and found before me a tangle of thorns and dead wood, impossible to pass through in silence. It was better to work back again and try the other side of the rocks. The way was clearer there, and I crept up to a rock four or five feet high, feeling certain from the sound that the fight would be in full view a few yards beyond.

With the rifle ready I raised myself slowly until my eyes were over the top of the rock. Some twenty yards off, in an open flat of downtrodden grass, I saw a sable cow. She was standing with feet firmly and widely planted, looking fiercely in front of her, ducking her head in threatening manner every few seconds, and giving angry snorts; and behind, and huddled up against her, was her scared, bewildered little red-brown calf.

For a few seconds I was puzzled and fascinated by the behaviour of the two sables. Then in the corner of my eye I saw, away on my right, another red-brown thing come into the open. It was Jock, casting about with nose to ground for my trail which he had over-run at the point where I had turned back near the dead wood on the other side of the rocks.

What happened then was a matter of a second or two. As I turned to look at him he raised his head, bristled up all over, and made one jump forward; then a long yellowish thing moved in the unbeaten grass in front of the sable cow, raised its head sharply, and looked full into my eyes; and before I could move a finger it shot away in one streak-like bound. A wild shot at the lioness, as I jumped up full height; a shout to Jock to come back; a scramble of black and brown on my left; and it was all over. I was standing in the open ground, breathless with excitement, and Jock, a few yards

285

off, with hind legs crouched ready for a dash, looking back at me for leave to go!

The spoor told the tale: there was the outer circle made by the lioness in the grass, broken in places where she had feinted to rush in and stopped before the lowered horns; and inside this there was the smaller circle, a tangle of trampled grass and spoor, where the brave mother had stood between her young and death.

Any attempt to follow the lioness after that would have been a waste of time. We struck off in a new direction, and in crossing a stretch of level ground where the thorn trees were well scattered and the grass fairly short, my eye caught a movement in front that brought me to an instant standstill. It was as if the stem of a young thorn tree had suddenly waved itself and settled back again, and it meant that some long-horned buck, perhaps a kudu or a sable bull, was lying down and had swung his head; and it meant also that he was comfortably settled, quite unconscious of danger.

I marked and watched the spot, or rather, the line, for the glimpse was too brief to tell more than the direction; but there was no other move. The air was almost still, with just a faint drift from him to us, and I examined every stick and branch, every stump and ant-heap, every bush and tussock, without stirring a foot. But I could make out nothing. I could trace no outline and see no patch of colour, dark or light, to betray him.

There I stood minute after minute – not risking a move, which would be certain to reveal me – staring and searching for some big animal lying half asleep within eighty yards of me, on ground that you would not call good cover for a rabbit. We were in the sunlight: he lay somewhere beyond, where a few scattered thorn trees threw dabs of shade.

I was hopelessly beaten, but Jock could see him well enough. He crouched beside me with ears cocked, and his eyes, all ablaze, were fixed intently on the spot, except for an occasional swift look up to me to see what on earth was wrong and why the shot did not come; his hind legs were tucked under him and he was trembling with excitement. There was nothing to be done but wait, leaving the buck to make the first move.

And at last it came. There was another light shake of the horns, and the whole figure stood out in bold relief. It was a fine sable bull lying in the shadow of one of the thorn trees with his back towards us; and there was a small ant-heap close behind him, making a greyish clot against his black back and shoulder, and breaking the expanse of colour which the eye would otherwise easily have picked up.

The ant-heap made a certain shot impossible, so I lowered myself slowly to the ground to wait until he should begin feeding or change his position for comfort or shade, as they often do. This might mean waiting for half an hour or more, but it was better than risking a shot in the position in which he was lying.

I settled down for a long wait with the rifle resting on my knees, confidently expecting that when the time came to move he would get up slowly, stretch himself, and have a good look round. But he did nothing of the kind. A turn or eddy of the faint breeze must have given him my wind;

for there was one twitch of the horns, as his nose was laid to windward, and without an instant's pause he dashed off. It was the quickest thing imaginable in a big animal: it looked as though he started racing from his lying position. The bush was not close enough to save him, however, in spite of his start, and through the thin veil of smoke I saw him plunge and stumble, and then dash off again; and Jock, seeing me give chase, went ahead and in half a minute I was left well behind, but still in sight of the hunt.

I shouted at Jock to come back – from force of habit: of course he could hear nothing. It was his first and only go at a sable. He knew nothing of the terrible horns and the deadly scythe-like sweep that makes the wounded sable so dangerous; and great as was my faith in him, the risk in this case was not one I would have taken. There was nothing to do but follow.

A quarter of a mile on I drew closer up and found them standing face to face among the thorns. It was the first of three or four stands. The sable, with a watchful eye on me, always moved on as I drew near enough to shoot.

The beautiful black and white bull stood facing his little red enemy and the fence and play of feint and thrust, guard and dodge, was wonderful to see. Not once did either touch the other. At Jock's least movement the sable's head would go down with his nose into his chest and the magnificent horns arched forward and poised so as to strike either right or left; and if Jock feinted a rush either way the scythe-sweep came with lightning quickness, covering more than half a circle and carrying the gleaming points with a swing right over the sable's own back. Then he would advance slowly and menacingly, with horns well forward ready to strike and eyes blazing through his eyebrows, driving Jock before him.

There were three or four of these encounters in which I could take no hand. The distance, the intervening thorns and grass, and the quickness of their movements, made a safe shot impossible; and there was always the risk of hitting Jock, for a hard run does not make for good shooting. Each time as the sable drove him back there would be a short vicious rush suddenly following the first deliberate advance, and as Jock scrambled back out of the way the bull would swing round with incredible quickness and be off full gallop in another direction. Evidently the final rush was a man-

oeuvre to get Jock off his heels and flanks as he started, and thus secure a lead for the next run.

Since the day he was kicked by the kudu cow Jock had never tackled an unbroken hind leg. A dangling one he never missed; but the lesson of the flying heels had been too severe to be forgotten. In this chase I saw him time after time try at the sable's flanks and make flying leaps at the throat; but although he passed and repassed behind – to try on the other side when he had failed at the one – and looked up eagerly at the hind legs as he passed them, he made no attempt at them.

It must have been at the fourth or fifth stand that Jock got through the guard at last. The sable was badly wounded in the body and doubtless strength was failing, but there was little evidence of this yet. This time the sable drove him steadily back towards a big thorn tree; but in the last step, just as the bull made his rush, Jock jumped past the tree and, instead of scrambling back out of reach as before, dodged round and was in the rear of the buck, before it could turn on him. There were no flying heels to fear then, and without an instant's hesitation he fastened on one of the hind legs above the hock. With a snort of rage and indignation the sable spun round and round, kicking and plunging wildly and making vicious sweeps with his horns; but Jock, although swung about and shaken like a rat, was out of reach and kept his grip. It was a quick and furious struggle, in which I was altogether forgotten; and as one more desperate plunge brought the bull down in a struggling, kicking heap with Jock completely hidden under him, I ran up and ended the fight.

*

It always took Jock some time to calm down after these tussles. While I was busy on the double precaution of fixing up a scare for the aasvogels and cutting grass and branches to cover the buck, Jock moved restlessly round the sable, ever ready to pounce on him again at the least sign of life. The slithering tongue and wide-open mouth looked like a big, red gash splitting his head in two; he was so blown, his breath came and went like the puffing of a diminutive steam engine, and his eyes with all the wickedness of fight – but none of the watchfulness – gone out of them, flickered incessantly from the buck to me; one sign from either would have been enough! It was the same old scene, the same old performance, that I had watched scores of times; but it never grew stale or failed to draw a laugh, a word of cheer, and pat of affection; and from him there came always the same responses, the friendly wagging of that stumpy tail, a splashy lick, a soft upward look, and a wider split of the mouth that was a laugh as plain as if one heard it. But that was only an interruption – his attention went back to the buck, and the everlasting footwork went on again.

I was still laughing at him, when he stopped and turning sharply round made a snap at his side; and a few seconds later he did it again. Then there was a thin sing of insect wings; and I knew that the tsetse fly were on us.

The only thought then was for Jock, who was still working busily round the sable. For some minutes I sat with him between my legs, wisping away the flies with a small branch and wondering what to do. It soon became clear that there was nothing to be gained by waiting. Instead of passing away the fly became more numerous, and there was not a moment's peace or comfort to be had; for they were tackling me on the neck, arms and legs, where the thorn-ripped pants left them bare to the knees. So, slinging the rifle over my shoulder, I picked Jock up, greatly to his discomfort, and carried him off in my arms at the best pace possible under the circumstances.

Half a mile of that was enough, however : the weight, the awkwardness of the position, the effort to screen him, and the difficulty of picking my way in very rough country at the same time, were too much for me. A tumble into a grass-hidden hole laid us both out sprawling, and I sat down again to rest and think, swishing the flies off as before.

Then an idea came which, in spite of all the anxiety, made me laugh, and ended in putting poor old Jock in quite the most undignified and ridiculous plight. I ripped off as much of my shirt as was not needed to protect me against the flies, and making holes in it for his legs and tail fitted him out with a home-made suit in about five minutes. Time was everything. It was impossible to run with him in my arms, but we could run together until we got out of the fly belt, and there was not much risk of being bitten as long as we kept up the running in the long grass. It was a long spell, and what with the rough country and the uncontrollable laughter at the sight of Jock, I was pretty well done by the time we were safely out of the 'fly'. We pulled up when the country began to fall away sharply towards the river, and there, to Jock's evident satisfaction, I took off his suit – by that time very much tattered and awry.

It was there, lying between two rocks in the shade of a marula tree, that I got one of those chances to see game at close quarters of which most men only hear or dream. There were no snapshot cameras then!

We had been lying there, Jock asleep and I spread out on

my back, when a slight but distinct click, as of a hoof against a stone, made me turn quietly over on my side and listen. The rock beside me was about four feet high, and on the other side of it a buck of some kind was walking with easy stride towards the river. The footsteps came abreast of us and then stopped, just as I was expecting him to walk on past the rock and down the hill in front of me.

I raised myself by inches, close to the rock, until I could see over it. A magnificent waterbuck bull, full-grown and in perfect coat and condition, was standing less than five yards away. He was so close that I could see the waves and partings in his heavy coat; the rise and fall in his flanks as he breathed; the ruff on his shaggy bearded throat, that gave such an air of grandeur to the head; the noble carriage, as with head held high he sniffed the breeze from the valley; the nostrils, mobile and sensitive, searching for the least hint of danger; and the eye, large and full and soft, luminous with watchful intelligence and yet mild and calm. It seemed almost possible to reach out and touch him. There was no thought of shooting. It was a moment of supreme enjoyment. Just to watch him : that was enough.

In a little while he seemed satisfied that all was well, and with head thrown slightly forward and the sure clean tread of his kind, he took his line unhesitatingly down the hill. As he neared the thicker bush twenty yards away a sudden impulse made me give a shout; and in a single bound he was lost among the trees.

When I turned round Jock was still asleep. Little incidents like that brought his deafness home.

*

It was our last day's hunting together; and I went back to the dreary round of hard, hopeless, useless struggle and daily loss.

There were only twenty oxen left when we reached the drift below Fig Tree. The water was nearly breast high and we carried three fourths of the loads through on our heads, case by case, to make the pull as easy as possible for the oxen, as they could only crawl then. We got one wagon through with some difficulty, but at nightfall the second was still in the river. We had carried out everything removeable, even to the bucksails, but the weakened bullocks could not move the empty wagon.

The thunder-clouds were piling up ahead, and distant lightning gave warning of a storm away up river; so we wound the trek-chain round a big tree on the bank, to anchor the wagon in case of flood. Reeling from work and weariness, too tired to think of food, I flung myself down in my blankets under the other wagon which was outspanned where we had stopped it in the double-rutted veld road; and settling comfortably into the sandy furrow cut by many wheels, was 'dead to the world' in a few minutes.

Near midnight the storm awoke me and a curious cold-ness about the neck and shoulders made me turn over to pull the blankets up. The road had served as a storm-water drain, converting the two wheel furrows into running streams, and I, rolled in my blankets, had dammed up one of them. The prompt flow of the released water as soon as I turned over, told plainly what had happened. I looked out

at the driving rain and the glistening earth, as shown up by constant flashes of lightning: it was a world of rain and spray and running water. It seemed that there was neither hope nor mercy anywhere. I was too tired to care, and drop-ping back into the trough, slept the night out in water.

In the morning we found the wagon still in the drift, although partly hidden by the flood, but the force of the stream had half floated and half forced it round on to higher ground. Only the anchoring chain had saved it. We had to wait some hours for the river to run down, and then to my relief the rested but staggering oxen pulled it out at the first attempt.

Rooiland, the light red ox with blazing yellow eyes and topped horns, fierce and untameable to the end, was in the lead then. I saw him as he took the strain in that last pull, and it was pitiful to see the restless eager spirit fighting against the failing strength. He looked desperate.

We outspanned in order to repack the loads, and Rooiland stood for a few moments alone while the rest of the cattle moved away; then turning his back on them he gave a couple of low moaning bellows and walked down the road back to the drift again. I had no doubt it was to drink; but the boys stopped their work and watched him curiously, and some remarks passed which were inaudible to me. As the ox disappeared down the slope into the drift, Jim called to his leader to bring him back, and then turning to me, added with his usual positiveness, 'Rooiland is mad. Umtagati! Bewitched! He is looking for the dead ones. He is going to die today!'

The boy came back presently – alone. When he reached the drift, he said, Rooiland was standing breast-high in the river, and then in a moment, whether by step or slip, he was into the flood and swept away.

The leader's account was received by the others in absolute silence. They were saturated with superstition, and as pagan fatalists, they accepted the position without a word. I suggested to Jim that it was nothing but a return of Rooiland's old straying habit, and probed him with questions, but could get nothing out of him. Finally he walked off with an expressive shake of the head and the repetition of his former remark, without a shade of triumph, surprise or excitement in his voice: 'He is looking for the dead ones!'

We were out of the fly then and the next day we reached Fig Tree.

That was the end of the last trek. Only three oxen reached Barberton, and they died within the week: the ruin was complete.

Our Various Ways

WHEN the trip was squared off and the boys paid, there was nothing left. Jim went home with wagons returning to Spitzkop; once more grievously hurt in dignity because his money was handed to my friend, the owner of the wagons, to be paid out to him when he reached his kraal. But his gloomy resentment melted as I handed over to him things for which there was no further need. The wagons moved off, and Jim with them, but twice he broke back again to dance and shout his gratitude; for it was wealth to him to have the reims and voorslag, the odd yokes and strops and wagon tools, the baking pot and pan and billies; and they were little to me when all else was gone. And Jim, with all his faults, had earned some title to remembrance for his loyalty. My way had been his way; and the hardest day had never been too hard for him. He had seen it all through to the finish, without a grumble and without a shirk.

His last shout, like the bellow of a bull, was an uproarious good-bye to Jock. And Jock seemed to know it was something of an occasion, for, as he stood before me looking down the road at the receding wagons and the dancing figure of Jim, his ears were cocked, his head was tilted a little sideways, and his tail stirred gently. It was at least a friendly nod in return!

A couple of weeks later I heard from my friend:

'You will be interested to hear that that lunatic of yours reached his kraal all right. But he is a holy terror. I suppose you hammered him into his place and kept him there; but I wouldn't have him as a gift. It is not that there was anything really wrong; only there was no rest, no peace.

'But he's a gay fighter! Below the Devil's Kantoor we met a lot of wagons from Lydenburg, and he had a row with one of the drivers, a lanky boy with dandy-patched clothes. The boy wouldn't fight – just yelled blue murder while Jim walloped him. I heard the yells and whacks, and there was Jim laying it on all over him – legs, head, back and arms – with a sort of ferocious satisfaction, every whack being accompanied by a husky suppressed shout: "Fight, Shangaan! Fight!" But the other fellow was not one for fighting; he floundered about, yelled for mercy and help, and tried to run away.

'I felt sorry for him and was going to interfere, but just then one of his pals called out to their gang to come along and help, and ran for his sticks. Jim dropped the patched fellow and went like a charging lion straight for the gang, letting out right and left; and in about five seconds the whole lot were heading for the bush with Jim in full chase.

'Goodness knows what the row was about. As far as I could make out from your heathen, it was because the other boy is a Shangaan and reads the bible. Jim said this boy – Sam is his name – worked for you and ran away. Sam said that he had never even heard of you, and that Jim was a stranger to him. But when the row began Sam first tried to pacify your lunatic. He knew Jim right enough – that was evident.

'I was glad to pay the noble Jim off and drop him at his kraal. Sam was laid up when we left.'

*

It is better to skip the change from the old life to the new – when the luck, as we called it, was out – for it is not the story of Jock, and it concerns him only so far that in the end it made our parting unavoidable.

So the new life began and the old was put away. But the new life, for all its brighter and wider outlook and work of another class, was not all happy. The new life had its hours of darkness too; of almost unbearable 'trek fever'; of restless, sleepless, longing for the old life; of 'home-sickness' for the veld, the freedom, the roaming, the nights by the fire, and the days in the bush! Now and again would come a sleepless night with its endless procession of scenes; and here and there in these long waking dreams came stabs of memory – flashes of lightning vividness: the head and staring eyes of the kudu bull, as we had stood for a portion of a second face to face; the yawning mouth of the maddened crocodile; the mamba and its beady hateful eyes, as it swept by before the bushfire; and the cattle, the poor, dumb beasts that had worked and died – they were not forgotten, and the memory of the last trek was one long mute reproach on their behalf.

All that was left of the old life was Jock; and soon there was no place for him. He could not always be with me, and when left behind he was miserable, leading a life that was utterly strange to him, without interest and among strangers.

While I was in Barberton he accompanied me everywhere, but – absurd as it seems – there was a constant danger for him there, greater though less glorious than those he faced so lightly in the veld. His deafness, which passed almost unnoticed and did not seem to handicap him at all in the veld, became a serious danger in a mining camp. For a long time he had been unable to hear a sound, but he was quick to notice anything that caused a vibration. In the early days of his deafness I had been worried that he would be run over while lying asleep near or under wagons, and the boys were always on the look-out to stir him up; but we soon found that this was not necessary. At the first movement he would feel the vibration and jump up.

In Barberton the danger was due to the number of sounds. He would stand behind me as I stopped in the street, and sometimes lie down and snooze if the wait was a long one – and the poor, old fellow must have thought it was a sad falling off from the real life of the veld. At first he was

very watchful, and every rumbling wheel or horse's footfall drew his alert little eyes round to the danger point. But the traffic and noise were almost continuous and one sound ran into another; and thus he became careless or puzzled and on several occasions had narrowly escaped being run over or trodden on.

Once, in desperation after a bad scare, I tried chaining him up, and although his injured, reproachful look hurt, it did not weaken me : I had hardened my heart to do it, and it was for his own sake. At lunch-time he was still squatting at the full length of the chain, off the mat and straw, and with his head hanging in the most hopeless dejected attitude one could imagine. It was too much for me – the dog really felt it; and when I released him there was no rejoicing in his freedom as the hated collar and chain dropped off. He turned from me without a sign or sound of any sort, and walking off slowly, lay down some ten yards away with his head resting on his paws!

I felt abominably guilty, and was conscious of wanting to make up for it all the afternoon.

Once I took him out to Fig Tree Creek fifteen miles away, and left him with a prospector friend at whose camp in the hills it seemed he would be much better off and much happier. When I got back to Barberton that night he was waiting for me, with a tag of chewed rope hanging round his neck, not the least ashamed of himself, but openly rejoicing in the meeting and evidently never doubting that I was equally pleased. And he was quite right there.

But it could not go on. One day as he lay asleep behind me a loaded wagon coming sharply round a corner as nearly as possible passed over him. The wheel was within inches of his back as he lay asleep in the sand. There was no chance to grab – it was a rush and a kick that saved him; and he rolled over under the wagon, and found his own way out between the wheels.

A few days after this Ted passed through Barberton, and I handed Jock over to him to keep and to care for until I had a better and safer home for him.

One day some two years later there turned up at my quarters an old friend of the transport days – Harry Williams. He had been away on a long trek to look for some supposed mine of fabulous richness, of which there had been vague and secret reports from natives. It was a trip of much adventure, but it was the end of his story that interested me most.

They had failed to find the mine; the rains had begun and the fever season set in; the cattle were worn out; the fever gripped them, and of the six white men, three were dead, one dying, and two only able to crawl; most of their boys had deserted; one umfaan fit for work, and the driver – then delirious with fever – completed the party.

The long journey was almost over, and they were only a

few treks from the store and camp for which they were making. But they were so stricken and helpless it seemed as though they must die within reach of help. The driver, a big Zulu, was then raving mad. He had twice run off into the bush and been lost for hours. Precious time and waning strength were spent in the search, and with infinite effort and much good luck they had found him and induced him to return. On the second occasion they had enticed him on to the wagon and, as he lay half unconscious between bursts of delirium, had tied him down flat on his back, with wrists and ankles fastened to the buckrails. It was all they could do to save him : they had barely strength to climb up and pour water into his mouth from time to time.

It was then at most two treks more to their destination; but they were too weak to work or walk, and the cattle were left to crawl along undriven. After half an hour's trekking, they reached a bad drift where the wagon stuck. The cattle would not face the pull. The two tottering trembling white men did their best, but neither had strength to use the whip; the umfaan led the oxen this way and that, but there was no more effort in them. To add to the horror of it all, the Zulu driver, with thirst aggravating his delirium, was struggling and wrenching at his bonds until the wagon rattled, and uttering maniac yells and gabbling incessantly.

The oxen stood out at all angles, and no two would pull together in answer to the feeble efforts of the fainting men. Then there came a lull in the shouts from the wagon and the white men looked round and saw the Zulu driver up on his knees freeing himself from the reims. In another moment he was standing up full height – a magnificent but most unwelcome sight. There was a thin line of froth along the half-open mouth; the deep-set eyes glared out under eyebrows and forehead bunched into frowning wrinkles, as for a few seconds he leant forward and scanned the men and oxen before him. Then as they watched him in breathless silence, he sprang off the wagon, picked up a small dry stick as he landed, and ran up along the span.

He spoke to the after-ox by name as he passed it; called to another, and touched it into place; and thrust his way between the next one and the dazed white man standing near it, tossing him aside with a brush of his arm. Then they saw how the boy's madness had taken him. His work and his span had called to him in his delirium; and he had answered. With low mutterings, short words hissed out, and all the sounds and terms the cattle knew shot at them – low pitched and with intense repression – he ran along the span, crouching low all the time like a savage stealing up for murderous attack.

Reaching the front oxen, he grasped the leading reim and pulled them round until they stood level for the straight pull out. Then down the other side of the span he ran with cat-like tread and activity, talking to each and straightening them up as he had done with the others; and when he reached the wagon again, he turned sharply and overlooked the span. One ox had swung round and stood out of line. There was a pause of seconds, and then the big Zulu called to the ox by name – not loudly but in a deep tone, husky with intensity – and the animal swung back into line again.

Then out of the silence that followed came an electrifying yell to the span : every bullock leaned to its yoke, and the wagon went out with a rush.

And he drove them at half-trot all the way to the store; the little dry twig still in his hand, and only his masterful intensity and knowledge of his work and span to see him through.

'A mad troublesome savage,' said Harry Williams, 'but one of the very best. Anyhow, we thought so; he saved us!'

There was something very familiar in this, and it was with a queer feeling of pride and excitement that I asked :

'Did he ever say to you "My catchum lion 'live''?'

'By gum! You know him? Jim. Jim Makokel'!'
'Indeed I do. Good old Jim!'

*

Years afterwards Jim was still a driver, working when necessary, fighting when possible, and enjoying intervals of lordly ease at his kraal where the wives and cattle stayed and prospered.

His Duty

AND JOCK?

But I never saw my dog again. For a year or so he lived
something of the old veld life, trekking and hunting, and
from time to time I heard of him from Ted and others.
Stories seemed to gather easily about him as they do about
certain people, and many knew Jock and were glad to bring
news of him. The things they thought wonderful and admir-
able made pleasant news for them to tell and welcome news
to me, and they were heard with contented pride, but without surprise.

One day I received word from Ted that he was off to
Scotland for a few months and had left Jock with another
old friend, Tom Barnett – Tom, at whose store under the
big fig tree, Seedling lies buried. Although I was glad that
he had been left with a good friend like Tom, who would

care for him as well as any one could, the life there was not of the kind to suit him. For a few months it would not matter; but I had no idea of letting him end his days as a watch-dog at a trader's store in the native country.

Tom's trouble was with thieves; for the natives about there were not a good lot, and their dogs were worse. When Jock saw or scented them, they had little chance : he fought to kill, and not as town dogs fight. He had learnt his work in a hard school, and he never stopped or slackened until the work was done.

So his fame soon spread and it brought Tom more peace than he had enjoyed for many a day. Natives no longer wandered at will into the reed-enclosed yard; their dogs ceased to sneak into the store and through the house, stealing everything they could get. Jock took up his place at the door, and hungry mongrels watched him from a distance or sneaked up a little closer when, from time to time, he trotted round the yard at the back of the building.

All that was well enough during the day. But the trouble occurred at night. The dogs from the surrounding kraals prowled about after dark, scavenging and thieving where they could – and what angered Tom most of all was the killing of his fowls.

The yard at the back of the store was enclosed by a fence of close-packed reeds, and in the middle of the yard stood the fowl-house with a clear space of bare ground all round it. On many occasions kraal dogs had found their way through the reed fence and killed fowls perching about the yard, and several times they had burgled the fowl-house itself. In spite of Jock's presence and reputation, this night robbing still continued, for while he slept peacefully in front of the store, the robbers would do their work at the back. Poor old fellow! They were many and he was one; they prowled night and day, and he had to sleep sometimes; they were watchful and he was deaf. So he had no chance at all unless he saw or scented them.

There were two small windows looking out on to the yard, but no door in the back of the building. Thus, in order to get into the yard, it was necessary to go out of the front door and round the side of the house. On many occasions Tom, roused by the screaming of the fowls, had seized his gun and run round to get a shot at the thieves. But the time so lost was enough for a dog, and the noise made in opening the reed gate gave ample warning of his coming.

The result was that Tom generally had all his trouble for nothing – but it was not always so. Several times he roused Jock as he ran out, and invariably got some satisfaction out

of what followed. Once Jock caught one of the thieves struggling to force a way through the fence, and held on to the hind leg until Tom came up with the gun. On other occasions he had caught them in the yard. On others, again, he had run them down in the bush and finished it off there without help or hindrance.

That was the kind of life to which Jock seemed to have settled down.

He was then in the very prime of life, and I still hoped to get him back to me some day to a home where he would end his days in peace. Yet it seemed impossible to picture him in a life of ease and idleness – a watch-dog in a house sleeping away his life on a mat; his only excitement keeping off strangers and stray dogs, or burrowing for rats and moles in a garden; with old age, deafness and infirmities growing year by year to make his end miserable.

I had often thought that it might have been better had he died fighting: hanging on with his indomitable pluck and tenacity; tackling something with all the odds against him; doing his duty and his best as he had always done. If on that last day of our hunting together he had got at the lioness, and gone under in the hopeless fight. If the sable bull had caught and finished him with one of the scythe-like sweeps of the scimitar horns. If he could have died – like Nelson – in the hour of victory! Would it not have been better for him – happier for me? Often I thought so. For to fade slowly away; to lose his strength and fire and intelligence; to outlive his character, and no longer be himself! No, that could not be happiness!

Well, Jock is dead! Jock, the innocent cause of Seedling's downfall and death, lies buried under the same big fig tree. The graves stand side by side. He died, as he lived – true to his trust. This is how it happened, as it was faithfully told to me:

It was a bright moonlight night – think of the scores we had spent together, the mild glorious nights of the Bushveld! – and once more Tom was roused by a clatter of falling boxes and the wild screams of fowls in the yard. Only the night before the thieves had beaten him again, but this time he was determined to be even with them. Jumping out of bed he opened the little window looking out on to the fowl-house, and, with his gun resting on the sill, waited for the thief.

He waited long and patiently. By-and-by the screaming of the fowls subsided enough for him to hear the gurgling and scratching about in the fowl-house, and he settled down to a still longer watch. Evidently the dog was enjoying his stolen meal in there.

'Go on! Finish it!' Tom muttered grimly. 'I'll have you this time if I wait till morning!'

So he stood at the window waiting and watching, until every sound had died away outside. He listened intently; there was not a stir; there was nothing to be seen in the moonlit yard; nothing to be heard; not even a breath of air to rustle the leaves in the big fig tree.

Then, in the same dead stillness the dim form of a dog appeared in the doorway, stepped softly out of the fowl-house and stood in the deep shadow of the little porch. Tom lifted the gun slowly and took careful aim. When the smoke cleared away, the figure of the dog lay still, stretched out on the ground where it had stood; and Tom went back to bed satisfied.

*

The morning sun slanting across the yard shone in Tom's eyes as he pushed the reed gate open and made his way towards the fowl-house. Under the porch, where the sunlight touched it, something shone like burnished gold.

He was stretched on his side – it might have been in sleep. But on the snow-white chest there was one red spot.

And inside the fowl-house lay the other dog – dead.

Jock had done his duty.

THE END

Bushveld Words and Pictures

The story of *Jock of the Bushveld* ends; yet much lives on. Jock's name has become familiar to generations of young people in Southern Africa and the roads he travelled are marked for all to see. The Bushveld as he knew it has changed; but there are parts where the game still roams free, protected by the foresight of those who thought to preserve something of this paradise for future generations. Some children have seen the bush and the animals that Sir Percy FitzPatrick wrote about; other children in other countries who read about Jock may find the background strange. Here are some explanations which may help them to understand:

The Veld

VELD: Open uncultivated land.

HIGHVELD: The high plateau in South Africa, about 5,000–6,000 ft (about 1,830 m) above sea-level, usually grassland.

MIDDLEVELD: The mixed country lying between the Highveld and the Bushveld.

BUSHVELD: Bush country; also called Lowveld or Low Country.

ANT-HEAP: Mound made by termites or 'white ants'; about 2–4 ft (0.6–1.2 m) in base diameter and height, but sometimes very much larger, up to 12 ft (3.6 m).

DONGA: A gully or dry watercourse with steep banks.

DRIFT: A ford.

KLOOF: A gorge, ravine.

KOPJE: A hill.

KRANS: A precipitous rock-face on a hill or mountain; a cliff, or crag.

MARULA: A tree of soft white wood, which is often carved into bowls, spoons, etc.; the fruit is eaten or fermented for drink.

POORT: A gap or gateway in a range of hills.

SLOOT: A ditch.

SPRUIT: A stream.

TAMBOOKIE GRASS: A very dense grass which sometimes has a height of 15 ft (4·5 m) and a stem diameter of 0·5 in. (1·2 cm).

VLEI: A small shallow lake; a swamp, marsh, bog.

WOODEN ORANGE: Fruit of the 'klapper' tree; wild orange, monkey orange.

Words of the Bush

ASSEGAI: A native spear.

BAAS: Master.

BILTONG: Meat cut in strips, slightly salted and dried in the open air.

DOUGHBOYS: Scones; frequently unleavened dough baked in the coals.

IMPI: An army or body of armed natives gathered for or engaged in war.

INDUNA: A head man, captain, chief.

INKOS: Chief – used as a term of respect in address or salutation.

KAHLE: Gently, carefully, pleasantly, well; 'Hlala kahle': farewell.

KAFFIR CORN: Sorghum, Indian millet.

KEHLA: A native of certain age and position.

KERRIE: A stick used for fighting, frequently knobbed; hence knob-kerrie.

KRAAL: An enclosure for cattle, sheep, etc.; also a collection of native huts, the home of a family, the village of a chief or tribe.

SAKUBONA: 'Good-day'.

SALTED HORSE: One which has had horse-sickness, and is thus considered immune; hence 'salted' is freely used as meaning acclimatized, tough, hardened.

SCHELM: A rascal.

SJAMBOK: Tapering rawhide whip made from rhinoceros, hippopotamus or giraffe hide; a horse-whip.

UMFAAN: A boy.

UMGANAAM: A friend.

UMLUNGU: A white man.

Historical References

CHAKA: The first of the great Zulu kings and founder of the Zulu military power.

DINGAAN: The second of the great Zulu kings; brother, murderer and successor of Chaka.

'MPANDE: The third of the great Zulu kings, 'Panda' the peaceful; brother of Dingaan.

KETSHWAYO: Fourth and last of the great Zulu kings; son of 'Mpande; leader of the Zulus in the great Zulu War of 1879.

THE GREAT WHITE QUEEN: Queen Victoria.

PIET RETIEF: One of the leaders of the Great Trek; he and his men, about a hundred in all, were treacherously murdered by Dingaan when peacefully negotiating with him at his kraal (1838).

ISANDHLWANA: The opening battle of the great Zulu War; the small British garrison of little more than 1,000 men were surprised by 24,000 Zulus and almost entirely annihilated; of the 598 officers and men of the 24th Regiment only six privates succeeded in escaping.

RORKE'S DRIFT: A small force of British, 104 men, under the command of Lieutenants Chard and Bromhead, saved Natal from invasion at Rorke's Drift where they drove off a force of 4,000 Zulus. They resisted innumerable attacks for over twelve hours; eleven Victoria Crosses were awarded for gallantry in that battle.

KAMBULA: Colonel Evelyn Wood repulsed the Zulu army at Kambula.

ULUNDI: The Zulus were decisively defeated at Ulundi (July, 1879), and their military power was broken.

Animals of the Bush

	Maximum height		Maximum weight		Record length of horns	
	in.	cm	lb.	kg	(to nearest inch)	(to nearest centimetre)
Buffalo	66	168	1,800	816	58	147
Kudu	60	152	650	295	71	180
Zebra	57	145	900	408	No horns	
Blue Wildebeest	55	140	570	258	32	81
Sable Antelope	54	137	525	238	61	155
Hartebeest	54	137	400	181	26	66
Waterbuck	53	135	600	272	39	99
Tsessebe	48	122	350	159	18	46

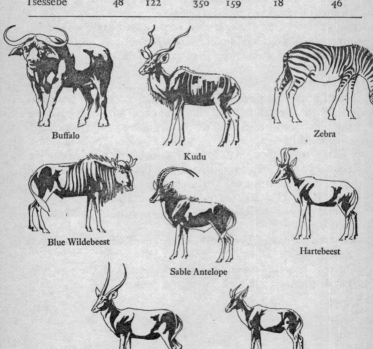

Buffalo

Kudu

Zebra

Blue Wildebeest

Sable Antelope

Hartebeest

Waterbuck

Tsessebe

| | Maximum height | | Maximum weight | | Record length of horns | |
	in.	cm	lb.	kg	(to nearest inch)	(to nearest centimetre)
Bushbuck	38	96	180	82	22	56
Impala	38	96	160	72	27	69
Reedbuck (Rietbok)	37	94	170	77	18	46
Springbuck (Springbok)	32	81	80	36	19	48
Oribi	26	66	45	20	7	18
Klipspringer	24	61	37	17	6	15
Stembuck (Steenbok)	23	58	32	14	7	18
Duiker	23	58	30	14	7	18

Bushbuck

Impala

Reedbuck (Rietbok)

Springbuck (Springbok)

Oribi

Klipspringer

Stembuck (Steenbok)

Jock

Duiker

DASSIE: A herbivorous rock-rabbit which lives among boulders and rocks; about 18 in. (45 cm) in length; maximum weight 9 lb. (4 kg).

Dassie

HYENA: Although a nocturnal animal it is often seen during the day; it feeds mainly on carrion; maximum height 30 in. (76 cm); maximum weight 155 lb. (70 kg).

Hyena

LAGAVAAN (LIKKEWAAN): Huge water lizard; Cape monitor; frequents rivers and streams and takes readily to the water; up to 8 ft (2·5 m) in length.

Lagavaan

MAMBA: The largest and swiftest of the deadly snakes of Africa, and one of the most wantonly vicious; attains lengths of 12 ft (3·5 m).

MEERKAT: A small mongoose; it preys on insects, mice and birds and is fond of eggs; about 26 in. (66 cm) in length.

Meerkat

WILD DOG (CAPE HUNTING DOG): It usually hunts in packs, and the prey is generally savaged while fleeing; maximum height 30 in. (76 cm); maximum weight 65 lb. (29 kg).

Wild Dog

Insect Life of the Bush

HOTTENTOT-GOD: A praying mantis; a source of many legends and superstitions because of its habit of remaining motionless

Hottentot-god

with head raised and front legs outstretched in what appears to be an attitude of prayer; in fact, a voracious carnivore which seizes its prey and holds it firmly while tearing it apart with its mandibles; the female devours the male during the mating process.

SCORPION: Easily distinguished from a spider by its clawlike pincers and the long upturned tail at the tip of which is the poisonous sting; nocturnal in habit, they live under stones, in crevices, under dead leaves, in dead wood, etc.

Scorpion

STICK INSECT: So named because of its resemblance to twigs of trees and shrubs on which it lives and feeds; some are further protected by sharp spines; many have no wings.

Stick Insect

TOCK-TOCKIE: A slow-moving beetle incapable of flight; it gets its name from its means of signalling by rapping its abdomen on the ground.

Tock-Tockie

TSETSE FLY: A grey fly, little larger than the common house fly; it is the vector of sleeping sickness in humans and Ngana in cattle.

Tsetse Fly

Bushveld Birds

AASVOGEL: A vulture; a large scavenging bird of prey with the head more or less bare of feathers; it subsists upon the carcasses of dead animals; has wonderful eyesight and soars at great heights to search for carrion.

Aasvogel

GO'WAY BIRD: The grey loerie; its characteristic call is a loud drawn-out 'go-way', hence the popular name; it also gives various catlike howls and shrieks.

Go'Way Bird

HONEY-BIRD: The honey guide; will guide honey-badgers and humans to bees' nests, uttering a harsh cry.

Honey-Bird

KORHAAN: The smaller bustard.

Korhaan

POU: The great bustard.

Pou

TICK BIRD: Oxpecker; usually found in association with domestic or wild beasts. It settles on the animal's back to pick off ticks and flies which it eats.

Tick Bird

A Transport Wagon

BUCKSAIL: Tarpaulin used for covering transport wagons.

DISSELBOOM: The pole or shaft of an animal-drawn vehicle.

NEKSTROP: The neck-strap, or reim, which, attached to the yokeskeys keeps the yoke in place; halter.

REIM: A stout strip of raw-hide.

TREK GEAR: The traction gear, chain yokes of a wagon.

VOORLOOPER: The leader; the man who leads the front oxen.

VOORSLAG: The strip of buck-hide which forms the fine end of a whip-lash.

YOKESKEY SKEY (JUKSKEI): The wooden cross-bar which, coupled by nekstrops, holds the yoke in place.

SPAN: A team of oxen, yoked in pairs numbering from two to twenty; usually fourteen or sixteen.

INSPAN: To yoke up, harness up.

OUTSPAN: To unyoke or unharness; also the camp where one has outspanned and places where it is customary to outspan.

DOUBLE SPAN: To double the number of oxen pulling one wagon (usually doubled to pull a heavy wagon up a steep hill or through a drift).

TREK: To move off or go on a journey; also a journey, an expedition; also the time, distance or journey from one outspan to another.

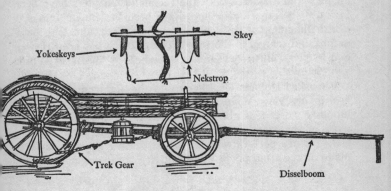

Note on the Abridgement

Jock of the Bushveld was first published in 1907 and was an instant and great success. Since then it has been read by thousands in many countries and has become a classic among animal stories. It is a long book and a certain amount of the background information and explanations are not as necessary now as they were for readers of seventy odd years ago; besides, the history of that period has appeared in detail in biographies and other works of history. We recently organized the publication of my father's biography entitled *The First South African* by A. P. Cartwright (Purnell & Son) which gives all the details of his life including the period covered in *Jock*.

Thus, the preface and first two chapters have been left out entirely and the book now starts with the birth of Jock and moves fairly quickly from his puppyhood to his adventures. Only one incident has been retained from the original second chapter: the story of Jim's capture of the lion cub. This is essential to his character build-up and has been put into the chapter 'Jim Makokel''. All the remaining chapters have been included, but the longer ones have been broken up into sections. Difficult passages have been re-arranged, and long paragraphs and sentences shortened. The glossary has been revised and in parts illustrated, and is now headed 'Bushveld Words and Pictures'.

We asked Dolores Fleischer to do the abridgement and she has, in my view, done a marvellous job with sympathy and humility. I feel it is no small undertaking to abridge a literary work of this standing, and she has managed to retain a complete picture of Bushveld life as my father drew it, and to maintain the atmosphere and sensitivity of the original.

CECILY NIVEN
Daughter of Sir Percy FitzPatrick